Pascual, Rafael del Pino, Eloi Pla
Puig, Mariano Puig, Xavier Pujol,
Francisco Riberas, Julio Rodríguez, Toni Ruiz, Carlos Torres, Jean-
Pascal Tricoire, Rafael Villaseca, José Viñals, George Yeo and Gildo
Zegna. Their experience and wisdom in governance offered many
good lessons from which my students and I received ideas and
inspiration on what makes a good board and a good board member.

This book is based upon eleven clinical studies of international
companies. I had the privilege to interview their chairpersons and/or
CEOs, as well as many board directors and senior managers. Their
openness and collaboration made a difference. Most of the
quantitative information used in the clinical studies is public, but
their personal views and observations are unique. I am very grateful to
them all for their time and generosity.

In my work on the clinical studies, I counted on some
distinguished coauthors. IESE professors Adrian Caldart and Josep
Tàpies were excellent cowriters of some of these cases. Míriam Freixa
helped me very effectively, by working with company data, while
keeping other duties at IESE running very smoothly. Roger Masclans
is an outstanding doctoral student who worked with data, information
and many interviews as well. Suzanne Hogseth did great work editing
the draft of the book. Eulalia Escolà and Louma Atallah are excellent
professionals who edit papers and cases, including the ones used in
this book. I am very grateful to them all.

My IESE colleagues John Almandoz, Gaizka Ormazabal, Pedro
Nueno and Joan Enric Ricart shared with me some extremely useful
suggestions to improve the quality of the text. I am very grateful to
them. Three anonymous referees offered very useful comments and
criticisms at an early stage of the book. They pointed out some
mistakes and weaknesses, and made very valuable suggestions.

Cambridge University Press editor Valerie Appleby has been a
great supporter of this project since its beginning, offering some
practical perspectives on the book's goals and some specific themes to
attract wider interest. I am very grateful for her great help. I am also

very grateful to her team at Cambridge University Press. Jessica Norman, Ragunathan Dhanuja, Hemalatha Subramanian, Catherine Rae and Tobias Ginsberg did an outstanding job in the book editing process.

The IESE Corporate Governance Center has been organizing for several years an annual corporate governance conference, in cooperation with the European Corporate Governance Institute (ECGI). The conference brings together leading scholars who present and discuss their research on corporate governance with other scholars, and with board directors and CEOs. It has become an important context in which to think about new corporate governance challenges and issues. I am very grateful to Professors Marco Becht and Colin Mayer, and ECGI board members, for their ideas and great collaboration in this conference. Marco and Colin always provide a unique perspective on corporate governance. The Social Trends Institute (STI) chairman, Professor Carlos Cavallé, has always provided insightful ideas for these conferences, as well as organizing STI's support.

IESE professors John Almandoz, Antonio Argandoña, Africa Ariño, Pascual Berrone, Tony Dávila, Marta Elvira, Fabrizio Ferraro, Mireia Giné, Gaizka Ormazabal, Joan Enric Ricart and Xavier Vives have been very active collaborators in the corporate governance conferences and other activities of the IESE Corporate Governance Center. Félix Sánchez is the managing director of this center and has helped me organize very efficiently the conference and other initiatives that have influenced this book. I am very grateful to them all.

I am grateful to IESE dean Franz Heukamp for his support in this and other projects, as well as associate dean Eric Weber and Christine Eckert, IESE's Research Division director.

Over the years I had the privilege of serving in or advising boards of directors of large and small companies, listed and privately held, including foundations, universities and international associations. The experience and positive example of other board members helped me understand better how boards function, what they should do to help their companies survive and develop, the importance of the human dimensions of boards, and what can make boards more effective. In serving on some boards, I developed the conviction that companies can be efficient economic organizations and effective institutions that can create economic and social progress. Competent boards of directors can make a great contribution to develop companies that will become respected social institutions.

Introduction

Over the past two decades, globalization, technology disruption, the 2008 financial crisis, activist shareholders and more recently, climate change, COVID-19 and new geopolitical risks have unleashed several earthquakes with deep and lasting effects on the business world and society. For most of the twentieth century, companies were institutions that helped create wealth, innovation and jobs, and raised the standards of living for many people. In a stable international context, firms played a key role in spreading economic growth and prosperity around the world. Unfortunately, the rising uncertainty unleashed by those trends has made the role of boards of directors in governing companies extremely complex.

In the 1990s, a new generation of boards of directors was born. Its key features were the increasing presence of external board members whose independence from the company and the CEO could provide the best advice for the firm's long-term development. National regulators quickly adopted new governance guidelines to improve the quality of the work of boards. In addition, in the aftermath of the 2008 financial crisis, new corporate governance reforms were introduced in most OECD countries in order to make boards more accountable. Unfortunately, the effects of those reforms on corporate performance were not as deep as intended, the overall quality of boards did not improve substantially and the new rules were unable to prevent major corporate governance crises, which pushed some firms to the brink of collapse.

Well-known companies such as ABB, Bayer, Boeing, Carillion, Deutsche Bank, General Electric (GE), Intel, Nissan, Thyssen, Uber, Wells Fargo, Wirecard and WeWork, among others, are recent victims of this devastating plight, with negative impacts on their reputation, market value and jobs. Their boards of directors had to orchestrate a corporate restructuring, with the formidable challenge of restoring trust among shareholders and other stakeholders.

The recent crisis at (GE) sheds light on the complex role of boards of directors. On June 12, 2017, GE appointed John Flannery as CEO in place of Jeff Immelt, who had held this position since 2001. The roots of the GE crisis go back to 2015, when it completed its $22 billion acquisition of the Alstom power business, a merger expected to create an industry giant. The acquisition of Alstom coincided with the peak of energy prices. The GE power business had underperformed ever since. This acquisition accelerated some of GE's strategic and financial problems and the board forced Immelt to step down in June 2017.

Shortly thereafter, Flannery announced that all GE divisions were under review and GE would write off $23 billion of its power business and reduce its workforce by 12,000 employees. In January 2018 GE also wrote off $6.2 billion in its insurance business. Flannery admitted that the board was considering the option of breaking up the company and additional divestment in light of its continuous market value decline and growing pressure from Trian, an activist hedge fund. GE's costly write-offs of its insurance and energy divisions nearly caused its demise.

On October 1, 2018, the board of directors decided that Flannery – their CEO of choice in June 2017 – was not the right person to lead the turnaround GE needed to survive its worst-ever crisis. Larry Culp – a recently appointed GE board member – was named the new CEO. For this icon of US industrial leadership, the way these events unfolded was devastating. On November 9, 2021, Culp finally announced that GE would break up into three companies: health care, energy and aviation. This was a dramatic decision that defined the end of the GE model and the closing of an era in US business.

Since 2008, GE was facing tremendous external and internal challenges. But did GE's board have the right capabilities to tackle them? In June 2017 the board was comprised of sixteen members plus the CEO, who also held the role of chairman. All of the members were

Contents

Figures

Tables

Acknowledgments

My professional interest in corporate governance goes back to my early days as a young IESE faculty member. IESE and the University of Navarra offered me the context where I developed the conviction that companies are not only effective economic institutions but human groups that need to be governed effectively to create prosperity. Boards of directors have a huge responsibility in achieving this purpose.

This book is the outcome of many years of collaboration with outstanding people. I am very grateful to colleagues with whom I taught corporate governance programs; in particular, IESE professors Carlos Cavallé, Herman Daems, Fabrizio Ferraro, Mireia Giné, Jordi Gual, Pedro Nueno, Gaizka Ormazabal, Joan Roure and Josep Tàpies, as well as Harvard Business School professors Jay Lorsch, Krishna Palepu and Suraj Srinivasan. This book uses many approaches and concepts that I learned – and keep learning – from them over the years. I want to thank my students in the IESE Advanced Management Program, Programa de Alta Dirección de Empresas (PADE), Global CEOs Program, Harvard Business School–IESE Value Creating Boards Program and the Board Directors Program for their contributions to collaborative learning and for sharing their experiences in board governance.

Over the years, I counted on the regular presence of some CEOs and board members as guest speakers at the IESE Executive Programs. I am very grateful to José María Alvarez Pallete, Isak Andic, Ibukun Asowika, Simón Pedro Barceló, Hans-Jacob Bonnier, Pere Botet, Nuria Cabutí, Paul Fribourg, Rosa García, José I. Goirigolzarri, Gonzalo Gortázar, Franz Haniel, Denise Kingsmill, Bruno de Leo, Antonio Llardén, Hansueli Maerki, Juvencio Maeztu, Luis Maroto, Tobías Martínez, Jordi Mercadé, Stanley Motta, Silvio Napoli, Carles

distinguished business leaders and served GE as independent directors. They had deep business experience, many of them at international companies, but the board was not very diverse. GE also had
in place all the board committees that regulation required. This crisis
was not driven by corruption or greed: Board members in no way
abused their position for personal gain. Overall, GE's board of directors had many of the qualities and attributes that corporate governance
regulation and the academic literature highlight as indicators of good
governance, but this was not enough to save GE.

The GE crisis brings into question the role of boards of directors
in times of rapid change. It serves as a powerful reminder of why
boards may falter and why companies fail in tackling disruptive
changes and radical transformation. A series of important shifts –
including technology disruption, climate change and the rising influence of activist investors in corporate boardrooms – have all put
incredible pressure on boards of directors. While the reasons behind
GE's failure are complex and not attributable to one single factor, they
nonetheless underscore the critical role of the board of directors in
strategy, transformation and CEO succession planning, particularly
during times of disruption.

I.I   THE EVOLVING ROLE OF BOARDS OF DIRECTORS
IN A TIME OF ACCELERATED CHANGE

Corporate governance crises are an intriguing phenomenon. Most of
the afflicted companies are listed firms, and as such, operate under the
close supervision of national regulators. They have strong disclosure
requirements. Following the 2008 financial crisis, capital markets
regulation substantially increased, with stricter transparency rules
and additional shareholder rights to vote on executive compensation
and other relevant decisions. In parallel, institutional investors' monitoring and engagement also grew. Activist investors became more
prominent around the world. All the key actors – regulators, investors
and capital markets institutions – took steps to improve the quality of
corporate governance.

Unfortunately, these efforts have not been enough to boost boards of directors' capacity to govern firms for the long term and develop strategies that create sustainable value. Most of those reforms were based on the notion that the role of the board is to monitor the management team, and design the incentives so that management makes good decisions that maximize shareholder value. With this paradigm, it is not a surprise to observe that many boards face a major challenge when their companies need to tackle huge problems that put their survival at risk. For a board, monitoring management is not enough in times of big disruptions. The board should get deeply involved in understanding the firms' challenges and work with the CEO to tackle them. While some corporate crises stem from unpredictable external factors, many of them originate in strategic decisions made by boards of directors themselves. A reasonable question emerges from these observations: Could these boards of directors been more effective in preventing a crisis?

The inability of boards to govern companies effectively has led to a widespread view among investors and scholars that the current board-of-director model is not working well. This model emerged in the 1990s in the EU, and was gradually adopted in many other OECD countries. Characterized by a majority of external, independent directors and a strong focus on compliance, this model is failing to deliver good governance.

Scholars, investors and regulators have recently suggested potential solutions for bolstering board effectiveness. Some investors and scholars would like to expand shareholders' voting power to decisions traditionally reserved for boards, such as strategic decisions. Some scholars suggest that boards of directors should adopt new governance practices, such as those used by private equity firms for their investees. Other experts say the answer lies in highly committed professional directors, hired and compensated as full-time employees. Most asset managers are placing a stronger emphasis on ESG factors as boosters of better governance. Finally, national regulators intend to strengthen the current model by increasing the number of external directors and enhancing accountability rules.

While most of these proposals offer useful insights – from steps to boost governance to how the boards' roles and functions should evolve to promote long-term success – many fail to clearly diagnose why the current model is falling short and offer a more holistic alternative. Moreover, most of these proposals make the assumption that boards should essentially monitor senior managers and protect shareholders' rights, as many corporate law systems define. Boards should do so, but legal duties fall short of what effective boards should do to govern the company.

Over the past two decades, scholars from diverse fields (finance, organizational economics, corporate law and strategic management) have assessed the quality of boards of directors by identifying key structural attributes and measuring their effects on corporate performance. The majority of empirical studies on boards of directors use some theoretical models of boards' structure and behavior, select large sets of data, establish some hypothesis on the relationships between structural factors of boards' and companies' performance and verify whether there is a relationship of causality between board structural dimensions and the firm's performance. In these studies, the most widely considered explanatory variables of the board structure include the number of external directors, board diversity, separation of chairperson and CEO roles and the organization and composition of board committees, among others. These are boards' structural attributes and they may be useful in improving the quality of board monitoring. Empirical evidence shows many of these factors as relevant qualities of effective boards, and national regulators use them to define the ideal board structure and composition. But, as I will discuss in this book, the real world of boards of directors offers a much wider perspective for effective board governance.

As in the case of GE, many companies that experienced a corporate crisis had boards with these attributes yet failed nonetheless. There is evidence suggesting that other important factors – beyond the board's structural attributes – may explain the quality of the board's governance. In particular, the effectiveness of boards in tackling firms' strategic challenges is one of them. This task requires specific competencies that the board as a whole should possess. These competencies include, among others, how the board discusses strategic issues, fosters a positive board culture, works with the CEO and functions as an effective team. These capabilities are different from the board's structural features used in most empirical studies.

The purpose of this book is to reflect on the challenges of boards of directors in highly disruptive contexts and how they should evolve to help firms more effectively create sustainable value. National corporate law systems highlight that the board should monitor financial performance, oversee the top management team and comply with all legal duties. Boards should do so. But these functions are not enough for boards to be effective, in particular, in times of deep change. I suggest that boards' work should consider structure and compliance issues, but should work on key tasks and develop the competencies necessary to address the firm's strategic challenges. This approach will help the board govern the firm effectively. Companies today face unprecedented challenges. Boards should adapt quicker in times of significant disruption. Compliance is extremely important, but boards mainly focused on compliance may not be doing enough to think in the firm's long-term development and meet their fiduciary duties. The additional pressures and uncertainty stemming from COVID-19 and its impact on firms only reinforces this sense of urgency.

I.2   TOWARD A HOLISTIC MODEL OF BOARDS OF DIRECTORS

The model of boards of directors presented in this book is based upon the notion of the board as the firm's steward. It is structured upon six central functions that define the board's governance core functions and the requisite competencies to help develop the company for the long term. Effective boards should develop key competencies to govern the firm, help top management tackle disruption and guide the firm's long-term development.

This perspective of boards is based upon clinical studies of international companies, developed through structured interviews with their chairpersons, CEOs, board members and senior managers. Companies' clinical studies provide a better understanding of the internal dynamics and evolution of an organization over a long period of time. Clinical studies offer a more holistic perspective of a company, by including the different views of the firm's senior managers and board directors. A call for prudence is indispensable: Conclusions from clinical studies should be taken with special care, avoiding the tendency to extrapolate and generalize. The data stemming from the clinical studies and key concepts from the strategic management and corporate governance academic fields are the foundations of the model of boards as the firm's stewards. This framework has the limits that emerge from the unique features of the companies considered in this book, but also provides some insights to reflect on the areas where boards of directors can improve their effectiveness.

The board as the firm's steward model requires some competencies that boards should develop to help govern companies in a highly uncertain context. These are competencies that the board as a group should have. The business evidence presented in this book highlights some of the most pressing strategic challenges companies are facing, the functions that boards should perform and the competences and capabilities boards should develop in order to effectively confront them. These challenges essentially question the firm's current strategy and business model, and force the board to rethink how the firm should evolve to survive and compete for the future.

Most of these board competencies have not been considered in recent research and integrated into board agendas, yet as the clinical studies show, boards can govern more effectively by developing them. These competences include, among others: an in-depth knowledge of the company's strategic issues and its global context; an understanding of the firm's corporate purpose; the alignment of expectations among shareholders, the board of directors and senior management team; the ability to interact and work with the CEO to define corporate strategy; the expertise in sustainability and digital change to support the CEO in corporate transformation; the integration of critical stakeholders' views; the dynamics of the board as a team; the management of boardroom diversity; or the capability to work on CEO succession plans and leadership development. Boards should identify and develop these competencies in order to successfully perform the functions that shareholders and other key stakeholders expect. These competencies are indispensable for boards to work effectively on six central functions and tasks that define this holistic model of boards.

The first board function is to define or review the firm's purpose, and make sure shareholders and major stakeholders are in alignment with it. A clear sense of why the company exists and is in business can help shareholders and core stakeholders to cooperate in achieving its purpose. Placing purpose at the heart of governance helps align different stakeholders better and gives a company a sense of orientation. Moreover, purpose can inspire and engage employees, and boost the company's customer appeal. The firm's purpose can help define a more specific mission for the board of directors itself beyond monitoring performance. Nevertheless, purpose should be integrated effectively into strategy and business model to truly help improve the firm's governance.

The second board function is to debate and approve the firm's strategy, by working in cooperation with the CEO. The board should have a firm grasp of the firm's challenges and provide a sense of strategic direction for the organization, employees, shareholders and all stakeholders. Companies are not static institutions; their environment changes – sometimes very rapidly – so they must also be able to adapt and evolve. Corporate transformation is an indisputable challenge in today's disruptive world. The CEO and senior management team should work on it, but the board should be engaged and discuss and support management in this complex process. Strategy is a function of the CEO and senior management team, but boards should govern it since it has a profound impact on the firm's long-term evolution.

The third board function is CEO and senior leadership development: to appoint, develop and assess the CEO and key members of the senior management team, and prepare their succession plans. Appointing a new CEO is one of the board's most consequential and complex decisions and is a critical part of the leadership development function. It requires board members to know senior managers well. Moreover, the decision on a CEO's exit – with a credible succession plan – is a delicate inflection point in the life of a company and a challenge for any board of directors.

The fourth function is to make the board an effective team of individuals who can work well together. A board of directors is a human group. A competent board should stay attuned to the human dimensions of the firm and care about board dynamics. Moreover, a solid understanding of what makes a board of directors an effective team and what defines the board's culture is critical for good governance. The style of work of the board of directors has a direct and indirect impact on the firm's culture. The board's capacity to shape the culture of both the firm and the board is a key capability, since they have a crucial impact on corporate performance.

The fifth board function is to engage proactively with shareholders and other key stakeholders. The board should work with the CEO on the main guidelines for shareholder engagement and some board members may even take part in it. In a complex and turbulent world, with the threat from activist investors circling many companies, the board should engage shareholders to understand their concerns and suggestions. In particular, most shareholders care about the quality of the firm's governance, and the board should be at the forefront of improving it. It is also important that the board makes sure that the company is engaging key stakeholders in an open way, cooperating with them in creating value and learning from them. The importance of having an overall view of the stakeholders in the firm's global value chain – from sourcing to the final customers – is highlighted in a special way in the recent major disruptions in global logistics created by current international political tensions and supply shortages. The board should engage shareholders and other critical stakeholders to govern the firm for the long term.

The sixth board function is to regularly assess the firm's financial performance and its overall impact in a holistic way. This involves the consideration of all footprints – positive and negative – that the company leaves through its activities, not only its financial performance. A competent board should be able to highlight the critical factors that shape the firm's overall performance and their internal connections, govern the company in coherence with them – not only by considering the share price, revenue or profit growth – and report accordingly. In assessing corporate performance and impact, the board should be able to clearly report the firm's contributions to and impact on its different stakeholders, including planet and local communities.

This model of boards of directors presents several attributes that can make boards more functional in addressing corporate challenges in times of rapid change. The first is that it focuses board members' work on governing the firm for its long-term development and serving as stewards of shareholders and other key stakeholders, as well as of the company itself. The board should understand how the firm can create economic value sustainably and work with the CEO to make it effective. This model is consistent with the expectations of large investors and national corporate law systems, yet broadens the board's scope of functions by including specific competencies for effective governance and value creation.

The second attribute is an emphasis on the board's ability to think strategically and encourage senior managers to adopt an entrepreneurial mindset in order to discover opportunities and promote the firm's long-term success. The board should not manage the company: This is the responsibility of the CEO. The board's function is governance and the CEO's function is management. At the same time, the board should learn how to collaborate with the CEO in order to effectively govern the firm and create value sustainably. This is a key competence for high-performance boards.

The third attribute of this model is its assumption that boards serve as the central actor in corporate governance, steering the firm's long-term direction, governing its main policies, mediating between different shareholders and stakeholders and engaging them. To this end, the board should ensure the firm has a corporate purpose beyond profits that serves as a beacon to its diverse stakeholders, and a strategy and business model consistent with that purpose that is capable of sustainably generating value. Since purpose and profits are both necessary, boards need to work closely with CEOs to create business models that guarantee their compatibility.

The fourth attribute of this model is the human dimension of the board of directors as a group. A board is made up of individuals who should work collegially together, even if their dedication to the company is limited. They should help create and monitor the firm's culture, based on professionalism, respect, accountability and trust. The company's culture is influenced by the board's culture. The board should also be aware of the firm's human dimensions, in particular with regard to leadership development, executive succession planning and corporate change. Board directors should learn how to promote a positive culture and work effectively as a team to help the organization excel.

1.3   BOOK STRUCTURE AND CONTENT

This book discusses how boards can become more effective in governing their firms in times of rapid change and in tackling critical challenges, among them, corporate purpose, sustainability, technology disruption and transformation, leadership development, diversity, board culture and the governance of the multi-stakeholder firm. It combines theory and clinical evidence from in-depth organizational studies of international companies, whose profiles are presented in Chapter 1. The book adopts an interdisciplinary approach. It is based on the strategic management perspective, and also borrows from the corporate finance and economics of organizations fields.

In each chapter, I discuss the challenges for specific companies and the dilemmas their boards faced in addressing them, and connect them with available theory and empirical evidence to present some governance guidelines.

Chapter 1 offers an overview of recent corporate crises and their relationship with the dominant model of boards of directors. I present a brief historical review of boards of directors and explore why the current generation of boards that was born in the 1990s has fallen short of its expectations. Understanding why this model has not been effective is relevant. In parallel, a close-up view of the inner workings of some boards sheds additional light on a conundrum overlooked by large–sample statistical studies. A board should understand their company's business and the industry in which it operates, make sure the company's long-term orientation is sound and expand its purpose beyond simple shareholder value maximization.

In this chapter, I introduce a basic proposition: Boards of directors and shareholders should assume that companies are not only efficient economic organizations, but also relevant and fragile social institutions whose long-term success and survival require good governance and effective boards. A dynamic society needs future-forward firms that innovate, invest and develop their talent pool, governed by boards of directors that provide strategic orientation beyond mere compliance. Boards should help address the firm's strategic challenges, define its priorities and make strategic decisions to promote its long-term success. In this way, boards can truly be the firm's stewards.

In Chapter 2 I discuss how boards can work on the company's purpose and shift their attention from profit maximization alone to become a purpose-driven organization. A corporate purpose offers a concise explanation of why a company exists and what it intends to do for customers, employees and society in a sustainable way. It provides a frame for shareholder and stakeholder expectations. With the growing emphasis on sustainability and ESG dimensions, firms need to develop an overall purpose-driven framework to ensure these pieces fit together and are well integrated into the firm's strategy.

Purpose is not an excuse for financial underperformance. Companies with purpose can better articulate goals and expectations and deliver good economic performance and shareholder returns. Purpose serves as a strong anchor for corporate goals, and enhances communication with shareholders and other stakeholders. Defining the right priority among different stakeholders is also a key task of the board. The board's function will evolve from merely overseeing and monitoring the CEO's efforts to serving as a steward of the firm's purpose and development. Boards should learn how to work with the firm's purpose, make it consistent with the firm's strategy and understand how their work can reinforce or erode corporate purpose.

In Chapters 3 and 4, I examine the role of the board in defining corporate strategy and working on corporate transformation. In Chapter 3, I argue that boards of directors should develop their own perspective on the future of the firm in collaboration with the CEO, and design the firm's strategy road map. In most industries, companies are experiencing disruptions as a result of technology, protectionism, climate change, geopolitical risks and new consumer preferences. The strategy road map should include various dimensions: what makes the firm unique, its value proposition for customers, the required capabilities and resources to compete, specific strategic choices to sustainably create economic value and the type of firm the board would like to develop in the long term.

The board of directors should provide a context where members can effectively reflect, discuss and approve the company's strategy. The board should not only approve the firm's strategy: It should offer an effective context for discussion and reflection on the strategy, business model and key decisions. Collaboration between the board and the CEO in this area is critical and can yield very positive effects on the firm's performance. The clinical studies presented also underline the importance of appointing board directors whose professional experience, strategic insights, diversity and personal commitment are able to facilitate board–CEO cooperation.

Against the backdrop of an increasingly complex business landscape, boards need to consider not only strategy, but also how to help companies adapt and transform. This is the theme addressed in Chapter 4. In the face of disruptive challenges, companies need to change. This chapter explores the board's role in the corporate transformation process when the pressure to change is intense, with particular emphasis on sustainability and digital transformation as two important drivers of major disruption.

In many industries, climate change, the global pandemic and other potential natural disasters and growing geopolitical tensions add to this pressure to adapt and compel CEOs and senior managers to rethink their company's strategy. Using the recent evidence of corporate transformations, I illustrate the unique role boards play in helping firms navigate this process, in collaboration with the CEO.

Chapter 5 examines the critical challenge of the CEO's appointment, development and succession plan. It also analyzes the role of the board in leadership development. Many corporate crises stem from a poorly managed CEO transition process. Boards that aspire to promote respected companies should focus on leadership development, talent management and succession plans. The ability to attract and develop stellar talent is a cornerstone of good governance and a driver of superior performance. This is a vital responsibility for board members and one that requires professionalism, dedication and deep knowledge of the firm and its people.

The board as a team and its interpersonal dynamics are the touchstones of effective boards of directors. In Chapter 6, I argue that the new generation of boards needs to go beyond monitoring senior managers to work harmoniously as a team capable of addressing the firm's challenges. The process of turning individual board directors into a high-performance team is complex. This chapter explores how the collegial dimension of the board's efforts can translate into effective teamwork and team development.

Moreover, the very nature of the boards of directors' role – limited dedication, diverse backgrounds and sporadic meetings – requires boards to work collaboratively with the CEO and the top management team. The board of directors appoints the CEO and, depending on the firm's statutes, confirms the key executive appointments the CEO wants to make. This decision should be founded on professionalism and trust. A constructive and highly professional relationship between the board of directors and the CEO is essential. Companies need to ensure that both the board of directors and senior management team are fully committed to making the company successful for the long term.

Effective boards should evolve from their emphasis on compliance and box-ticking to promoting a healthy corporate culture that underpins individual and corporate behavior. This is the theme examined in Chapter 7. Corporate culture can serve as a driver of employee engagement, inspiration and creativity and competitive advantage. This is a delicate issue: The board does not define corporate culture, yet can still enhance and protect it, and ensure that the company possesses a culture that fosters collaboration, customer orientation, initiative, accountability, transparency, diversity, inclusiveness and integrity, all of them qualities that helps develop the organization for the long term.

In Chapter 8, the spotlight is shareholder and stakeholder engagement. Boards that govern for the long term should actively engage shareholders – or oversee the interaction with them – learn from their suggestions and assure that the company has an adequate shareholder structure to carry out its activities and purpose. Boards should also understand how key stakeholders interact and create joint-value with the company, and how it can learn from them. In Chapter 8, I discuss the types of positive relationships the board of directors should establish with shareholders and relevant stakeholders to develop the company for the long term.

Among the board's responsibilities is to ensure the company has the right type of shareholders to pursue its purpose. A major assumption in many corporate governance studies is that shareholders are homogeneous and have the same preferences. The evidence indicates the contrary: Shareholders are heterogeneous. There is a wide variety of shareholders: family offices, pension funds, passive investors, private equity firm, hedge funds or governments, among others. Each shareholder is unique, with distinct time horizons and motivations. The board of directors needs to consider this diversity. It also should choose the best shareholders for the firm, in terms of commitment, time horizons and stewardship. Boards of directors should engage and work with shareholders in a collaborative way, by offering them a clear and complete overview of the firm's performance, challenges and foreseeable evolution.

Effective boards should assess the overall economic and social impact of their companies. In Chapter 9, I discuss how boards can set goals and policies and regularly disclose information about the firm's financial and nonfinancial performance. In particular, boards should make sure that corporate purpose, as well as environmental and social dimensions, are well defined and coherently integrated into the firm's strategy, business model, culture and people development policies.

Financial and nonfinancial information should be disclosed and presented in a holistic and connected framework. In this way, shareholders and stakeholders will have deeper appreciation of the firm's progress toward fulfilling its goals and purpose. At present, there is a heated debate about how to define standards for nonfinancial information and environmental, social and governance (ESG) factors. Effective boards should take regulation into account, while making efforts to establish their own ESG objectives that are consistent with their strategy and business model, and disclose them in a clear manner.

Chapter 10 presents a summary of the reflections and learnings stemming from the clinical studies and their implications on how to develop the boards of directors of the future and the functions that they should embrace to govern companies effectively.

Companies are confronted with unprecedented challenges that threaten their survival. The quality of good corporate governance and the work of boards of directors are more relevant than ever. Societies need dynamic and successful companies that can have an overall positive impact. Boards of directors can effectively help firms achieve their purpose and explicit goals. By supporting a firm's success in creating and spreading prosperity, boards will contribute to make companies more respected institutions in society.

I The Changing Nature and Functions of Boards of Directors

On March 29, 2019, Tim Sloan, CEO of Wells Fargo, announced he would step down immediately as the bank's chief executive. He had held that position since October 2016 when the bank's cross-selling and fake account scandal became public. Some senior managers in the retail bank unit of Wells Fargo had set ambitious sales objectives and introduced aggressive compensation incentives, pushing salespeople to increase cross-selling of financial products and open millions of unauthorized checking and credit card accounts. Customers were also overcharged for some services they had never purchased (Srinivasan et al., 2017).

Earlier that month, Sloan had appeared before the US House of Representatives Financial Services Committee and the Office of the Comptroller of the Currency to offer his views on the Wells Fargo scandal. His comments sparked sharp criticism among US lawmakers. They took issue with his failure to acknowledge any personal responsibility and were unconvinced that he was the best fit to continue as Wells Fargo's CEO. Two weeks later, under intense pressure and growing scrutiny from shareholders and media, Sloan announced his resignation.

A financial scandal devised by some of the bank's senior managers was overlooked by the board of directors, reflecting a poor managerial oversight system. The scandal evolved from some aggressive sales objectives into a full-fledged corporate governance crisis. It developed into the banking sector's largest reputational crisis since the Lehman Brothers bankruptcy in 2008. After a long search process, on September 27, 2019, the Wells Fargo board announced the appointment of Charles Scharf, former CEO of Bank of New York Mellon, as the new CEO.

The Wells Fargo crisis marked a turning point in the United States corporate world after the 2008 financial crisis. With a reputation as a well-managed, reliable bank that had escaped unscathed from the 2008 crisis, Wells Fargo was considered a model of what a good retail bank should look like. But the seeds of the scandal had been sown years earlier in the bank's retail business before surfacing in 2016.

Several facts help explain the nature of this crisis. The first relates to regulatory changes in the United States. They were designed to make banks more accountable and less prone to risk-taking, yet had not worked in the case of Wells Fargo. Second, this crisis would not put the bank's future in jeopardy – Wells Fargo had neither a problem of liquidity nor solvency – although regulators would limit its growth and strategic choices in the future. The third was the board of directors' failure to monitor top management and prevent the crisis. Even if most individual board members were unaware of and opposed to these practices, some of the board's central functions in the bank's governance – taking care of the long-term development of the bank and monitoring top management – were not working properly. Regulators would eventually put tremendous pressure on the bank, reshape its board of directors and cap its growth.

This crisis raises several questions about the bank's corporate governance. How effective was the Wells Fargo board in working on strategy, corporate growth and executive compensation before the scandal emerged? How did the Wells Fargo board shape the values and goals of the bank? How did it monitor corporate culture? How was culture related to executive compensation? Which mechanisms were in place to oversee risk management? Finally, why did the board take so long to recognize that it was ultimately responsible for this crisis?

The Wells Fargo governance failure may seem extreme, yet it reflects many challenges that boards of directors grapple with in the twenty-first century. The work of boards of directors has become extremely complex. Investors are putting more pressure on boards and CEOs. The business environment is more uncertain. Disruptive technologies are making business models obsolete, and, in many cases, boards lack the necessary capabilities to deal with this disruption. Climate change is a growing challenge and an important risk for companies. Activist investors are circling companies in search of quick profits through spin-offs and restructuring. Meanwhile, there is an increasing number of regulatory issues on board agendas, as well as growing pressure from public opinion, social media and social activists.

There is some evidence that the quality of management has improved dramatically in many countries and industries over the past decades (Bloom and Van Reenen, 2007; Bloom, Sadun and Van Reenen, 2012). Unfortunately, the same cannot be said of the quality of boards of directors. In fact, the number of recent corporate crises suggests that improving boards' effectiveness is still a work in progress.

The Wells Fargo, General Electric and other corporate governance crises reveal deficiencies in the dominant model of boards of directors and highlight the need for a deep renewal to make boards more effective institutions (Monks and Minnow, 2011; Lipton, 2017; Bainbridge, 2018; Gilson and Gordon, 2019). The current model of boards emerged and became the paradigm in the 1990s, particularly in listed companies. It was the answer that investors and regulators offered when facing changes in ownership, the growing dispersion of shareholders in recent decades and the rising role of institutional investors as shareholders. Investors wanted CEOs and top managers to be held more accountable to the board, and consequently introduced changes in the board structure, composition, functions and duties. Unfortunately, the success of these changes in improving governance has been limited.

In this chapter, I review the recent evolution of boards of directors, the emergence of the current model of boards and its core characteristics. I also discuss why this model has been unsuccessful in helping firms deal with change. In the final section, I present the fundamental elements of a new model of boards of directors to improve its functionality, which will be developed in the rest of the book.

I.2 CORPORATE OWNERSHIP AND THE ROLE OF THE BOARD OF DIRECTORS

The evolution of boards of directors since the 1990s is not only the story behind the demise of managerial capitalism (Chandler, 1977, 1990; Cheffins, 2019) and the rising influence of boards of directors; it is also the story of a major shift in ownership around the world, in particular, the United States and Western Europe (Franks and Mayer, 2017), and subsequent changes in corporate governance and regulation (Zingales, 1998; Gordon and Gilson, 2019). Shareholders have the legal capacity to appoint and remove board directors, and – within corporate law – give the board some key governance functions. Shareholders' engagement and capital markets regulations have shaped the way boards work (Gilson, 2018; Rock, 2018; Cheffins, 2019; Dasgupta, Fos and Sautner, 2021).

Between the 1950s and 1990s, households held the majority of shares in listed companies in most countries. Table 1.1 shows the evolution of ownership of listed companies in the United States between 1950 and 2020. In 1950, the household sector held 92.8% of shares in US listed companies. This figure was 45.6% in 2000 and 38.3% in 2020 (Dasgupta, Fos and Sautner, 2021). During those years, in the absence of large, relevant shareholders influencing boards of directors, these institutions essentially served as advisory boards to the CEO, with the exception of companies with very large shareholders that shaped the firm's strategy – for instance, family businesses or state-owned firms (Carter and Lorsch, 2003; Millstein, 2017). This model of boards reflected the fragmentation of shareholders (with many individuals owning shares in listed companies), the separation of shareholders and boards and the accumulation of power by CEOs at the expense of boards. For the most part, this period saw high

Table 1.1. *Shareholders of US listed companies (%)*

Shareholders	1950	1990	2000	2020
Household sector	92.8	56.5	45.6	38.3
Mutual funds	1.6	7.1	18.3	20.8
Closed-end funds	0.9	0.5	0.2	0.2
Exchange-traded funds	0.0	0.0	0.4	6.6
Private pension funds	0.0	16.2	11.2	5.4
Federal, state and government pension funds	0.0	8.1	7.7	5.3
Insurance companies	2.6	4.1	6.2	1.9
Foreign sector	1.6	6.9	9.3	16.4
Other	0.4	0.7	1.1	5.1

Source: Dasgupta, Fos and Seitner (2021). Federal Reserve Statistical Release Data: Flow of Funds Data, United States. The Household Sector includes Bank Personal Trusts. In percentage of market value.

economic growth in Western countries, product innovation and better general management (Bloom and Van Reenen, 2007). In this growth context, boards basically approved the decisions made by CEOs and top managers. It was the heyday of managerial capitalism.

US company ownership started to change in the 1970s and 1980s, with the growing importance of institutional investors. The most relevant are mutual funds, exchange-traded funds (ETF), insurance companies, public pension funds and private pension funds. By the end of 2020, these institutional investors owned directly more than 40 percent of US shares in listed companies, while the household sector only held 38.3 percent (Dasgupta, Fos and Sautner, 2021). Many shareholders in US and British family–owned firms accelerated their divestment from those firms by selling their shares to investment funds or going public (Franks and Mayer, 2017). Today, family business still remains a relevant feature of the US economy, but not in large, listed companies, where institutional investors and pension funds collectively control large shareholdings (Villalonga and Amit, 2009; OECD, 2021).

The rising power of institutional investors as shareholders (Rock, 2018; Bebchuk and Hirst, 2019; Fisch, Hamdani and Solomon, 2020) stems from the growth of mutual funds and index-based funds. The experience of active investors in picking up some stocks and charging clients expensive fees, was replaced by large passive investors such as BlackRock, Vanguard, State Street and Fidelity, among others. These companies offer final clients a cheap way to invest in listed companies, and their success is one of the remarkable features of contemporary capital markets.

At the same time, the growing dominance of institutional investors has created a corporate governance conundrum. Institutional investors are becoming large block holders in listed companies. This has engendered some potential antitrust issues and highlights the need that these investors get involved in corporate governance as responsible owners (Azar, Schmalz and Tecu, 2018; Azar, 2020; Fisch, Hamdani and Solomon, 2020; Hill, 2020a; Azar and Vives, 2021). Large institutional investors offer individual investors good financial opportunities, but their vast size and lack of regular engagement policies as shareholders are problematic. They invest in thousands of companies and try to interact constructively with boards of directors, but most do not have the capabilities to engage with them on a regular basis (Rock, 2018; Bebchuk and Hirst, 2019; Fisch, Hamdani and Solomon, 2020). In many cases, they need to follow the advice of proxy advisory firms for specific decisions to be voted in shareholders' meetings.

A different corporate ownership evolution can be observed in Continental Europe, Asia and Latin America. By the end of 2017, families and individuals still owned 45.70 percent of shares in more than 28,000 companies in 85 countries (OECD, 2021). Families were by far the largest type of owners of companies around the world (see Figure 1.1). Countries such as Germany, Switzerland, France, Italy and Spain still show today a very significant presence of families as shareholders in large, listed companies. International firms such as Henkel and BMW in Germany; Schindler and Roche in Switzerland;

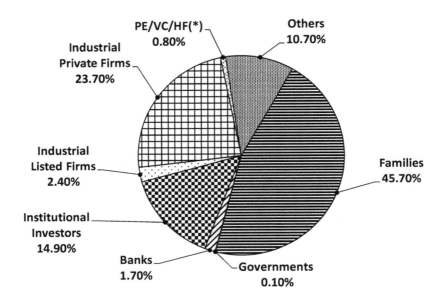

FIGURE 1.1 Corporate ownership in eighty-five countries
Source: OECD Capital Market Series Dataset (2017, 28,643 Companies)
(*) PE: Private Equity. VC: Venture Capital. HF: Hedge Funds

Prada and Fiat in Italy; L'Oréal and Bouygues in France and Acciona, Inditex, Ferrovial and Gestamp in Spain are all listed companies whose founding family still controls a substantial percentage of shares. This provides these firms with a shareholder of reference that signals a clear commitment to a long-term horizon. In Asia and Latin America, family businesses are also very relevant, although the government as the shareholder of reference is still important.

This model of ownership with families as shareholders has several implications for corporate governance. The first is that these families are shareholders with a significant stake in the firm's equity. They dedicate time to governance functions. In most cases, the family has representatives on the board of directors and an influence on the firm's values and long-term orientation. In well-governed companies, families with a controlling stake know they should exercise self-control and not abuse their position.

Second, families as shareholders mostly have long-term horizons and many of them think in terms of generations (Palepu and Nueno, 2014; Masclans, Tàpies and Canals, 2020). This feature offers companies shareholder stability and longer time frames when considering strategic decisions. Companies with long-term shareholders may be slightly slower in terms of adaptation and change but offer stability. Both attributes, adaptability and stability, may be positive capabilities for companies at different stages of their development.

Industrial foundations have recently emerged as important shareholders in some large companies in Continental Europe (Thomsen et al., 2018). Foundations received the company's shares from the founders and became their owners, often with a large, controlling stake. This is the case for companies such as Ikea, Bertelsmann or CaixaBank, in which significant shareholdings are in the hands of a foundation. Although they also have governance challenges, these foundations provide a long-term horizon and are adept at aligning the interests of the firm's different parties.

Private equity and venture capital firms (Gompers, Kaplan and Mukharlyamov, 2016) are a new generation of investors that provide equity and an exit option to the previous shareholders (Neckebrouck, Meuleman and Manigart, 2021). They have grown fast over the past thirty years, first in the United States and later in Europe and Asia. When they invest, they tend to become shareholders of reference in these companies. Private equity firms follow a model of corporate governance that, in general, aligns shareholders, boards and senior managers better, although their time horizons are shorter.

As a result of these ownership shifts, shareholders have become more heterogeneous over the past three decades (Aguilera et al., 2017). The discussion on how to improve the quality of governance through better boards of directors also needs to understand the identity of shareholders and their commitment to the firm. Shareholder expectations of boards of directors evolve as the nature and preferences of shareholders become more diverse. Different shareholders have, among other attributes, different earnings expectations, appetites for risk and time horizons. Each shareholder has its own motivations to get involved in corporate governance and have an active presence in the board of directors. In particular, large institutional investors are learning how to actively engage with companies without having a seat on their boards. Boards of directors should take these factors into account. Considering shareholder heterogeneity is relevant because an important duty of boards is to ensure the company has the ownership structure and the type of shareholders that its purpose and activity require. In good companies with competent boards, shareholders' views should be discussed in the boardroom. And boards should also make sure that the firm's shareholders support the company's development.

The increasing diversity of shareholders, each with unique expectations and time horizons, has emerged almost at the same time as globalization and technology – and has reshaped industries and companies over the past decades. Disruptive technologies and new ways to organize production and distribution of goods and services have eroded traditional companies' competitive advantages, new entrants have challenged incumbents, corporate performance has decreased and the complexity of boards of directors' strategic challenges has grown dramatically.

Changes in ownership over the past few decades without a stronger shareholders' engagement made the independence of board directors and other dimensions of the board structure the dominant features of this new generation of boards since the 1990s. Boards of directors moved from managerial capitalism and being CEO-centered to assume the critical role in the firm's governance. Unfortunately, directors' independence and other qualities are not enough to guarantee that boards are able to play this vital role in governance in times of disruptive changes.

I.3   THE EMERGING GENERATION OF BOARDS OF DIRECTORS IN THE 1990S

Through the 1990s, most boards of directors – particularly in listed companies – were essentially advisory boards that confirmed the decisions made by top management. Despite a growing scholarly and regulatory consensus that the main functions of the board were monitoring top management and governing the company, the fact is that few boards executed effectively these functions. Only in certain corporate crises that required restructuring and turnaround processes did the board of directors play a leading role. This advisory model fell into disfavor. The main reason was that it was not adequately fulfilling its goal to monitor management and, more importantly, did not govern the long-term development of the firm. The CEO was in charge of the company and controlled the board. There was no clear role for the board and the monitoring of top management was ineffective.[1]

The growing shareholders' diversity, the emergence of large institutional investors and the increasing role of capital markets forced a reconsideration of the role of boards of directors in the early 1990s. Investors were concerned about protecting their investments and governments started to regulate corporate governance to defend shareholders' rights.

The legal tradition of boards in the United States and EU share some common notions on the functions of the board of directors, yet with relevant differences that influenced how boards evolved. In the United States, the dominant legal tradition is shaped by Delaware's jurisdiction, the state where most US-listed companies are incorporated. According to the General Corporation Law of the State of

---

[1] Notorious corporate crises such as the Penn Central collapse in 1970, with illicit payments, highly leveraged transactions and a board of directors that neither anticipated nor functionally managed the crisis, marked a turning point in corporate governance and drove the need for more effective boards of directors (Securities and Exchange Commission Task Force, 1972; Cheffins, 2019). In Germany, the Siemens governance crisis in the late 1990s was also an inflection point in governance.

Delaware, "[t]he business and affairs of every corporation organized under this chapter shall be managed by or under the direction of a board of directors" (n. 141a). The board of directors is the center of this corporate governance model. Court decisions over the years have confirmed the preeminence of the board of directors in the firm's governance.

Delaware and other state jurisdictions establish that board directors have two basic duties, which highlight their centrality in governance. The duty of care specifies that a board director must exercise diligence in acting as a board member. This duty includes the study of the affairs the director should know about and the decisions that the board should make.[2] The duty of loyalty requires that a director shows undivided loyalty to the company it serves, putting the firm's interests above personal interests in business issues.

In the United States, the renewal of boards of directors also got some momentum from the private sector that confirmed the centrality of boards in the firm's governance. In 1978, the Business Roundtable published "The Role and Composition of the Board of Directors of the Large Publicly Owned Companies," which highlighted that the board is the ultimate corporate authority. It endorsed the principle of the board-centric approach to governance. In 1988, the American Law Association published its own set of principles of governance based on the Delaware legal tradition that expanded the 1978 Business Roundtable report.

In the EU, the trigger for the renewal of corporate governance and the board's role was the "Report of the Committee on the Financial Aspects of Corporate Governance" (Cadbury et al., 1992), published in the United Kingdom. It was prepared by the committee chaired by Sir Adrian Cadbury, with the support of the UK Financial Reporting Council, the London Stock Exchange and the accounting profession in the aftermath of the United Kingdom's 1986 financial

---

[2] Board directors are supposed to use their best business judgment to make decisions. In specific cases, courts will defer to board directors and their business judgment.

"big bang." This report advocated the central role of the board of directors in the firm's governance and adopted some Delaware principles but also highlighted its own identity. It stated that public companies

> should be headed by an effective board which can both lead and control the business. Within the context of the UK unitary board system, this means a board made up of a combination of executive directors, with their intimate knowledge of the business, and of outside, non-executive directors, who can bring a broader view to the company's activities, under a chairman who accepts the duties and responsibilities which the post entails
>
> *(n. 41)*.

This report paved the way for many of the corporate governance codes approved over the past two decades in most countries, including the influential OECD Principles of Corporate Governance (1999). Many of these codes are based upon the Cadbury report and assume that boards made up of independent board members offer the best system for improving the quality of governance and eventually, the firm's long-term performance. This pathway for boards looked very reasonable, but was insufficient to guarantee companies' long-term success since it did not take into account some of the board of directors' holistic responsibilities.

I.3.1   The New Model of Boards of Directors: Core Attributes

The first attribute of the new board of directors' model is the majority of external, independent board directors without professional connections with the company and its top management. In the previous model, many boards were comprised by the firm's senior executives. Independent directors are supposed to guarantee that the board is not constrained by managers' conflicts of interest or preferences.

The second attribute is the division of work within boards through the creation of specialized board committees. The most significant are the audit committee, the executive compensation committee and the nomination committee, each with a president and a majority of external directors. By emphasizing these committees, regulation clarifies some of the board's main duties. All board members share the same legal responsibility yet hold different roles within the board to make it more effective.

The third attribute is the recommendation to separate the role of the chairperson from the role of the CEO. This feature is dominant in the EU but still highly debated in the United States. The chairperson's main function is to take care of the firm's governance and board leadership. The CEO's mission is to manage the company. The empirical evidence around the advantages and disadvantages of this separation is not very clear (Finkelstein, Hambrick and Cannella, 2009), although there is a widespread assumption, based upon individual cases and situations, that this division of functions may be a prudent governance decision in many companies.

The fourth attribute is that shareholder primacy has been the firm's dominant goal in different governance codes, with some exceptions, such as the German Code of Corporate Governance (2005), chaired by Gerhard Cromme, and the 2003 Spanish Code, chaired by Enrique Almada. Both codes highlighted the role of the board in developing the company for the long term and creating value sustainably. The past three decades have been the peak of the doctrine of profit maximization as the goal of good governance and shareholders' primacy. The recent UK Unified Code (2018) emphasized the value of corporate purpose and the need to pay attention to other stakeholders in governing the company. This may be a turning point for the definition of the firm's goals from a legal perspective.

The fifth attribute is the evolution of executive compensation, which is proposed by the board compensation committee, approved by the board and eventually voted on by shareholders. Over the past two decades, the standard executive contract has defined an executive compensation system dependent upon the company's financial goals. It is based on the assumption that economic incentives genuinely connect top managers' motivations with shareholder gains (Bebchuk and Fried, 2004; Edmans and Gabaix, 2016). In many cases – particularly in the United States – these incentives are huge and tend to be linked to the share price rather than to the cash generated. The fact is that executive compensation levels have been growing quickly, both in good and bad years, and have at times been based on schemes that are neither easy to understand nor related to the firm's performance. They are under attack by proxy advisory firms and some investors, and have provoked public outcry. There is widespread agreement that the current system does not work. The recent inclusion of ESG goals will make this system even more complex.

The sixth feature of this model is compliance. The complexity of leading companies in competitive industries on a global scale makes the role of the board very important and its task herculean. Board members might not have the time to deeply understand the company's strategy. They might not know senior managers well. There are also constraints in board meeting agendas and compliance issues require a lot of attention. The information provided is selected by the chair of the board and the CEO. The chairperson defines the board meeting's agenda and time allocation of each issue with the CEO.

Codes of good governance and other regulatory frameworks state that the board should know about certain issues – financial performance, strategy and executive compensation, among others – and that it should discuss these issues often. Top management reports to the board on these matters and how the company meets legal compliance. All in all, these duties are related to what organizational scholars would define as the formal organization. But corporate performance also depends on how the informal organization functions: how board directors work together as a team, the depth of their strategic discussions, the quality of the information they receive from the CEO and their interactions with her.

The final feature is that investors still rely on market forces for good governance. In the 1980s and 1990s, hostile takeovers with massive amounts of debt contributed to discipline management follies, such as diversified conglomerates that were not creating value. Activist investors play a similar role today. Their strategies are controversial and may create other problems for companies in which they invest, as the cases of iconic companies such as Xerox and Yahoo! attest.

1.3.2 Board Structure: Is It Enough to Create an Effective Board?

In the 1990s and 2000s, most listed companies in the United States and Western Europe gradually adopted many of the attributes of the new board of directors' model. This became the reference and also extended its influence on family firms and other privately owned companies. While this model had some potential advantages, the GE crisis briefly described earlier highlights some problems.

GE had successfully weathered the effects of the 2008 financial crisis thanks to very prudent financial management and the support of key investors. In 2015, GE completed the $22 billion acquisition of Alstom's power business to form an industrial behemoth in energy. Soon afterward, some investors noted that the company was using more cash than it was generating (Crook, 2018; Colvin, 2019). In May 2017, GE reported that its power unit had a negative outlook and that orders were down. CEO Jeff Immelt was forced to step down in June 2017 and John Flannery replaced him. In the following months, the board declared that all GE divisions were under review and announced very large write-off in its long-term insurance business and its power business. The exorbitant costs of the write-off moved the company to the verge of collapse. Eventually, on October 1, 2018, the board of directors fired Flannery after fifteen months on the job and named Larry Culp – a recently appointed GE board member – as the new CEO.

The dramatic GE crisis is relevant for corporate governance. GE was considered a paradigm of success among large US companies. Its managerial and leadership style was studied in universities and companies around the world. Its board was made up of external, independent members, most of them successful business leaders. It was structured according to recent corporate governance criteria. It was weak in terms of diversity but had most of the qualities known as indicators of a good board.

The GE board context make the GE crisis even more difficult to understand. Why did the board fail to see GE's quickly deteriorating performance? Why did the board approve in 2015 the highly expensive acquisition of Alstom at a time when most energy observers considered energy prices to be at their peak? What did the board think about GE's financial situation and the fact that the company was unable to generate the cash necessary to face future liabilities? Is it reasonable for a good board of directors of a company renowned for its ability to generate great leaders to support three different CEOs in such a short period of time?

Even for former GE board directors, it is difficult to get the full picture of what happened at the company. GE's board structure was fine, but the scale of the GE governance crisis was monumental. GE is still a unique company with leading technologies and many of its businesses will probably survive after the November 2021 breakup in three companies. But the nature of its recent governance crisis sheds light on why boards of directors today might not work effectively.

I.3.3   The Declining Effectiveness of the New Model of Boards of Directors

Unfortunately, the notion of boards of directors made up of independent directors did not live up to its promise. Many boards of directors failed to fulfill their job: to help develop the company for the long term and protect investors. It is also important to note that the crisis of boards of directors I describe is essentially a crisis of boards in listed companies with dispersed ownership and external board directors. In this book, I also discuss the experiences of family businesses or listed companies with large shareholders. These cases reveal a deeper shareholder commitment and better alignment between shareholders and boards of directors.

The reasons for the failure of the current model of boards of directors are diverse. This model does not consider the role of the board in strategy. Board directors should have a good knowledge of the business, the broader political and social trends and the firm's strategy. Some recent corporate crises (Deutsche Bank, Yahoo! and WeWork, among others) stemmed from mediocre business strategies. Boards also need to better understand the global political and social context in which they operate. The recent crises of large tech platforms like Facebook and Uber are rooted in a lack of understanding of the wider political, economic and social context where these companies operate. In some cases, board directors may not be prepared for a deep discussion on strategic issues with the founders or the top management team.

The second reason is that this model does not pay attention to the delicate issue of CEO development and succession. John Flannery at GE, Travis Kalenick at Uber or the four CEOs between 2011 and 2018 at Deustche Bank, among others, are cases of corporate governance crises related to how boards managed the CEO appointment process. Some of these CEOs had good qualities yet were not fit to lead as chief executive of a complex organization. The hiring, development and firing of the CEO and the top management team is a central duty of the boards. Unfortunately, boards spend little time on this task.

The third reason is the assumption of the lack of collaboration between the board of directors and the CEO and top management team. Agency theory introduced the hypothesis of the diverging interests of top managers and shareholders, and the need to align managerial goals with financial incentives (Ross, 1973; Jensen and Meckling, 1976). But agency theory has transformed a hypothesis into an undisputed assumption in corporate governance. This hypothesis downplays a condition of good governance: A company needs both a good board of directors and a good senior management team. They should work in tandem to develop the firm for the long term and guide it with a clear sense of purpose.

The fourth reason is the lack of proper shareholder engagement and stewardship, in particular, in companies with dispersed shareholders. Boards need committed shareholders, especially in companies that depend on long-term investment. Shareholders should behave as responsible owners of shares and make sure that boards of directors fulfill their duties with professionalism and integrity.

The evidence of the past two decades shows that regulatory enforcement and capital market discipline are not enough to improve the quality of boards. There is also a clear need to rethink the role of boards in a new era defined by heightening competitive forces, technology disruption and new geopolitical risks. The interaction between companies and regulators will become more demanding and intense – as Facebook, Google and Uber, among others, are currently experiencing in both Europe and the United States. Companies cannot be only efficient optimizers. In times of trade wars or global health crises, companies need a certain degree of flexibility and resilience and the ability to change quickly. Boards should work with senior managers to achieve this. There is certain evidence that a growing number of board directors agree on the urgent need to change.[3] Board members express that their boards should focus more on strategy and disruptions, CEO and leadership development, and should care about the firm's purpose, the board as a team and the firm's culture. The need to renew boards of directors is urgent and designing a clear reform pathway is indispensable.

1.4   RETHINKING THE MODEL OF BOARDS OF DIRECTORS

The growing perception that the current model of boards – based on external, independent board members – has a limited functionality to help govern companies effectively has opened up the discussion on how to improve the model. I will briefly introduce some of them.

---

[3] See the 2022 IESE Survey on Boards of Directors, the 2021 KPMG Views from the Boardroom Survey and the PwC 2021 Annual Corporate Directors Survey.

The first proposal for boards of directors' reform is a natural evolution of the current model. It suggests better stock-based incentives for executives and giving shareholders more voting powers. Some scholars (Bebchuk, 2005, 2008) and institutional investors support this view. The improvement will arise from better enforcement of contracts with top managers, expanding shareholders' powers and giving boards new responsibilities through regulation. These reforms include better alignment of boards of directors and CEO compensation to long-term performance plans, opening up new avenues for activist investors to have stronger influence, giving shareholders a bigger say on strategic decisions – including climate change policies – and shareholder democracy to allow them to vote on some strategic issues.

Expanding shareholder democracy entails giving shareholders the right to vote on more decisions in annual shareholders' meetings. However, this may not always be a winning proposition for many companies that need to make strategic decisions for the long term. Few shareholders allocate the necessary time to get to know the company and its challenges well. Wider shareholder democracy may be a useful concept for some decisions, but the analogy between a company and a democratic political system is limited. A company is a business, but not only a business. It is also an organization, a human reality, whose people help create economic value in a specific industry context through coordination of activities. Without a good understanding of these realities, higher direct shareholder democracy may be inefficient to govern a company in order to create long-term value, as the effects of some cases of shareholders' activism (Hewlett Packard, Xerox or Yahoo!, among others) show.

Gilson and Gordon (2019) made a different proposal inspired by the private equity industry. Many private equity firms have a phenomenal track record in increasing the firm's value in relatively short periods of time (Gompers, Kaplan and Mukharlyamov, 2016). A key element in their strategy is the use of a special type of boards of directors, which stands out in terms of its structure, composition, commitment and functions. In this case, the private equity company names directors with extensive experience in a specific industry, who spend a considerable amount of time with the CEO to understand what needs to be done to operate a successful turnaround and improve the company's long-term growth prospects. Board directors' compensation will also be linked to the financial performance of the company and, eventually, to the equity value at the time of the private equity firm's exit. Gilson and Gordon propose a slightly different approach, in which independent board members work with directors appointed by the private equity firm. They also suggest linking board members' compensation to long-term value creation, as occurs in companies owned by private equity firms.

The private equity version of boards is an interesting suggestion to improve boards' quality. Its main attribute is that it requires board members to substantially increase their time commitment to the firm and board issues. While the private equity model may be a suitable solution in some cases, shareholders' time horizons create a problem for some companies. By their very nature, private equity firms and their investors have limited time horizons, with the intention to sell the company to other investors or launch an IPO (Gompers, Kaplan and Mukharlyamov, 2016). This may not be the best time frame and not even the best solution for many firms. This proposal also depends too much on financial compensation and incentives, and does not address deeper issues such as the necessary role of boards in the firm's long-term development. Moreover, an emphasis on the executive compensation incentives paid to board members may create new agency problems, with directors focused on their own financial compensation.

An alternative proposal suggests professional board directors (Pozen, 2010). It proposes that the current model of boards of directors, whose members work only part time and frequently also serve on the boards of other companies, be replaced by a board with professional, external board members with a higher time commitment to each company. In this model, a board member would only sit on one or two boards, with a high dedication to each company – at least ten days a month – and a long-term contract and executive compensation more closely tied to financial performance. This proposal is interesting but has some drawbacks, such as the decreasing engagement of shareholders in boards of directors. This model does not solve the agency problem and still relies on executive compensation as a motivational force.

Bainbridge (2018) makes a more radical proposal to avoid the failures of the current model of boards: the outsourcing of the major governance functions to external, specialized companies. Instead of individuals elected by shareholders to serve on boards, companies will choose a board service provider (BSP). This is a company with the explicit purpose of offering other companies the corporate governance services that they need, including its board of directors. The BSP will be the final decision maker in any company. The proposal is very radical and difficult to implement, even in listed companies, in particular, when firms have large shareholders – families, family offices or pensions funds. These shareholders usually want to have some seats on the board of directors. Some national corporate law systems protect their rights to do so.

A final proposal comes from some institutional investors and regulators. Over the past years, investors have been asking companies they have invested in for additional disclosures of nonfinancial information. Initially, investors' demands were focused on the firm's model of governance, in particular, executive compensation, board composition or board committees. Carbon footprint and some social issues recently joined the list of factors (environmental, social and governance factors) that companies should disclose. Institutional investors started to ask for this type of information because they understood that there are nonfinancial issues that have or may have an economic impact on the firm's performance; they wanted to know more about these risks and eventually ask companies to reduce them. Regulators also joined them in setting some new standards for firms in some of those areas. These initiatives are necessary in some cases. Unfortunately, they are not enough to improve the quality of

governance, because they do not address some of the corporate challenges discussed in this chapter and that boards should tackle. There
is a need to rethink the role and functions of boards of directors in a
more holistic way.

I.5 IN SEARCH OF A NEW MODEL OF BOARDS OF DIRECTORS

The current model of boards, based on independent directors with a
limited dedication to the firm, is not effective in helping firms tackle
strategic challenges. Moreover, it is a model based on a key agency
theory hypothesis: the design of mechanisms and incentives to monitor CEOs so that they maximize shareholders' returns (Friedman,
1970; Jensen and Meckling, 1976; Fama and Jensen, 1983). This
assumption does not reflect well the reality of heterogeneous shareholders and their interactions with the board. But it has been partially
translated into many corporate law systems that define the functions
of the board in this way.

Other alternative views of boards, such as the board as an institution that provides resources (access to capital markets and other
investors) to the company (Pfeffer, 1972; Pfeffer and Salancik, 1978) or
the board as a strategic decision-making institution (McNulty and
Pettigrew, 1999) never became the main hypothesis in corporate
governance studies.

In this section, I will briefly review the major forces that shape
the changing model of boards of directors: the firm's global context
and competitive challenges, the firm's history and specific context,
the nature of shareholders and key stakeholders and the role and
interaction of scholarly ideas and regulation (Figure 1.2). Some of
these forces (the interaction between ideas and regulation) have been
discussed in the previous sections. In particular, in this section I will
describe some of the competitive challenges that define the firm's
context. I will also introduce a more holistic notion of the firm, which
is important for corporate governance. Finally, I will discuss the role

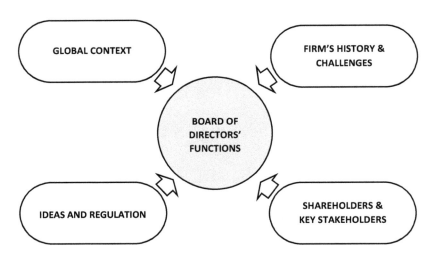

FIGURE 1.2 Board of directors' functions: Driving forces

of shareholders and key stakeholders – in particular, the CEO and senior management team – and their interaction with the board.

These concepts and factors are important for the holistic model that I will present in Section 1.6, because they reflect major forces that shape the way boards are designed and behave. In particular, these notions take into account new board capabilities, the notion of the firm as a relevant social institution and the firm's basic relationships with shareholders and other parties, including the relationship of the board of directors with the CEO and top management team. They consider what regulators and investors expect from boards of directors, but go beyond them.

1.5.1 Firm's Global Context: Complex Challenges and New Competencies

The increasing complexity of the business world makes the role of the board of directors more demanding. Understanding the nature of the challenges corporate governance will face in the coming years is a critical step in rethinking the functions and capabilities that boards need to develop (Klarner, Yoshikawa and Hitt, 2021).

The companies profiled in this book offer a glimpse of some of the most pressing challenges that boards are facing and the need to develop the required competencies to effectively tackle them. The first is the strategic complexity that companies need to navigate in order to remain competitive in a changing world driven by technology, protectionism, climate change or changing consumer behavior.

The second challenge is the new dynamics of competition and technology disruption in many industries. The current software revolution and the emergence and dominance of platform-based companies have intensified industry rivalry and given rise to new sources of competitive advantage. Board directors should have adequate knowledge and experience on these issues to make good decisions. Moreover, in firms driven by software and other intangible resources and capabilities, people and leadership development have also become top priorities for boards.

Investing in people and leadership development are relevant areas, and boards of directors need to work on them in cooperation with the CEO. This is the third challenge that boards need to tackle. This goes beyond the boards of directors' duty regarding CEO succession plans. In today's economy, intangible assets like software, customer intimacy, brand and reputation are more important than ever (Haskel and Westlake, 2018). They are created and driven by people. In the past, people development was defined and implemented by the CEO and the senior management team. As the battle for talent intesifies, boards need to understand and support people development in cooperation with the CEO.

The fourth challenge is the fight against climate change and pressing social issues like race and gender discrimination. Boards are compelled to take environmental, social, diversity and other non-financial issues into consideration. Some of these themes are or will be mandatory; others may be optional. Boards should make sure that there is a coherent integration of these issues into the firm's strategy and business model, the development of a multi-stakeholder strategy and the definition of new metrics and indicators to track relevant quantitative and nonquantitative factors. This new reality makes the work of boards of directors more complex.

The fifth challenge is that shareholders expect good financial performance and predictable growth in the companies where they invest. Unfortunately, growth has become an elusive goal amid stagnated productivity, flat or decreasing populations in advanced economies and increasing political risk in emerging markets. The likely outcome of rising geopolitical tensions, lower global integration and relocation of activities in global value chains will probably lead to lower volumes of foreign direct investment and financial flows. This may slow down GDP growth and increase volatility in the coming years.

While tackling these external challenges, boards also face an important internal challenge: the need to reconsider the collaborative nature of their work and the development of a professional, constructive and collaborative relationship with the top management team. A board of directors is a collegial team of professionals with a collective decision-making process. All the problems that teams face – coordination, free-riding, group thinking, trust, leadership, etc. – are compounded by the fact that boards of directors are made up of people whose dedication to the company is limited. Boards will not be effective in corporate governance unless they recognize the need to operate as a team. They also need to understand that they do not manage the company: this is the CEO and senior managers' responsibility.

The board of directors should establish a collaborative, professional and transparent relationship with the CEO and the senior management team, offering them support and also ensuring the management team is fully aligned with the long-term goals and governance criteria defined by the board. This perspective on the work of boards of directors essentially diverges from the current model of boards. In the following chapters, I present evidence of successful companies that have effectively developed this positive relationship. It can impact how employees work in teams, the degree of collaboration in corporate initiatives and the company's ability to innovate and come up with better and profitable ideas for its customers. In the end, the culture of the board of directors permeates and affects the culture of the organization.

1.5.2   A More Holistic Perspective of the Nature of the Firm

Creating a new mission for the board of directors requires some explicit assumptions regarding the notion of the company, its purpose and the role shareholders and other stakeholders play in its future (Mayer, 2013; Hart and Zingales, 2017; Henderson, 2020). Since the 1970s, shareholder primacy has been a key principle in governance and maximizing shareholder value became the undisputable goal of the firm. Both the new challenges confronting firms and the limitations of the shareholder primacy paradigm require a deeper reflection on what a firm is and which goals it should have for an effective governance.

In this section, I present some assumptions and notions on companies that I observed in the organizations examined in this book. Some of them have also been highlighted in the academic literature (Simon, 1976; Holmstrom, 1982; Freeman, 1984; Holmstrom and Tirole, 1989; Holsmtrom and Milgrom, 1991; Milgrom and Roberts, 1992; Hart and Moore, 1995; Roberts, 2007; Porter and Kramer, 2011; Ricart i Costa and Rosanas, 2012; Mayer 2013; Hart and Zingales, 2017; Tirole, 2017; Zingales, 2017; Edmonson, 2018). Many of these notions soften the hypothesis of maximizing shareholder value, and can help reflect deeper on the role of boards in governance.

The first assumption is that companies are relevant social institutions that create wealth and jobs, generate investment and innovation, promote community prosperity and foster social dynamism. They need to be competitive in order to survive. Companies are complex institutions with different parties contributing to them (Freeman, 1984; Milgrom and Roberts, 1992; Roberts, 2004; Argandoña, 2008; Barney, 2018). Shareholder value is only one indicator of their successful development. Corporate governance needs to consider these diverse parties and their contribution to the firm's long-term value creation.

The second assumption is that companies require the collaboration of various parties who bring distinct assets, resources and capabilities to a common project (Holmstrom and Milgrom, 1991; Milgrom and Roberts, 1992; Barney, 2018). Today's economy has been defined as "capitalism without capital" (Haskel and Westlake, 2018), in which talent, ideas and intangible assets are more important than physical assets. In this context, collaboration and trust are indispensable.

Cooperation among individuals in companies is usually organized around teams. In agile organizations, teams are the central block. The theory of the firm based on team production is more relevant in this context (Alchian and Demsetz, 1972; Blair and Stout, 1999). These teams require people who have the necessary capabilities to execute the different tasks, as well as the attitudes to work cooperatively. The effectiveness of teams requires certain conditions, such as clarity in the mission and goals, trust and coordination (Katzenbach and Smith, 1993; Edmonson, 2012, 2018) among others.

The third assumption is that companies will benefit from defining and working with a corporate purpose that expresses their reason for being and describes their distinct personality, values and uniqueness. As Mayer (2018) points out, a corporate purpose defines why a firm exists, helps coordinate the different goals and expectations of stakeholders and integrates them at a superior level.

The fourth assumption is that most companies need capital to invest for the long term (Barton and Wiseman, 2014). The investment needed for decarbonization, energy transition or communication infrastructures, among others, is colossal and requires long time-horizons. Companies with long-term investments also require investors with long-term horizons. Boards should make sure the company has the investors with the time perspective it needs.

The fifth assumption is that good management matters (Bloom and Van Reenen, 2007). Good governance requires effective managers who will coordinate the efforts of the different parties, help develop and implement strategy, engage people and direct them toward the common purpose. Managers are not only agents of investors who aspire to maximize shareholder value. Rather, they should aim to develop the company for the long term, create value for all and assure that the different parties that contribute to the company – and not only shareholders – are considered. Effective boards of directors should make sure that a company has a very competent senior management team.

The sixth assumption is that a company also needs a board of directors that represents and balances diverse shareholder and stakeholder interests, but also that offers an independent view that helps protect the firm (Carter and Lorsch, 2003; Gilson and Gordon, 2019). The board should make sure the company is well governed, with a focus on its long-term development and an understanding of how competitive advantages are generated, particularly those related to talent development, innovation and corporate culture.

The final assumption is that companies contribute to society by designing a competitive value proposition for their customers. In this process, they innovate, provide goods and services, create jobs, pay taxes, offer educational opportunities to employees and respect the environment, among other contributions. Companies leave behind many impressions in their interactions with stakeholders. Society offers companies the right to operate and a stable social context, including a rule of law, education and health-care services. Companies cannot survive in decrepit societies and should contribute to them beyond their direct economic impact. Competitive companies need dynamic societies and should contribute to creating them. It is the proper role of the board of directors to reflect on the company's interactions with different stakeholders and their lasting effects, and the overall impact of its actions on the wider society.

In the context defined by these assumptions, the role of boards of directors is truly relevant. More specifically, the evidence presented in this book is that boards should become stewards of the company's long-term development. If this is the board's mission, the indicators of performance should change. Financial performance is indispensable, but there are other goals that companies should consider. These include, among others, customer service and satisfaction; employee engagement and development; environmental sustainability; innovation and new products and services; and a corporate culture that is healthy, fair and inclusive. Boards that consider these dimensions will help create economic value, respect stakeholders and also benefit shareholders.

This model of boards of directors describes a governance institution that thinks and acts for the firm's long-term success. Boards are accountable to shareholders and other stakeholders. They make decisions to enhance the firm's purpose and its long-term development. They work with top managers collaboratively, promote an inclusive and humane culture and help make companies respected institutions in society. Boards should work effectively with top managers. The board of directors and the top managers are the two engines that drive the firm (Canals, 2010a).

1.5.3   Central Relationships with Shareholders and Stakeholders That Define the Board's Role and Functions

Corporate law describes boards of directors' duties toward the company they serve, shareholders and other stakeholders. In general, national jurisdictions have defined board duties as those relevant to protect the company and its shareholders.

The board should comply with the law, but good governance goes beyond compliance. A more holistic view of the board of directors should consider shareholders' interests, but also take into account other stakeholders. The notion of shareholder primacy in corporate governance comes from the identification of ownership of a company's shares with ownership of the company and the right to residual claims (Jensen and Meckling, 1976; Grossman and Hart, 1986). This notion is clear, but rather simple in reflecting the complexity of a company and the function of coordinating and sustaining different stakeholders to make the contributions that the company needs.

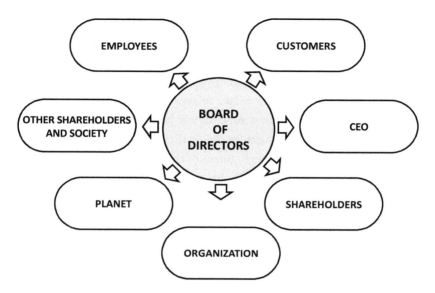

FIGURE 1.3 The board of directors: Its key relationships

In governing the firm, the board should manage these relationships effectively and with fairness, since they are essential for the firm's long-term development. In Figure 1.3, I present the essential relationships of the board with some stakeholders. Some of these relationships derive from the firm's nature and activities, and the board's specific duties (for instance, with shareholders or employees) as defined in different jurisdictions. Other relationships emerge from the firm's activities and exchanges with other stakeholders. Effective boards should understand them well and nurture them, in particular, relationships with customers and employees. These relationships have a direct impact on the firm, not only on costs, but also on revenues – for instance, interactions with customers, reputation and its competitive advantages.

The firm's core relationships are with employees and customers. Employees work at a company to make a living, but with the purpose of serving customers. The board should not manage the specific relationships with customers or employees; this is the responsibility of the top management team. But the board should make sure that the goals, policies, dominant values and culture, as well as decisions regarding the basic relationships with employees and customers, are coherent with the firm's purpose and governance. The reason is that the company exists to serve customers. Firms should engage people and customers. An effective board should use indicators of performance that shed light on the quality of this engagement. This notion has clear implications in terms of the amount of time the board dedicates to reviewing people policies, talent development and customer service and satisfaction.

The second relationship is with the CEO and top management team. Appointing a CEO is one of the most transcendental decisions that a board can make. In this regard, I refer not only to the hiring and firing of the CEO (Monks and Minnow, 2011; Larcker and Tayan, 2017), but also the development, assessment and mentoring of the CEO and the top management team, including the board's succession plans. Monitoring the CEO and the top management team is the legal duty of a good board of directors, but its responsibilities also include their development and collaboration. Moreover, it is fair to say that the board of directors of most of the companies profiled in this book assume their chief duty is to help develop the company in collaboration with the CEO and the senior management team.

The third relationship is with shareholders. This has been the dominant perspective in corporate governance, but boards need to move beyond maximizing shareholder returns in the short term to help create value sustainably for the long term. This requires a board that knows well the firm and its business, fully understands how the firm creates and sustains its competitive advantages and works with the CEO to reinforce them.

The board should also make sure the company has the type of shareholders it needs for its future development. Shareholders are diverse. Boards of directors have the final responsibility to find the right shareholders and engage them. The goal, eventually, is that shareholders become good stewards of the firm's purpose by providing stable capital in return for confidence in the firm's management. This is particularly complex in listed companies, but even in these cases the board should reflect on it. The board should foster engagement and constructive dialogue with shareholders.

The fourth relationship of the board of directors is with the company as an organization. The board should understand the company and its business, formal and informal organization and culture. Board members should get to know key people in the organization in order to assess their competencies, as well as their customers. The board should also understand the firm's external context, industry, competitors, strategy and corporate culture, and what makes a company unique for its employees. In addition, the board needs to consider its impact on the organization and the firm's long-term ability to compete and succeed.

The fifth relationship is with the planet and natural environment. Companies and governments are coming to terms with a deteriorating environment caused by human actions. The levels of atmospheric pollution, the depletion of species and natural resources, and the promotion of unnecessary consumption are important obstacles to achieving a sustainable society. This is an important reason why governments should regulate the firm's environmental impact and define a level playing field for all, in an internationally coordinated effort. At the same time, companies should disclose their real environmental impacts and associated costs, and strive to minimize them. By doing so, they will gain the respect of investors, customers and employees.

The sixth relationship is with society, in particular, the local communities where the company operates. The company impacts society through a variety of channels: wealth generation, job creation, new investment, R&D, employee education and development and tax payments, among others. Companies make a contribution through these actions. It is also true that companies benefit from social goods that society provides such as education, health care, public infrastructures and a stable social environment. One can argue that companies pay taxes to support these public goods, but this is not always the case. It is not a matter of adding new responsibilities to companies. Rather, it is a question of understanding that companies need healthy societies in order to operate successfully in the long term. Firms are key players in these societies, and as such, they are part of the solution to improve them. Companies should be respected institutions because they are efficient and promote the common good.

1.5.4 A Central Relationship: The Dynamics between Boards of Directors and CEOs

The interaction between the board of directors and the CEO and senior managers is a key relationship and an indispensable feature of good governance. Boards of directors focus on the governance of the corporation for its long-term development and work with the CEO on purpose, strategy and major corporate policies. The CEO assumes the board's goals and main guidelines, and manages the company to reach them. Just as a bird needs two wings to fly, good governance requires the cooperation of both. The quality of the interaction between the board and the CEO is a defining feature of good governance and shapes the effectiveness of boards.

In Table 1.2, I present a simple model to explain the nature of some interactions between the board of directors and the CEO, and their potential outcomes depending on their respective level of professional commitment and capacity for mutual engagement. The different scenarios highlight the potential threats, as well as the opportunities for good governance. The first – and worst – scenario is defined by a mediocre top management team and a weak board of directors; they are neither professionally competent nor engaged with one another in a collaborative way. Under these circumstances, the company is adrift, even if the business is doing fine for a while from an economic viewpoint. Neither the board of directors nor the CEO are up to the challenge of developing the firm for the long term. This is the worst-case scenario for the firm's potential development.

Table 1.2. *Interactions between the board of directors and senior management*

		Senior Management	
		Mediocre	**Competent**
Board of Directors	**Weak**	• Governance failure • Corporate decline	• Managerial capitalism • Corporate diversification
	Strong	• Weak management • Leadership development gap	• Long-term horizon • Trust

Shareholders should shake up the board and the board needs to renew the top management team.

The second scenario is defined by a board of directors that apparently shows professionalism and a top management team that lacks competence. In the end, this situation mainly reflects a board problem since it is unable to diagnose the firm's managerial competencies earlier and the CEO is unable to effectively manage the company. The board is responsible for this situation; its structure and composition may be good, but is not functional enough. Making sure that the company has a very competent CEO and top management team is the top responsibility of the board of directors. Some corporate crises such as the GE case described earlier may be an outcome of this combination of factors.

The third scenario reflects a case in which the senior management team is competent and engaged, but the board of directors is professionally weak and not deeply committed to the company and its duties. This was the case of managerial capitalism seen in many boards before the reforms of the 1990s. The company may perform well in the short term, but a weak board could lead to future crises that may emerge from divisions among board members when facing complex challenges or the rising of activist shareholders. A good management team is not enough to offset a mediocre board of directors in the long term.

The fourth scenario emerges when both the board of directors and the top management are fully engaged with the company and are professionally competent in their respective jobs. In this case, the firm's governance and management foundations are very good. The board should develop some policy guidelines that help establish and sustain constructive relationships between the board and the CEO. Even in this case, the company needs clear governance principles to enable both board directors and top managers to understand their respective roles and collaborate well for the long-term success of the firm.

A board of directors in a company with a strong management team also has some challenges. In this case, some of its top priorities are how to develop and lead the management team, how to think about top management succession, how to challenge the team to tackle new initiatives and how to develop functional ways to work together. Leading a good management team is also a challenge for a board.

The interaction between the board and the top management team is critical for good governance, as I will discuss in Chapter 7. The board should be active, but not act alone, and board members need to be engaged while working as a team and in collaboration with the top management. Boards should take the lead in setting up some principles for board–CEO relationships: how the CEO should work with the board, encourage the CEO and the top management team to come up with new ideas to be approved by the board and how to integrate different managerial perspectives on the firm's future.

1.6 THE BOARD OF DIRECTORS AS THE STEWARD OF THE FIRM'S DEVELOPMENT

In this book, I present a holistic model of boards of directors in which the board serves as the steward of the firm's long-term development,[4]

---

[4] The notion of stewardship in management (Davis, Schoomarn and Donaldson, 1997) and in the institutional investors world (Katelouzou, 2019; Gordon, 2021) and the

a function that assumes that the firm should create economic value sustainably for shareholders and key stakeholders.[5] This model considers that the board has the central governance function, should tackle the firm's strategic challenges and should play a mediating role among different stakeholders (Blair and Stout, 1999). It involves a renewal of the functions of the board so that it acts as a credible trustee for shareholders and other stakeholders. The notion of the board as steward also highlights the need to protect not only investors, but also the company itself and its future development. In this context, shareholders play an important role. A better corporate governance system also means that shareholders – in particular, relevant shareholders – should discover what serious engagement with the firm entails and should spend time learning about the company if they want to have an effective voice in their affairs.

The main attributes and assumptions of the steward's model in relation to the current model of boards of directors are summarized in Table 1.3, organized in four blocks: the changing business landscape, shareholders, companies' goals and boards of directors' functions. The table offers a first glimpse of the steward model's features in relation to the traditional model's features.

The majority of empirical studies on boards of directors establish some hypotheses on the relationships between structural factors of boards of directors and companies' performance, select large sets of

investment management community (Cossin and Boon Hwee, 2016) has a long tradition. Unfortunately, it has not been widely used in studying boards.

[5] This model is developed based upon some relevant scholarly foundations: the role of boards in strategy (McNulty and Pettigrew, 1999); the company as a multi-stakeholder institution (Freeman, 1984; Rosanas, 2008; Bower and Paine, 2017; Henderson, 2020); the diversity of shareholders (Hart and Zingales, 2017; Franks and Mayer, 2017); the company based on purpose (Bartlett and Ghoshal, 1994; Stout, 2012; Henderson and Van den Steen, 2015; Mayer 2018; Quinn and Thakor, 2019; Edmans, 2020); board collaboration with the CEO and the board as a team (Hambrick, 1987; Holmstrom and Milgrom, 1991; Blair and Stout, 1999; Hackman, 2002; Finckelstein, Hambrick and Canella, 2009; Edmonson, 2012, 2018); or the role of executive incentives in governance (Bebchuk and Fried, 2004; Edmans and Gabaix, 2016), among others.

Table 1.3. *Boards of directors: The current model and the steward model*

	The Current Model	The Steward Model
Business Landscape	• Stability • Occasional change • Externalities not considered • Passive stakeholders	• Complexity • Continuous disruption • Volatility • Climate change • Activist consumers and employees
Firms' Shareholders	• Homogeneous • Low commitment	• Heterogeneous • Good stewards
Companies' Goals	• Profit maximization • Shareholders' primacy	• Long-term value creation • Shareholders and stakeholders
Board of Directors	• Agent of shareholders • Oversight • Focus on profits • Compliance • Board structure • Monitor CEO • Complex reporting	• Steward of purpose • Strategy, long-term value • Profits and overall impact • Corporate culture • Board as a team • Collaborate with the CEO • Accountability

data and try to verify whether there is a relationship of causality among factors. Some of those studies have been very useful in pointing out relevant factors that can help improve the quality of governance. Unfortunately, many of them are not able to provide a holistic perspective of what makes boards of directors work. This book takes a different pathway. I worked on detailed, longitudinal clinical studies of international companies, with dozens of structured interviews with their CEOs, board members and senior managers. The use of clinical studies – or longitudinal case studies – has been documented and presents some advantages, as well as challenges (Eisenhardt, 1989; Pettigrew, 1990; Eisenhardt and Graebner, 2007).

Companies' clinical studies may offer a better understanding of the internal dynamics and evolution of an organization, with a longer time horizon. They allow the observation of a more holistic perspective of a company, by including the different views of the firm's senior managers and board directors. They may offer some clues on which policies and practices work and which ones do not work in a specific company. A call for prudence is indispensable here: Conclusions from clinical studies should be taken with special care, avoiding the tendency to extrapolate and generalize.

The longitudinal clinical studies in this book were based upon personal structured interviews with chair persons, CEOs, board members and senior managers.[6] Table 1.4 offers a summary of the firms' profiles. The questions selected for those interviews were grouped into major categories: companies' strategic challenges as perceived by the board; how the board works on those challenges; how the board cooperates with the CEO in tackling those challenges and defining the firm's strategy; how the board works as a team; the role of CEO and people's development; the culture of the board and the culture of the firm; how the board engages shareholders and key stakeholders; and how the board assesses the firm's overall impact beyond financial performance.

I organized and structured the data from those interviews in a model that highlights the main functions that boards should assume to help firms deal with disruptive challenges effectively. I tried to connect them with previous academic contributions on this theme.

This model is based on the features of the companies considered in this book, and any generalization should consider those

---

[6] The clinical studies consist of eleven international companies from seven countries. They were based on seventy-eight structured interviews with the companies' CEOs, board members and senior executives, conducted between 2014 and 2020. They also use available public information. All clinical studies except one were summarized and are available as shorter case studies, nine of them at IESE Publishing and one at Harvard Business School Publishing.

Table 1.4. *Clinical company studies: Profiles*

Company	Country	Industry	Shareholders
Almirall	Spain	Pharma	Family and listed
Amadeus	Spain/France/ Germany	Software	Listed company
Bertelsmann	Germany	Publishing and media	Foundation
Cellnex	Spain	Telecoms infrastructure	Listed company
Fluidra	Spain/US	Pools	Family and listed
Henkel	Germany	FMCG	Family and listed company
Ingka	The Netherlands	Furniture and retail	Foundation
Puig	Spain	Fashion and fragrances	Family business
Schneider Electric	France/China	Energy management	Listed company
Unilever	United Kingdom/ The Netherlands	FMCG	Listed company
Werfen	Spain	Medical diagnostics	Family business

attributes, but it provides some insights that reflect on areas where boards of directors can actually improve their effectiveness. It is consistent with the notion of boards as defined by corporate law in most OECD countries. It is a model that is also shaped by the firm's global context, the firm's current challenges, its major shareholders and key stakeholders and by ideas and regulation, as highlighted in Figure 1.1.

In this book, I argue that effective boards should think and act as good stewards beyond monitoring and compliance. Boards should shift their attention from improving short-term results toward long-term value creation, with good strategic thinking. To achieve this goal, boards should move from control to purpose and corporate culture, as major drivers of organizational performance. Boards also should evolve and move from oversight of the management team to leadership development policies and practices.

These wider perspectives define some critical tasks and functions that boards should undertake, beyond monitoring CEOs. Boards should develop the competencies to undertake these tasks and functions. The current emphasis of diversity on boards is right as it highlights the need that boards have for board members with different backgrounds and professional experiences. This is one of the signals of board members with the required competencies to serve on a board. But the board itself should develop practices and have as a team the competencies to govern the firm (Cheng, Groysberg, Healy and Vijayaraghavan, 2021) and help it tackle its main challenges. The quality of boards' competencies will help improve the quality of the boards decision-making or CEOs advisory function, and eventually have a positive impact on the firm's overall performance. Figure 1.4 presents the logic behind the notion of boards of directors' functions and tasks presented in this book and their connection with directors' competencies, board of directors' competencies, board decisions and impact.

The model of the board of directors as the firm's steward presented in this book is based on six major board functions (see Figure 1.5): define and approve a corporate purpose; establish a long-term orientation for the firm through strategy and corporate transformation; select and develop the CEO and senior management team, and prepare credible succession plans; define the culture, agenda, dynamics and guidelines of the board as a team; engage shareholders and critical stakeholders; monitor performance and assess the firm's overall impact.

A board of directors will be able to undertake these tasks and functions if individual board members have certain capabilities and

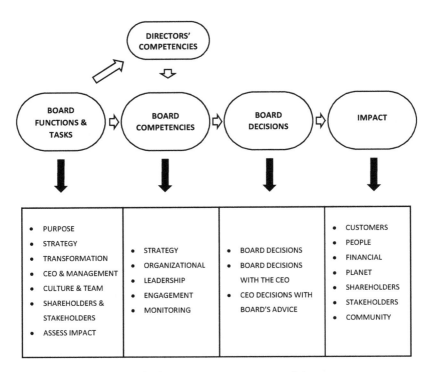

FIGURE I.4 Boards' functions, competencies and decisions

personal attributes. Individual board members' capabilities are very relevant, but are not enough. The board is a team made up of diverse individuals. They should work collegially as a team and the board should develop some competencies to be able to undertake successfully its functions. The main capabilities of the board stem from some of the major functions of the board: strategic, organizational, leadership, engagement and monitoring. The experience of the boards reviewed in this book is that the board's competencies are shaped by the board's main functions and tasks. This is the fulcrum of this book, although in discussing the board's tasks and functions, some implications for boards' competencies will ensue.

The first function is the firm's purpose. The board should understand and discuss why the firm exists and establish in cooperation

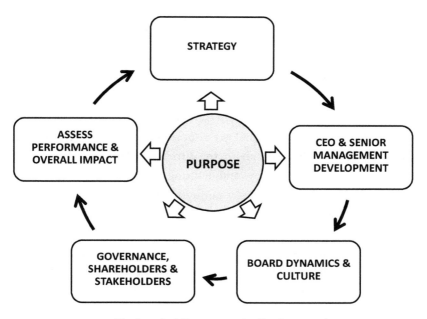

FIGURE 1.5 The board of directors as the firm's steward

with the CEO the specific customer needs the firm wants to serve in a profitable and sustainable way. Profits are a condition of success and survival but are not the specific purpose of a company (Drucker, 1973; Ghoshal, 2005; Stout, 2012; Mayer, 2018). A clear purpose can facilitate a better clarification and integration of the motivations that different parties bring to a company. It can also motivate employees and attract the talent the firm needs. It will help firms communicate better with their customers. It will clarify with investors the type of company they are investing in. Defining purpose may be easy, but implementing purpose is truly complex. Purpose is a new, central function of a board of directors.

The second function of the board of directors is to offer the firm and its shareholders and other stakeholders – for instance, customers or suppliers – a long-term orientation. The board is the responsible party for the firm's development, which requires that it spends time reflecting with the CEO on the firm's strategy. The board should not overstep and replace the senior management team in this key function but rather work with the CEO and her team. The board should not only approve a strategic plan prepared by the senior management team: It should work with the team to discuss it, check assumptions by asking the right questions, help think about scenarios, debate goals and policies and help the CEO get a more holistic perspective of the firm's future. By thinking about the firm's challenges and strategic options in an integrated way, and defining mechanisms to track execution, the board will be better equipped to help the CEO face the firm's challenges.

Strategy is not static. It involves dynamism. If market conditions change, the board should challenge the senior management team on whether the firm should change its strategy. Corporate change and transformation used to be processes that companies undertook once in a while. Amid the current disruptive climate in the business world and society, companies need to change more often and boards need to ensure the CEO is helping steer the course needed for the firm's survival.

The third board function is the process of CEO and senior managers' appointment, development, compensation and eventual succession. The choice of a new CEO is one of the most influential decisions that a board can adopt. It is also one of the most complex ones. Choosing the wrong CEO is also a prime reason why companies get into trouble. As with strategy, individual board members may have experience in choosing CEOs, but it is not the most common type of expertise in boards of directors. Moreover, success in CEO nominations is also related to a process of leadership development in the company, including senior managers and those who report to them, which becomes a key area the board should pay attention to. In the end, senior leadership development is closely connected with the firm's people development policies. Successful strategy and transformation processes depend very much on their interaction with an effective leadership development practice.

The fourth board function is related to board dynamics, the human and interpersonal dimensions of companies. A central aspect of the human perspective of boards of directors is the human reality of the board itself. The board is a group of directors who meet only occasionally, with a part-time dedication to the company and ambiguously defined goals beyond the generic duties of care and loyalty. The question of whether the board can work as an effective team is a core issue in corporate governance that has received little attention in the academic literature. The evidence presented in this book points to the high relevance of this factor for the board's effectiveness.

A company is made up of people with concrete tasks and responsibilities, who should be respected, engaged and developed with the board's support. Corporate culture is a key dimension in talent attraction and development. Moreover, corporate culture can have an impact on setting goals, defining corporate strategy and designing compensation schemes for managers and employees, as the Wells Fargo experience illustrates. Investors and regulators are increasingly concerned about how the board of directors monitors and shapes the firm's culture.

The fifth function of the board as the firm's steward is to guarantee that the company has the functional and clear governance system to develop it for the future and attract the right shareholders who understand the firm's purpose and strategy. The board – through the chairman, CEO or CFO – should define clear guidelines to engage with shareholders, beyond some financial commitments regarding dividend policies or other financial dimensions. Loyal shareholders should make the effort to know the company well, and boards of directors should make sure that their concerns are taken into account, even if the decisions that some shareholders may advocate are not considered by the board. The board, not shareholders, should govern the company, but shareholders, as well as other significant stakeholders, have a say on the company's development. The board should also provide clear guidelines on how senior managers should engage key stakeholders.

The sixth function of the board of directors is to assess the firm's overall impact, including financial performance. Companies should disclose information following the guidelines defined by regulators for each jurisdiction. Nevertheless, a board has the duty to explain which goals the firm pursues, how they meet shareholders' and different stakeholders' expectations, the firm's strategy and strategic decisions and how they support the firm's purpose. The board should use an integrated – and simple – framework to report the firm's performance, including relevant financial and nonfinancial dimensions. This is a demanding function for boards of directors, but a consequence of a more holistic view of boards involved in defining a purpose for a company, crafting strategy, developing people and supporting the firm's culture. The board should regularly assess its effectiveness in advancing the firm's purpose and diverse goals.

This model of boards of directors defines an aspiration for boards that meets their legal duties of monitoring top management and the firm's performance but transcends these goals. Moreover, it defines key areas and drivers that are indispensable to achieve these goals. This model also helps consider boards from the perspective of the professional competencies that board members, and the board as a team, require in order to be effective. In some cases, boards' nominating committees use a list of needed board competences – such as finance, digital transformation and cross-cultural skills – and how capable different board members should be in each one of them. This is useful but may not suffice. The board should make sure that it can successfully manage major business and social challenges. This model can help the board reflect on them.

In Table 1.5, I present a simple framework that relates each main board function and the board's professional competencies. These areas are organized in four categories: knowledge and experience, capabilities, soft skills and personal attitudes and values (Canals, 2012). The board can use this framework to assess regularly the level of competency of the board and individual board members in these basic functions.

Table 1.5. *The board of directors: Key functions and competencies*

	Knowledge	Capabilities	Soft Skills	Personal Attitudes
1. Purpose • Notion of purpose • Integration into strategy • Purpose and values				
2. Corporate Strategy • Strategic challenges • Strategy • Transformation				
3. CEO and Senior Managers • CEO • Senior management • Leadership development				
4. Human Side of Boards • Corporate culture • The culture of the board • The board as a team				
5. Governance • Engaging shareholders • Managing stakeholders • Quality of governance				
6. The Firm's Overall Impact • Financial performance • People and leadership • Customers • Planet • Suppliers and other stakeholders • Local communities				

In the following chapters, I will present and discuss the key functions of the board as the firm's steward. This framework includes yet transcends compliance. I present and develop this model through propositions based on theory and empirical evidence from companies examined in this book. In each chapter, I develop ways in which boards can work on the firm's strategic challenges in collaboration with the top management team. In this process, some relevant principles and notions for boards of directors emerge. The first is that firms are relevant social institutions that have – or possibly have – a purpose, as well as explicit goals to achieve. Defining and nurturing a corporate purpose is a pathway for companies to foster strategic thinking, customer loyalty and employee development, as well as manage diverse shareholder and stakeholder expectations, establish boundaries on what to do and what not to do and structure key strategic decisions. Boards of directors should play a role in all of these realms and protect the firm's purpose.

The second principle is that the board should help develop the company as an organization for long-term value creation. Board members should encourage long-term thinking and offer a perspective of where the company should be in a few years' time; understand the industry in which the company operates, its customers and competitors; discuss the company's strategy and business model with the top management team; and define an aspiration and set some goals for the type of company that it wants to be.

The third principle is that boards should look after the survival and successful transformation of companies, which are currently under tremendous pressure to change. The role of the board in transformation is unique, although very different from the roles of the CEO and top management team. Defining the board's responsibilities and functions in corporate transformation is among the critical features of a good board of directors.

The fourth principle is getting the right CEO and senior management team for the firm. Boards that aspire to develop companies for the long term should move beyond financial goals and metrics, and support the development of the CEO, management team and talent pool, as well as succession plans. People make a difference and boards should help companies in moving from financial performance to investing in people to boost innovation and performance. People development is indispensable for a competitive and dynamic company. Boards of directors should also get involved and oversee this process.

The fifth principle is that corporate culture and values are important attributes of good companies. Culture is considered to be the responsibility of the CEO and senior management team. Nevertheless, the sheer importance of culture in fostering a positive work context means the board needs to understand, assess and shape it. Boards that think long term need to move beyond compliance to promoting a healthy corporate culture that encourages positive individual and corporate behavior. Collaboration is a key ingredient of a healthy culture. Boards should shift from monitoring the CEO to collaboration. CEOs and senior managers are accountable to the board of directors and the entire team, and boards are accountable to shareholders, regulators and the entire organization. Boards need to go beyond monitoring management and become a team capable of working with the top management to develop the firm for the long term.

The sixth principle is that effective boards should engage actively with shareholders, listen to them, learn from their suggestions and make sure the company has the shareholder structure that best supports the company's purpose. It should also engage relevant stakeholders in a constructive dialogue and gain their views and commitment to the long-term development of the firm.

The seventh principle is to ensure that environmental (E) and social (S) policies are coherently integrated in the corporate purpose, strategy and people development strategy. The board should also support effective and transparent governance guidelines (the G factor). The example set over the years by successful companies that have taken ESG dimensions seriously shows that integrating these dimensions into the firm's strategy is a key success factor.

Finally, financial performance is indispensable, but boards should also help assess the firm's overall impact. Economic performance needs to be complemented by other performance indicators related to the firm's talent pool, customers, pattern of learning and innovation and contributions to addressing externalities, such as carbon emissions. Boards need to consider both financial and nonfinancial goals.

Boards of directors that develop their function following these guidelines will have a deeper and more positive impact on companies and society. I define these boards as the firm's stewards, institutions that think and act long term, with entrepreneurial initiative and collegiality, and are accountable to shareholders and stakeholders. They truly support the firm's long-term development.

1.7 FINAL REFLECTIONS

In this chapter, I examined the evolution of boards of directors over the past few decades and presented some arguments for the renewal of the role of the board of directors. The combination of new corporate challenges, technology disruption, dispersed ownership, investor activism and environmental and social issues drives the need for change in boards of directors. The CEO and top management team play a critical role in leading the company. The collaboration between the board and the CEO requires a new perspective: how the board and top management team – led by the CEO – can work together in a more cooperative and productive way for the company's long-term development.

The current model of boards of directors should evolve toward a more holistic perspective of the board's role and functions, focused on the firm's long-term development. The board as the firm's steward model offers a holistic framework to assess and design the functions, agenda and work of boards of directors. It focuses on central functions and responsibilities of boards of directors overlooked in the current model, such as their role in forging corporate purpose, strategy, corporate culture and leadership development.

This model of boards includes some key functions that define the core areas the board should support: corporate purpose, strategy and transformation, appointing and developing the CEO and key managers, nurturing the firm's culture, developing the board as a team and assessing the firm's impact.

In particular, I highlight the human, interpersonal relationships of the board, both among board members and between the board and the senior management team. It is very relevant to consider the board as a team, a group with its own decision-making process, which needs to be effective in order to fulfill its mission. In any company, the CEO and senior managers are not only agents to be monitored; they serve as key actors in developing successful companies. Interaction and collaboration between the board of directors and the top management team based on professionalism and integrity are essential for good governance.

2　Boards of Directors and Purpose

From Monitoring to Stewards of the Firm's Purpose

2.1 THE VALUE OF PURPOSE IN THE FIRM'S LONG-TERM ORIENTATION: CORPORATE TRANSFORMATION AT INGKA[1]

The role of the board of directors in recent corporate crises at Bayer, Boeing, Facebook, GE, Volkswagen, WeWork and Wirecard, among others, offers a reminder that the quality of the boards' work matters. Asset managers with significant shareholdings are asking boards to be more accountable for the firm's strategy and its environmental and social impacts. Moreover, the list of ESG (environmental, social and governance) factors that investors want boards to consider keeps getting longer.

Corporate purpose can help boards by providing a coherent framework to address some of these issues. Some experts and investors even suggest that companies adopt a formal purpose beyond profitability. Regulators in France and the United Kingdom recently passed laws requiring listed companies to adopt a statement of purpose. Is this the right way forward for companies? Can purpose improve the quality of governance and the work of boards? If so, how can it be implemented effectively?

Empirical evidence on the impact of corporate purpose on performance is increasingly clear.[2] Companies that include dimensions of purpose in their strategy also show slightly higher economic

---

[1] This section is based on Masclans and Canals (2021).

[2] According to most of these studies, companies that include some dimensions of purpose in their strategy and business model also show slightly superior economic performance. See, among others, Edmans (2011); Eccles, Ioannou and Serafeim (2014); Flammer (2015); Ferrell, Liang and Renneboog (2017); Ioannou and Serafeim (2019) and Gartenberg, Prat and Serafeim (2019).

performance. The challenge for companies is no longer a question of why purpose is important, but how boards of directors can adopt purpose effectively.

Over the past decade, some companies have forged fresh paths by introducing the notion of purpose in their strategies and business models, moving beyond statements of purpose to truly integrate this principle into their strategy and operations. Ingka is one of them.

In June 2020, Ingka's CEO Jesper Brodin and deputy CEO Juvencio Maeztu were pondering how to rethink fundamental corporate governance questions and deliberate them with the board of directors. Ingka was the retail arm of Ikea, the world's largest furniture maker. Ikea and Ingka had a strong sense of mission in society, inspired by their founder, Ingvar Kamprad. Ikea was one of the world's most advanced companies in terms of its environmental impact and inclusiveness. Both Brodin and Maeztu were proud of this achievement, but felt the company could do an even better job by introducing corporate purpose into the heart of Ingka's strategic decision-making.

Moved by a strong entrepreneurial drive, Ingvar Kamprad founded Ikea in 1943 in Småland, in the south of Sweden. It started off as a mail-order business for pencils, postcards and similar merchandise. Kamprad soon entered the furniture manufacturing market and explored innovative solutions such as furniture design, self-assembly and advertising in order to differentiate its products from competitors. In 1951, Ikea published its first furniture catalog and in 1953, opened a showroom where customers could experience its products before ordering them. In the early 1960s, Kamprad's sense of innovation disrupted the furniture industry in Sweden and other European countries.

Kamprad believed Ikea's sense of mission and corporate values would serve as the company's key drivers. In 1976, he published the booklet "The Testament of a Furniture Dealer," in which he summarized Ikea's mission: "To create a better everyday life for the many." He also highlighted the core values that should guide Ikea's operations. These values were still present in 2021 and were aimed at guiding all managerial decision-making. Kamprad also had a specific perspective on governance. In 1977, he divided the ownership of Ikea into two companies: Ingka, which included the retail business, and Inter Ikea, which included the management of the Ikea concept, brand and franchise system. He also established two foundations as the sole shareholders: the Interogo Foundation, the owner of Inter Ikea; and the Stichting Ingka Foundation, the owner of Ingka.

Ikea's business model and ownership structure helped the company thrive, with high organic growth from the 1980s through the 2000s. Ingka was initially responsible for product design, supply chain and production, logistics, retail, store management and sales growth, and became a linchpin in Ikea's business success. It focused its strategy on a unique retail model in different markets, while maintaining Ikea's vision and culture. Ingka was strongly committed to sustainability, which played a central role in its business model. Innovation was also a core pillar in Kamprad's model. Ingka managers pushed for innovation in product design, packaging and logistics. The company offered products adapted to ever-changing customer needs.

The mission of Ikea's founder permeated the firm's culture and values and underpinned myriad decisions. Ingka's management team had developed a series of questions to articulate its purpose around Kamprad's vision and to assess the strength of the firm's purpose. The first question was: Is the notion of purpose well articulated? The second question was: Does this notion of purpose inspire our people? The results of several employee surveys reflected a deep understanding of the firm's purpose and its role in engaging people and providing meaning to their daily activities. At the same time, these surveys underscored areas for improvement.

The third question was: Is purpose integrated into Ingka's strategy and operations? In recent top management meetings, there was a shared view that the concept of purpose was well defined and inspired people, but could be better integrated in strategy and operations.

The fourth question was: Do our people and customers recognize our purpose? The founder's approach was to share little about the company and surprise customers with the final product. But there was also the sense that a company with nearly 200,000 employees could do much more to better communicate its purpose and new initiatives.

With the aim of strengthening the link between purpose and values, Brodin and Maeztu held many meetings with managers in 2019. Various initiatives were adopted to make purpose more explicit within the organization. The first involved a deep reflection on corporate growth and furniture sales. This led to an assessment of new business models, including selling secondhand furniture, renting furniture and offering furniture repair services. A core consideration was how far Ingka should diverge from its current focus on furniture and basic elements for homes.

A second initiative, as the company advanced its digital business operations, was to define a set of ethical rules that would govern the use of customer data. Ingka made a clear commitment to not use data to sell more to current customers. It justified the use of data to get to know customers better, but not to offer them goods or services that might fit their profiles.

A third initiative sought to boost Ingka's engagement with its stakeholders. Senior managers believed the company should become an activist voice in major social issues such as climate change, diversity and inclusiveness.

A fourth initiative focused on how the notion of purpose could help renovate the traditional retail business. Amid changing consumer behavior, an upsurge in online sales and the emergence of new competitors, business growth in stores had been diminishing since 2014. In this area, the challenge was to make sure customers kept returning to Ikea stores thanks to an outstanding value proposition.

Ingka's journey had been very successful. The role of mission in its evolution was accepted by all major stakeholders as a fundamental pillar. At the same time, Ingka had to undergo a fundamental transformation process that involved greater investment in online sales, with a different business model and lower margins. This entailed less investment in traditional stores and city centers.

The evolution to become a multichannel company was also urgent. Yet the governance criteria and mechanisms, including financial criteria, were anchored in the traditional retail model. This led to numerous reflections on how the company should evolve, how it should adapt its governance to adopt new business models and the role of Ingka's purpose in this process.

Defining corporate purpose and articulating corporate strategy, policies and activities around purpose, as well as new performance measurement systems, are responsibilities of board directors and CEOs. These are complex tasks. The experience at Ingka suggests that introducing corporate purpose at the core of a company is a long-term commitment and requires strongly determined board and CEO, excellent management and constant renewal. In this way, corporate purpose can become a powerful engine in the transformation process of a company.

Based on clinical cases of specific companies, this chapter offers a framework to help boards of directors and senior management teams effectively discuss and adopt corporate purpose. I review the origins of corporate purpose in Section 2.2. The different perspectives of the notion of purpose are discussed in Section 2.3. In Section 2.4, I present a framework with the basic elements to articulate a notion of purpose for boards of directors. In Section 2.5, I introduce a model to help boards of directors' work on corporate purpose and discuss the potential impact of purpose on the board's decisions, including strategic acquisitions or divestments, hiring and developing CEOs and senior managers and executive compensation.

2.2   THE ORIGINS OF CORPORATE PURPOSE

The notion of purpose has relevant roots in the field of management.[3] It includes the work of pioneering management thinkers in the first

---

[3] Corporate law also has a rich tradition in dealing with corporate purpose. For a wider view of corporate purpose in corporate law, see Stout (2012), Mocsary (2016), Fisch and Solomon (2020) and Rock (2020), among others. In this chapter the focus is on the field of management.

half of the twentieth century (Barnard, 1938; Drucker, 1955) and other scholars in more recent decades, including Selznick (1957); Andrews (1971); Donaldson and Lorsch (1983); Bartlett and Ghoshal (1994); Khurana (2004); Canals (2010b); Birkinshaw, Foss and Lindenberg (2014); Mayer (2013, 2018); Gartenberg, Pratt and Serafeim (2019); Quinn and Thakor (2019); Blount and Leinwand (2019); Henderson (2020) and Edmans (2020), among others.[4] Henderson and Van den Steen (2015) and Henderson and Serafeim (2020) have further opened this debate in the field of organizational economics.

As Davoudi, McKenna and Olegario (2018) pointed out, the original concept of the corporation in Roman Law included a sense of purpose: "From the *piae causae* of Ancient Rome to Medieval monasteries and the City of London, corporations have been purveyors of education, civic administration, public works, philanthropy and spiritual engagement for millennia." In the Renaissance and the modern era, some European governments gave corporations the license to operate under the condition of providing goods for society or its citizens in a fair way. Until the mid-nineteenth century, this was the condition under which companies were created, with investors offering a certain degree of state protection and limited liabilities (Fisch and Solomon, 2020; Rock, 2020).

With the industrial revolution, the development of capitalism and new growth opportunities triggered by technical change, the role of profits in financing new ventures and motivating entrepreneurs became more powerful. The emergence of stock exchanges and the growing number of listed companies reinforced the importance of financial performance and investors' protection. But this motivation never excluded the action and motivation of entrepreneurs with the

---

[4] With a clear interdisciplinary approach, with scholars from the fields of corporate finance, corporate law, organizational economics and strategic management, IESE and ECGI organized the 2020 Conference on Corporate Governance around the theme "Can Corporate Purpose Improve Corporate Governance?" The main contributions were published in the *Journal of Applied Corporate Finance*, 2021, 33 (2).

drive and desire to wield a positive social impact through their business. As O'Toole (2019) documented in his excellent book about enlightened capitalists, the past two centuries have seen many entrepreneurs use business to address some of the world's most chronic and entrenched problems, outside the realm of philanthropy.

At the heart of these businesses, there was a core ideology on higher purpose beyond making money. The value of ethical principles was not only connected with the notion of purpose, or the hypothesis that ethics is good for business. In many cases, ethics was understood as a set of principles to show respect for every person, employee or customer. For the leaders of those businesses, respect for human dignity and service to the common good were principles that transcended other criteria or management practices. These entrepreneurs also considered philanthropy a good practice, but sought to have a positive social impact through their companies' operations.

This view of companies and entrepreneurs and their connection with society was implicit in the development of capitalism in Western Europe in the nineteenth and twentieth centuries. Even in countries and industries where shareholder profitability was the foremost criteria, it was assumed that businesses should contribute to society as an implicit notion in the social contract between companies and society. Governments gave companies the license to operate in exchange for providing social good, while avoiding social harm. As Drucker (1973) observed years before the CSR movement, "[f]ree enterprise cannot be justified as being good for business; it can be justified only as being good for society."

The profit motivation always played a role in capitalism, but in the United States, a stronger notion of shareholder primacy was emerging. Berle (1931) and Berle and Means (1932) sparked an important debate on the growing dispersion of ownership in US–listed firms in the early 1900s and the power of CEOs and senior management in defining the company's goals and strategy. The primacy of shareholders – the paradigm in governance – started to gain support in part, as a reaction to protect minority shareholders from senior management follies. However, the notion of minority shareholders without legal protection in the Berle and Means perspective does not reflect the reality of ownership today. In the United States and Western Europe, professional asset managers own nearly 65 percent of the shares of listed companies and have specific responsibilities and leverage to remove CEOs and board directors if they deem it appropriate (Rock, 2020; OECD, 2021).

Around the same time as Berle and Means' contribution, Dodd (1932) expressed a different view of the firm: Companies are not simply vehicles to generate shareholder returns but social entities whose interests are shared by multiple groups or constituencies. This is one of the early foundations of the multi-stakeholder view of the firm. Dodd's definition of the firm suggests that companies have some common interests that different parties pursue. Drucker (1955) expanded on this reasoning, considering that the purpose of a firm is to have and serve customers. Berle and Means supported the notion of shareholder primacy. Dodd and Drucker, the stakeholder vision. Each perspective focused on a specific goal: either profit maximization (shareholder primacy perspective) or value creation for all (the multi-stakeholder view). In between these extremes, different options can be found, including combinations of profit and purpose – or purpose and profit, depending on the individual's perspective.

In the 1970s and 1980s, shareholder primacy and profit maximization gained traction with Friedman (1962, 1970), Ross (1973), Jensen and Meckling (1976) and Fama and Jensen (1983), among others. These ideas gained strength in the 1980s, with the explosion of hostile takeovers and highly leveraged MBOs. The radical deregulation of capital markets in the United States and the United Kingdom in the 1980s, and increasing pressure to place shareholder primacy above any business activity – a trend originated in academia (Rappaport, 1986; Jensen 1989) and in the investment banking world – contributed to its acceptance (Cheffins, 2019). Maximizing shareholder value became the new business mantra. Outsourcing, first, and globalization and offshoring, later, were considered drivers of higher corporate performance, irrespective of their longer term impact on companies and societies at large. Shareholder returns became the overwhelming metrics of success. The opening of emerging markets and the internet revolution in the mid-1990s gave incredible power to these ideas. In this context, employees were gradually viewed primarily as human resources. Work could be outsourced and individuals could be readily hired and fired, without other considerations beyond effectiveness and financial performance.

The goal of maximizing shareholders' value, coupled with the savings glut in global capital markets in the 1990s and the early 2000s, increased the pressure on companies to increase short-term economic value for shareholders. The global economy became more integrated, dominated by finance and disrupted by digital technology. Companies such as Amazon, Facebook and Google led a huge disintermediation process, provoking the obsolescence of innumerable firms operating as retailers or distributors of goods and services. The prevalent lax monetary policy and aggressive bank lending during this time made it easier for companies and families to increase their borrowing, and pushed lenders and investors to misallocate financial resources by mispricing risk.

The eruption of the 2008 financial crisis brought the world economy to the brink of collapse and, for a while, the excess of irrational borrowing and lending appeared to end. But the global savings surplus and lax monetary policies of previous years still left investors in search of profitable destinations for their savings. Investors viewed companies as mere assets in their portfolios, putting the pressure on companies to deliver short-term profits.

An upturn in unemployment and precarious working conditions, together with declines in income and social welfare coverage, were a lethal combination for many citizens in many countries following the 2008 financial crisis. Social and political activists in the United States and Europe began targeting companies that had cut jobs and reduced investments while simultaneously boosting profits or cash dividends to their investors, as well as banks that had sought government bailouts. Against this backdrop, populism began to reemerge in many Western countries.

The overall impact of the principle of shareholder maximization has been controversial. The debate about whether it created benefits for the many or only for the few (e.g., the top 1 percent) is still an open question and a source of heated debate triggered in particular by Piketty (2014). Investors and, to some extent, boards of directors have focused too much on short-term performance at the expense of long-term sustainable value creation (Barton and Wiseman, 2014; Bower and Paine, 2017). In developed countries today, a widespread view among the public is that companies have become institutions that are disconnected from people and generate low levels of trust (*Edelman Trust Barometer*, 2020, 2021). As Hill (2020b) pointed out, the debate has become a binary contest.

The pressure to replace the paradigm of shareholder value maximization by notions of purpose is growing among asset managers. Impact investors such as Norges Bank, TCI, ValueAct Capital and Hermes, family offices and large asset managers such as BlackRock, Vanguard and State Street, among others, emphasize the need for companies to come to terms with a more complex reality. These asset managers invest in all industries across economies and cannot externalize social and environmental costs. For this reason, they are pressuring firms to consider the ESG–related costs and risks of their operations. Moreover, large asset managers have started calling for companies to define a purpose, look after the environment, explain how they nurture a positive corporate culture and report on ESG factors. They have embraced the view that purpose and corporate culture shape behaviors and might eventually impact the firm's capability to create sustainable economic value.

Regulators are also stepping in. A prime example is the Global Financial Stability Group, a group of thirty-five central banks that wrote a letter in April 2019 asking banks and financial institutions to include climate change risks in their estimates of overall risk, as well as the impact of climate change in the risk profile of each bank. This initiative was accepted by major central banks around the world and unleashed a wave of actions. The European Central Bank announced that it would conduct the first climate risk stress tests for Eurozone banks in spring 2022. The steps taken by the United Kingdom's Financial Reporting Council (2018) and the French 2019 governance code encouraging boards of directors to reflect on their firms' purpose also mark an inflection point in the matter of purpose at the regulatory level.

Driven by investors, asset managers and regulators, these forces are tipping points for corporate governance. They are pushing boards of directors to define their firm's purpose and think more deeply about their wider social impact.[5] As Mayer (2018), Eccles and Klimenko (2019) and Henderson (2020) point out, regulators and investors will put additional pressure on companies in the coming years to include these social and environmental dimensions in their reporting. Nonetheless, most asset managers and shareholders need to change their mindsets, investment criteria and frameworks. In parallel academia, investment banks and consulting firms should offer new paradigms for decision-making.

An important driver behind the push to reconsider the role of purpose is the evolving perception of companies in society. Firms' reputations have scarcely recovered since the 2008 financial crisis and the trust gap between firms and society remains wide. Younger generations hold increasingly unfavorable views about companies due to

---

[5] The August 2019 Business Roundtable statement on corporate purpose underlines this change in perception in society and how business leaders in large US companies react. This statement supports the view of the company as a multi-stakeholder institution that should consider the interests of different stakeholders, not only shareholders. With this statement, the Business Roundtable reverted to its 1981 positioning on multi-stakeholder institutions, a position that changed in 1997 when it clearly pivoted toward the notion of shareholder primacy. The World Economic Forum (2020) issued a statement highlighting the importance of companies becoming multi-stakeholder organizations, going back to some previously expressed in 1973. See Bebchuk and Tallarita (2022) for a critical view of these statements. Mayer (2020) provides support for stakeholder management.

their perceived indifference toward the social and environmental problems generated through their activities. They see that large, established organizations might not offer a sense of purpose about what they do. If companies want to continue to attract talented professionals, they need to understand these social and environmental factors. The role of companies in society is an important driver in motivating and engaging young professionals. The COVID-19 crisis might offer companies the opportunity to change course and set things right. Otherwise, their reputations might be at risk for another heavy blow.

It is in this business context that companies such as Ingka, Unilever and Schneider Electric, among others, have become increasingly relevant because their core decisions are guided by a clear sense of purpose. The experience of these firms is pertinent since they are helping forge new performance and accountability paradigms, while serving as groundbreaking references for other firms. These organizations are not perfect. They do not provide definitive models or approaches, but instead offer useful insights on how corporate purpose can anchor business activities and operations, and connect with strategy, culture and organizational design. In the end, these companies reveal the innovative power of management and its capacity to develop strong pillars of respect, social commitment and accountability to shareholders and stakeholders. These factors provide solid foundations for sustainable reputation and performance.

2.3 CAN WE AGREE ON A NAME? DIFFERENT PERSPECTIVES ON CORPORATE PURPOSE

Over the past few decades, the dominance of the shareholder value maximization paradigm has overshadowed the role of purpose in management theory and practice. The recent interest in purpose has inspired a multitude of initiatives – companies expressing their purpose in unique ways – in tandem with scholars' efforts to define this concept and extrapolate its implications for boards of directors, management and regulators.

A growing number of CEOs are adopting this approach.[6] As the long-standing CEO of Medtronic, Bill George observed, "[t]he real bottom line of the corporation is not earnings per share, but service to humankind" (Melé and Corrales, 2005). In this section, I highlight complementary notions and approaches to corporate purpose. In the following section, I describe the core elements of corporate purpose relevant for corporate governance.

There is no unique, widely accepted notion of corporate purpose. Moreover, the notions of purpose and mission have often been used interchangeably by management scholars in recent decades.[7] Both terms seek to ask the vital questions of why a firm exists and how it plans to achieve its explicit goals. Some management scholars described these questions as the purpose of the firm (among others, Barnard, 1938; Drucker, 1955; Selznick, 1957; Andrews, 1971; Collins and Porras, 1996; Kouzes and Posner, 2017). Other authors used the notion of mission[8] (Drucker, 1973; Pearce and David, 1987; Duane Ireland and Hitt, 1992 or Kaplan and Norton, 2001, among others).

---

[6] See the interesting discussions on corporate purpose and the firm's goals between Bengt Holmstrom and Paul Polman, and between Colin Mayer and Luigi Zingales, in the IESE ECGI 2020 Corporate Governance Conference (Holmstrom and Polman, 2021; Mayer and Zingales, 2021).

[7] In the management literature, mission and purpose have been widely used over the past decades to refer to the same reality. The Oxford Dictionary offers some useful distinctions. It defines purpose as "the reason for which something is done or created, or for which something exists." This noun comes from Latin, "propositum," which refers to something that has an end. It defines mission as "a strongly felt aim, ambition or calling." This noun comes from the verb "mitto," to charge someone with a specific end.

[8] The firm's purpose is different from a vision statement. Purpose explains why a company exists. The firm's vision expresses an aspiration on what the firm is trying to become (Collins and Porras, 1996) through specific decisions and policies. Each perspective complements the other. Kamprad' s vision for Ikea – to create a better life for the many – is more a reflection on purpose than a business vision, even if his colleagues still refer to it as the founder's vision. A corporate purpose is not about the projected financial benefits of a certain competitive positioning or an efficient business model. It is an explanation of why a company exists, what it aspires to do for its customers and people, its impact on society, and how it tries to balance these ends while also creating economic value.

Some notions of purpose highlight serving customers as the first priority (Drucker, 1955). Others underscore the role of employees and their motivation and engagement (Henderson and Van den Steen, 2015; Gartenberg, Prat and Serafeim, 2019). Some scholars suggest that purpose does not intrinsically entail a pro-social aim for the firm (Henderson and van den Steen, 2015). Other authors go a step further and support this pro-social stance. As Quinn and Thakor (2019) suggest, purpose is something perceived as producing a social benefit over and above the tangible pecuniary payoff shared by the principal and the agent. This is an open question and one that should defer to the business judgment of the company's board of directors.

In practice, the origin of purpose in each company is unique. In some firms, corporate purpose is defined by the firm's founder (Ingka). In others, it was up to the firm's top management and board of directors to define or renew it (Unilever and Schneider Electric). The rest of this section explores relevant perspectives on the notion of purpose, based upon different goals and stakeholders.

2.2.1 Purpose as Serving Customers First

Drucker (1955) offers a good starting point. He explains that, in general, the purpose of a company is to attract a customer while making a profit to cover the risk of business activities and avoid losses. Management should aim for this goal and employees should work in a coordinated and engaged way to serve customers. Two decades later, Drucker (1973) described the relationship between purpose and objectives: "[A] business is not defined by its name, statutes or articles of incorporation. It is defined by the business' mission." Drucker offers a simple view of purpose but one that contains a number of important components: a focus on explicit objectives, people engagement, the need for efficiency and economic value creation and the role of management. It is also a notion that can embrace a pro-business or a pro-social slant – or a combination thereof – in the firm's orientation, but is not bound by the notion of shareholder value maximization.

2.2.2   Purpose as the Function That Company Aspires to Perform in Society

Mayer (2018) proposes that "the purpose of the corporation is to do things that address the problems confronting us as customers and communities, suppliers and shareholders, employees and retirees." Profits are not the purpose of the corporation but an outcome. This definition leads to a broader perspective on purpose. He also points out that corporate purpose is neither a definition nor an aspiration: It is a specific perspective on a problem that the company wants to solve.[9]

Companies may use purpose to publish anodyne statements that serve for public relations but have little impact on the company's management or performance. When considering corporate purpose, board directors and CEOs should be wary of these good intentions. While these declarations may be noble, they may create new problems if not implemented well, including their perception as mere "window dressing" and the negative reputational impact this connotes. The growing importance of purpose in corporate governance has sparked a wave of initiatives to ensure its proper place in the governance structure.

Purpose should not be reduced to a statement or guidelines. It is a central pillar of the firm's corporate governance and management model. Companies should be explicit about the specific contribution they aspire to make: how they address concrete needs with a business solution. Corporate purpose should offer clarity on a firm's contribution and underpin its strategy, organizational culture and business model. Strategy, organization and policies should be articulated around the unique value proposition or service it seeks to provide to customers (Canals, 2010a).

---

[9] *The Principles for Purposeful Business* (2019), an innovative project sponsored by the British Academy and led by Colin Mayer, defined the purpose of business as "to solve the problems of people and planet profitably, and not profit from causing problems." A corporate purpose defines how an organization helps people and society address some challenges and tries to minimize the problems that companies can create.

2.2.3 Purpose, Employee's Identity and Reputation

Henderson and Van den Steen (2015) define purpose as the firm's concrete goal or objective beyond profit maximization. This notion is simple, yet also clearly highlights purpose as a goal or project that surpasses financial performance. As a result, it is possible to infer that maximizing shareholder value or economic profits, in and of itself, is not a purpose. More specifically, Henderson and Van den Steen present a model that explains how firms can create value through purpose by supporting impact investment or other social dimensions of their activities, as well as by reinforcing employees' identities and reputation. This view offers a specific channel through which purpose can be translated into higher economic performance.

Using this definition of purpose, Gartenberg, Prat and Serafeim (2019) elaborate on the relationship between purpose and performance. This notion allows these authors to measure the beliefs of employees in the meaning and impact of their work. These two features – meaning and impact – capture two dimensions of corporate purpose and its relevance for employees. This is interesting because they include how purpose shapes employees' attitudes and engagement, which can make a true difference in the life of any company, including a positive impact on performance.

2.2.4 PURPOSE AS A MORAL RESPONSE TO THE FIRM'S CHALLENGES

Bartlett and Ghoshal (1994) connected purpose with the firm's wider responsibilities. Purpose is "the statement of a company's moral response to its broadly defined responsibilities, not an amoral plan for exploiting commercial opportunity." They support a shift from strategy, structure and systems to a model built on purpose, process and people. The primary role of top management, in their view, is not to set strategy, but instead to instill a sense for shared purpose. A key challenge in this definition is whether a board of directors or senior managers are subjected to the shareholder primacy principle – as some scholars and corporate lawyers suggest – or whether they have the discretion to exercise their business judgment and consider other stakeholder expectations with a view for long-term value creation (see Fisch and Solomon, 2020; Rock, 2020).

A corporate purpose provides an umbrella for the distinct motivations that individuals in an organization may have. Different people bring a variety of motivations to their daily work. As Barnard (1938), Selznick (1957), Pérez López (1993) and Ghoshal and Moran (1996), among others, pointed out, individuals may experience different types of motivation. The first is extrinsic motivation, defined by the pursuit of external goals such as money, status, reputation or recognition. The value of these motivations is related to the decision maker's satisfaction derived from these external factors. The second is the intrinsic motivation to achieve goals pursued for their own sake, because they generate positive outcomes in and of themselves, such as learning, satisfaction for getting things done or a sense of accomplishment. This motivation is not related to external factors. Pérez López (1993) also defined a third type of motivation: transcendent motivation, by which people do things for the sake of serving others. They generate personal satisfaction when other people are able to benefit from one's work or contribution. This notion is consistent with the empirical results of Gartenberg, Prat and Serafeim (2019).

Corporate purpose does not exclude extrinsic motives. Good organizations need them. Purpose simply frames them through a wider lens. In any organization, work with others in a cooperative and coordinated way is indispensable since the company exists to serve customer needs. Serving customers not only requires knowledge and financial resources, but capabilities that enable people to serve customers sustainably. Purpose can help people work collaboratively and may develop unique corporate advantages. This may be one of the reasons – together with investors' unique preferences and choices – behind the growing number of asset managers who include purpose as a criterion to assess the quality of the firm's corporate governance, as well as the upsurge in investors focused on impact investment (Yan, Ferraro and Almandoz, 2018). In this way, a corporate purpose helps integrate these different motivations into an overarching goal for the company, one that transcends financial indicators. While these are vital for its development, they are not the only measure of organizational success.

In time, purpose will encourage positive attitudes and contribute toward a virtuous circle: Purpose drives motivation, motivation increases engagement, engagement boosts cooperation among colleagues, engagement and cooperation foster innovation and better customer service and better service leads to higher sales and performance.

2.2.5 Purpose and Stakeholders

Purpose helps articulate the notion of a multi-stakeholder company (Freeman, 1984; Melé, 2009; Porter and Kramer, 2011; Bower and Paine, 2017; Lipton, 2019). As examined in the case of Ingka, corporate purpose – when placed at the heart of the organization and interweaved into its strategies and policies – sheds light on the role of the firm's different stakeholders. It can help the firm better align stakeholder expectations by offering clarity on the company's intentions and how it considers different stakeholders' contributions.[10]

Salter (2019) introduces an interesting dimension related to stakeholders' expressions of purpose. He supports the principle of reciprocity as the foundation of relationships among different stakeholders. Reciprocity is closely connected to collaboration in the workplace and required for organizations to be effective. Originally defined by Aristotle,[11] this principle opens up a new perspective in corporate

---

[10] See Bebchuk and Tallarita (2021a) for a summary of problems related to the stakeholder view of the firm.

[11] Some of the basic notions on companies and individuals are associated with different schools of philosophy. See Aristotle, *Ethics to Nicomach*. Melé (2009) offers useful frameworks on how Aristotle's notions of fairness and justice can help develop the notion of corporate purpose and in time, make companies more human.

purpose by allowing expressions of purpose to reflect the interests of different parties. Each party may have different interests. Each party has different minimum goals of fair returns. Companies – especially public companies with dispersed shareholders – are free to pursue a wide variety of purposes; their only constraint are duties toward different parties. Reciprocity enhances commitment and collaboration.

2.2.6   A Holistic Notion of Purpose

Purpose expresses a company's reason for being and the customer needs it aspires to serve in a profitable and sustainable way and with a positive impact on all stakeholders (Canals, 2010a, 2010b). By using this notion, corporate purpose should make explicit why the company exists, what it strives to achieve in serving its customers, how it relies on its people and other stakeholders, how it aims to operate and simultaneously create economic value and what impact its operations have on the planet and society. This definition of purpose allows the inclusion of ESG factors that a company needs or wants to consider, but goes beyond these factors and aims to integrate them into the firm's strategy.

2.4   CORPORATE PURPOSE: KEY NOTIONS FOR BOARDS OF DIRECTORS AND SENIOR MANAGERS

In the debate on corporate purpose, the real challenge for companies is not the convenience of corporate purpose. The impact of purpose indicators on corporate performance is positive. The challenge is how boards of directors and senior managers effectively articulate purpose to enhance governance and management. This chapter began by discussing the role of purpose in Ingka's transformation. The following section explores the role of purpose at Unilever. Ingka and Unilever's experiences provide some interesting approaches on how to articulate corporate purpose.

2.4.1   Unilever: Purpose and Strategy

Paul Polman, CEO of Unilever, was pondering the firm's challenges and how to sustain corporate growth in preparation for his April 4, 2017,[12] meeting with investors. In the wake of an unsolicited and failed takeover attempt of Unilever by Kraft Heinz in February 2017, the need to update the firm's strategic framework was more relevant than ever.

Under Polman's leadership, Unilever embarked on an ambitious initiative in 2010 aimed at merging business performance with wider social impact: the Unilever Sustainable Living Plan (USLP). This was a radical management innovation that included the firm's social impact as a central element of its corporate strategy. This plan was also the main pillar in making Unilever a multi-stakeholder company, a concept in which Unilever was a pioneer and a trailblazer.

Unilever had its roots in two Dutch companies founded by Van den Berg and Jurgens, two entrepreneurs and butter merchants who diversified into margarine, a new butter alternative; and in a British company set up by William Lever, a British entrepreneur who began producing an inexpensive household soap in the late 1890s. In the 1920s, Van der Berg and Jurgens joined their businesses and created Margarine Unie. Lever had conversations with the new Dutch company and in 1927, they merged both companies. Unilever started to operate as one on January 1, 1930. William Lever always held the firm belief that a company would grow if it operated well and with ethical principles, an approach that he defined as shared prosperity or "doing well by doing good."

Unilever owned more than 400 brands in nearly 200 countries, with a total revenue of €52.7 billion in 2016. Its portfolio of brands was outstanding, including some of the best brands in the industry – Dove, Rexona, Lipton, Knorr and Magnum, among others – each with annual

---

[12] See Canals (2019) for the recent evolution of Unilever and the connections between corporate governance and corporate purpose. Paul Polman's quotes in this chapter are taken from Canals (2019). See also Polman and Winston (2021).

revenue above €1 billion. But the 2008 financial crisis coincided with a sense at Unilever that it was time for a change, after years of stagnating sales and declining margins and profits.

Polman was the first CEO to come from outside of the company. In April 2009, after four months of intense work and armed with ideas and suggestions from hundreds of managers and employees, customers and shareholders, he made some pivotal decisions. He reorganized his team and announced Unilever should double the size of its business and realize 75 percent of this growth from emerging countries. Emerging markets already represented nearly 45 percent of total revenues in 2009, higher than competitor firms. He also unveiled the Unilever Sustainable Living Plan (USLP), which denoted a completely new strategy. It planned to integrate strategy and business activities with the company's broader impact on society. The plan was inspired by an ambitious notion: "Unilever has a clear purpose: to make sustainable living commonplace."

The Sustainable Living Plan was presented to investors and other stakeholders in 2010. Unlike many corporate social responsibilities initiatives, the plan took responsibility for the total value chain. It included targets to be achieved by 2020: help more than 1 billion people improve their health and hygiene; double the proportion of the portfolio to meet the highest nutritional standards; halve the greenhouse gas impact and water consumption; and sustainably source 100 percent of its agricultural raw materials. These goals were very ambitious, but an even bigger challenge was reaching them not only by business units or geographies, but along the entire value chain. As Polman put it, "[y]ou might outsource your supply chain but you cannot outsource your responsibilities."

What distinguished these initiatives from other firms' effective socially responsible action plans was not their scope and ambitions. Instead, it was Polman and the board of directors' determination in steering the company in this direction, while providing the board with information and persuading them to follow this route. For this reason, USLP was at the center of Unilever's strategy: engage consumers, drive growth, reduce costs, inspire employees and sustain innovation. As Polman shared,

> [t]he world is at a point that it needs decisions to help solve some big social problems. It is not enough for companies to say that they contribute to a better world. Companies are important social players and need to come up with solutions and be part of the solution. They must strive to be a net contributor to a world that gives them a reason to exist. After all, businesses cannot succeed in societies that fail nor can they be bystanders in a system that gives them life in the first place.

Polman and his team were very committed to developing Unilever as a multi-stakeholder company, with the drive and determination to serve customers well, generate profits and meet the company's sustainability plans and goals while having a wider impact on society. At the same time, Unilever also wanted to serve shareholders well. Polman explained this concept in a clear way:

> Unilever is a company defined as a multi-stakeholder corporation. We serve all stakeholders, not only shareholders. It is important that we deliver very good financial results and offer shareholders a good financial return, but strategy discussions at the board level need to have this perspective in mind. We need to serve customers first. If we do this well, we can also serve well shareholders and other stakeholders. We like to call our model one of long-term compounded and responsible growth.

Unilever's clear purpose was expressed in the company's values and helped reinforce them: integrity, respect for every person, making a positive impact, working in cooperation with partners and continuous improvement, among others. Top management expected these values to guide the company's daily operations, particularly management systems: how top executives managed, how they were held accountable and how managerial performance was assessed. Polman expected culture and values to shape people's decision-making. "It is very relevant to see how values influence major strategic decisions, like acquiring another company or investing in a new category or in the network of suppliers in the value chain," he said. "We try, for example, to see the social impact in everything that we do, the capital allocation process and the potential development of our people."

He considered that Unilever could succeed only with a long-term horizon for serving customers. This was the reason why immediately after taking over as CEO in 2009, he announced Unilever would stop offering quarterly earnings guidance and frame compensation for the longer term. He wanted shareholders to focus on the long term, not the short term. By putting pressure on managers in the short term, Unilever might miss long-term opportunities. Polman also believed that companies should help solve major societal problems, such as climate change, poverty, food security and youth unemployment, through its main activities. They could not be solved by governments alone or by companies focused on myopic quarterly goals. These global challenges required public–private coalitions and a long-term focus. This was a defining moment of his tenure at Unilever because he shaped how he wanted to work with shareholders from his own perspective: by delivering economic value but also focusing on other dimensions in a company that he defined as a "multi-stakeholder company." He was one of the first CEOs to illuminate the devastating effects of short termism and the shareholder primacy focus, which so many listed companies used as a basis for their activities. As he asked rhetorically, "[i]f business does not have a deeper purpose to serve society, then what is its purpose?"

Polman was also realistic about how to work with investors:

> We need to work on those long-term issues and, at the same time, be able to deliver value to our shareholders. In the long term, we can guarantee better returns if we help tackle those big issues because we will discover new opportunities. I have also tried to convey a sense of urgency about performing financially. We need to

execute our sustainability plan well and deliver financial results. It does not mean "trust us and we will come back in 10 years." No. We are committed to delivering well every year, year in, year out and so we have done this. Our own people are so mission-driven that they understand that our model depends on it.

Although progress had been complex and the path ahead appeared uncertain, Unilever's board of directors, employees and investors agreed Unilever had led a successful transformation since Polman's arrival in 2009. A key pillar in his leadership was to develop a deeper sense of corporate purpose in a company long guided by social values that had never been explicitly integrated into its strategy and organization. The new purpose helped connect the different business functions and business units, giving meaning to Unilever's different activities around the world. The Unilever case also shows that purpose takes into account ESG factors, but its scope goes beyond these.

2.4.2   The Notion of Purpose for Boards of Directors and Senior Managers

The Unilever and Ingka experiences on purpose help unbundle the notion of corporate purpose and its use by boards of directors and senior managers. Corporate purpose expresses why a company exists and how it plans to serve some customers' needs or solve customer challenges in a profitable and sustainable way. In this section, I present a framework with the crucial dimensions of corporate purpose as a guide for boards of directors and senior managers (see Figure 2.1).

2.4.2.1   A Challenge to Be Solved or a Need to Be Served

A good purpose is not only a statement with positive, aspirational intentions: It needs to drill down on the challenge the company aims to tackle, and the type of need or problem it aspires to solve. A good purpose needs to define a goal that engages people and dimensions that require a business solution. Without a challenge, a purpose may

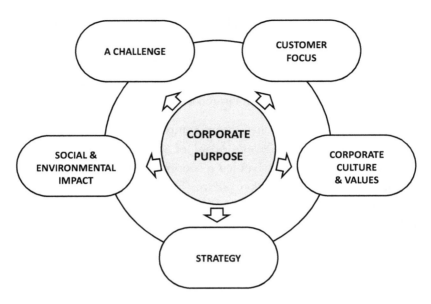

FIGURE 2.1 Corporate purpose: A framework

lose its drive. The challenge may not have a very high aspirational goal, but has to relate to other people's needs. It may include concrete customer demands that need to be addressed, the unresolved concerns of current consumers, efforts to optimize the purchasing journey (including lower prices) or the ambition to reduce the firm's environmental footprint.

Schneider Electric, the French provider of energy and digital solutions for enhanced efficiency and sustainability, promises energy usage to be safe and reliable, efficient and sustainable, open and connected. Over the years, it has offered effective solutions to improve energy usage, including the design of software to reduce energy consumption by companies, families and individuals. From its origins as an engineering and manufacturing company of products and services for the efficient use of electricity, Schneider Electric has become a company that uses software and connectivity to make buildings and manufacturing plants more energy efficient and miti-gate their environmental impact.

In this process, its purpose of managing electricity efficiently to reduce its consumption and its global environmental impact has placed Schneider Electric at the forefront of sustainability and the fight against climate change. This focus has been key in redesigning strategy, reconfiguring its business model and, more importantly, deeply engaging its people to solve specific problems around the use of electricity. It has also become an employer of choice among engineers, computer scientists and other professionals for its technical capabilities and concern for clean energy (Masclans and Canals, 2019).

2.4.2.2   The Firm's Purpose to Serve Customers

The dominance of efficiency in organizations and society has shifted the focus on performance, leaving little space for the human perspective of work in organizations. In this context, companies should make an explicit commitment to serve customers in a fair, respectful way by trying to address their needs. Schneider Electric offers a good lesson. In its efforts to help customers use energy more efficiently through innovative products, it has adopted a strategy aimed at easing their transition to sustainable energy sources. While this was not easy for Schneider Electric, its top management was able to generate a broad variety of innovative solutions for customers while applying efficient energy management criteria.

Companies with purpose should serve customers in a fair and professional way, while at the same time show respect for people, reduces the firm's negative environmental and social impact and contribute to society by delivering tangible and intangible benefits. Corporate purpose can help companies become respected institutions and generate an atmosphere of trust and goodwill.

2.4.2.3   Purpose Shapes Corporate Culture

The Ingka experience shows how the founder's vision influenced both the firm's strategy and its culture. In 2020, when the senior management team was considering how to renew Ingka's corporate purpose, they realized it was not simply a matter of crafting or rewriting a statement. It was a complex process that eventually had to influence corporate strategy and corporate culture.

Corporate culture is the implicit code of behavior that individuals follow in their professional activities within an organization. This code does not emerge because certain norms and rules have been written, but because employees have assumed them (Kotter and Heskett, 1992; Guiso, Sapienza and Zingales 2015; Schein, 2017; Groysberg, Lee and Price, 2019).

If the firm's purpose engages employees and encourages them to work toward concrete goals, its culture must reflect this purpose and inspire them to genuinely achieve a solution for the challenge defined.

When a purpose is intertwined in the firm's culture, it can help change behaviors. An important distinction can be observed in organizations between a deeply impactful purpose and a vague and generic statement of purpose. Time will tell whether the purpose will have a positive impact. But if purpose does not become part of the corporate culture, its impact will probably be superficial and short-lived.

2.4.2.4   *Purpose Should Influence Strategy to Create Sustainable Value*

A corporate purpose needs to shape the business strategy. Strategy, goals and policies have to form a coherent system that helps the firm serve customers.

The Unilever Sustainable Living Plan was more than a strategic framework guided by a statement of purpose. It opened up new initiatives related to the firm's product development, supply chain, sourcing and operations around the world, with the explicit goals of reducing carbon emissions and water consumption, and making sourcing in specific emerging countries more sustainable. Strategy was not etched in stone. Purpose helped nurture a sense of aspiration and a spirit of innovation around the basic challenges that Unilever sought to resolve, as well as stimulated the initiative and creativity of its globally dispersed employees.

The experience of companies that have successfully defined their purpose suggests that the hardest part of the process is translating it into strategy and the business model. The real challenge in purpose is clarity and implementation through different policies. Some key questions can help boards in working with purpose to create sustainable value:

- How can the firm nurture individuals' sense of meaning?
- How does the firm define its strategic goals? Are they coherent with purpose?
- How does purpose influence the activities and policies defined in the business model?
- Which indicators of performance does the company use?
- Are measurement and rewards systems defined by corporate purpose?

Methods to monitor goals and reporting systems are important for companies that define a corporate purpose. If a company continues to measure performance using the same economic indicators as before or persists in prioritizing short-term economic results, the impact of purpose will be limited. On the other hand, if purpose helps top management redefine goals and establish indicators that truly reflect the company's progress regarding its purpose, it will help align strategy and shape people's behavior.

2.4.3   Purpose and Stakeholders' Goals

Corporate purpose expresses the goals and specific impact the company aspires to achieve. Its board should assess whether the firm is reaching these goals. When purpose is included, some criteria will not have the quantitative nature of financial indicators. It should comprise both quantitative and nonquantitative indicators to help the board of directors and the senior management team in defining its expectations from the adopted notion of purpose and assessing the firm's performance.

In recent years, the consideration of ESG dimensions has converged toward corporate purpose. Purpose has a wider scope than ESG factors, although it can reinforce them. As explored in this chapter, some notions of purpose may lead to special definitions of ESG objectives. The important thing is not the intervention of regulators to step in and define how purpose should be assessed. The challenge for each company, its board of directors and its senior management team is to define the firm's purpose, integrate it into strategy and operations, and make explicit specific dimensions of purpose, which may encompass dimensions of ESG factors.

An example of an incomplete application of ESG factors can be seen in rating agencies and asset managers that overlook important social dimensions (the "S" factor) in their assessments of firms' success. The "S" factor should not only disclose the firm's fight against any type of discrimination or issues of health and safety. It should also consider the quality and diversity of employees, their professional competences and development, the level of trust in an organization and the positive attributes of corporate culture. In management research, there is a long tradition of stressing the importance and impact of these dimensions on economic performance (Drucker, 1973; Pfeffer, 1997; Ulrich and Brockband, 2005). In order for ESG indicators to drive better governance, they should move beyond financial indicators and quantitative analysis and embrace qualitative dimensions, particularly those linked to customer satisfaction, employee engagement and development. In Chapter 5 I recommend that companies place their own people and people development as key dimensions to be considered in governance.

2.5   THE ROLE OF THE BOARD OF DIRECTORS IN NURTURING AND IMPLEMENTING CORPORATE PURPOSE

Some investors are encouraging companies to define their purpose. Many are also paying greater attention to ESG dimensions and companies' wider impact on society. The asset management industry in particular has become more concerned about the role of purpose and how companies include ESG dimensions in their reporting. If large investors are serious about it, their attitude could be game-changing and make purpose an indisputable pillar of corporate performance. Boards of directors are experiencing this growing pressure.

Regulatory pressure on specific aspects of corporate purpose is also increasing. New efforts include a light approach by some national regulators that want ESG factors included in their corporate governance annual reports. This is the case of policies demanding an explicit statement of purpose, such as those recently approved in the United Kingdom and France, or similar advances, such as Germany's latest code of corporate governance.

But as Lipton (2019) suggests, companies should adopt a positive attitude in this realm and avoid a passive stance in the face of these broad trends. Boards can be drivers of change and companies can act as a positive reference in society. They should not wait for new regulation to be implemented. It is better for companies to adopt a proactive attitude, strive to manage their stakeholders more holistically and emphasize purpose by including ESG dimensions in their strategy, goals and policies. This approach also considers the benefits of a diversity of methods in defining and implementing corporate purpose.

In this section, I review several policies and practices regarding corporate purpose that boards of directors should consider and adopt (see Figure 2.2). These practices go beyond the prescription of writing a brief statement of purpose. This could be useful in some cases, but only when the statement reflects a deeper reality, is integrated into the firm's business strategy and business model and signals the willingness to move forward.

The notions and practices presented here stem from the experience of the companies analyzed in the book. An interesting aspect of these dimensions is their clear connection with the board of directors' functions and responsibilities, because they fall under their legal responsibility, help clarify the firm's strategy, or are considered as a good practice. As with other board functions, working on purpose is primarily the work of the CEO and management team. The board should help the CEO by reviewing purpose and ensuring that the

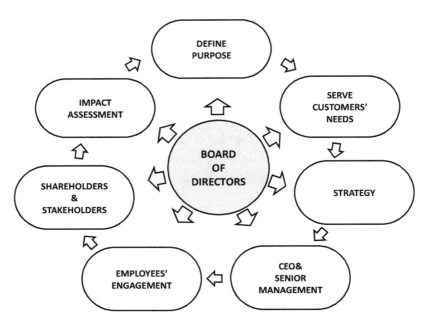

FIGURE 2.2 The role of the board of directors in corporate purpose

project is comprehensive and actionable, linked with corporate strategy and corporate culture and influences hiring and people development. The board may add specific areas of expertise and evidence, and offer advice on how its principles and metrics can be effectively shared with shareholders and other stakeholders. In this respect, communication with the investor community is not the sole responsibility of the CEO or the CFO; the board should take this responsibility seriously and act accordingly. Purpose offers a wider perspective of the role and duties of boards of directors. In the end, it gives boards of directors a unifying and useful sense of long-term direction that can be shared throughout the organization.

2.5.1   Understand, Define and Renew the Firm's Purpose

The importance and impact of corporate purpose require boards of directors to spend time to understand it and explore its implications on the firm's strategy, business model, strategic decisions, organizational design, CEO and senior management hiring, people development, employee behavior and performance and compensation systems, among other policies and factors.

Framing a discussion around purpose requires skillful preparation by the chairperson and the CEO. They need to put forth the right questions and challenges in front of the board, and prepare relevant information that members can analyze before the board meeting. The boards of Ingka and Unilever, among others, have undergone this process several times. Doing this effectively helps the board better formulate other strategic decisions.

If the style, quality and tone of questions are indispensable attributes of good board debates, they are even more important in the board's discussions on purpose. Some board members may prefer to discuss strategic decisions or ways to improve the firm's financial performance. Purpose has the potential to integrate people and encourage initiatives that help enhance the firm's reputation and eventually improve its economic performance. Purpose may also impact the company's ability to attract and retain people, which is a core success factor for any organization. This wide scope of perspectives requires additional efforts on behalf of the chairperson and CEO in preparing and running board meetings on this topic.

There are several questions that may help improve the quality of the debate and clarify expectations regarding the board's role in this area (see Table 2.1). Some of these questions relate to the basic structure of purpose as presented in Figure 2.1. The first question is: Does the board understand the firm's purpose and its implications for the governance and management of the firm? This is a key question, a pillar to help board members understand how corporate purpose connects with strategic decisions (Younger, Mayer and Eccles, 2020).

The second question: How does the company serve customers and address their needs? Do the company's offerings truly enhance their lives? If the answer is no, the company has a problem, and the challenge of attaining sustainable economic performance might not be an issue of productivity or efficiency.

Table 2.1. *Some questions on the firm's purpose for board of directors*

- Does the board of directors understand the firm's purpose and its implications for governance and management?
- What specific customer need is this company serving? What role do customers play in strategy and innovation?
- Why would talented people want to work at this company?
- Why do investors want to invest in this firm? Which time horizon do they have?
- What is the overall impact of the firm's purpose?

The third question: Why would talented people want to work in this company? Hiring and retaining good CEOs and senior managers are crucial functions of the board of directors. Attractive compensation plans and professional projects are major factors of engagement for managers. Nevertheless, individuals have a broad range of motivations, as observed by the growing trend among high-performing professionals who aspire to work in socially motivating ventures. Boards of directors should understand the reasons behind the CEO or manager's interest in joining the company. It may also reveal much about the individual's motivations and personal fit with the company's purpose and culture.

The fourth question: Why would investors like to invest in this company and what is their time horizon? Financial performance may be an important motivator. But the revolution in the investment community and its growing interest in corporate purpose and ESG factors appear to be irreversible trends. A productive discussion on purpose has to generate a better set of reasons and indicators to convince investors to commit to the company.

The fifth question: What is the firm's overall impact on society? There are clear impacts connected with customer service and satisfaction, economic performance and employee retention and development. Boards also need to consider other environmental and social factors that make a company a respected institution in the community where it operates. These include job creation, involvement in education, re-skilling and training – especially current and potential employees – fiscal contribution and the company's ability to serve as a dynamic hub for local communities. Respected companies consider these dimensions (Canals, 2010a) and boards of directors need to gauge the quality of their organizations in this highly relevant area.

2.5.2 Connect Strategy and Strategic Decisions with Purpose

The quality and strength of a company's purpose do not reside so much on their level of aspiration but on how they connect with strategy, strategic plans and decisions and implementation. Strategy is a very important area of responsibility for the board of directors, to be shared with the CEO and top management team. A positive impact of corporate purpose is how it nurtures and improves the quality of strategy discussions. For this reason, the board should look at corporate purpose as an essential pillar for formulating and executing strategy.

Paul Polman and his team designed the Unilever sustainability plan as a fully integrated component of its strategy and business model, including product design, sourcing, operations, logistics, manufacturing and distribution. Their primary goal was assuring the Unilever Sustainable Living Plan would cover the totality of the firm's supply chain and not shift the responsibility for sustainability and environmental impact to third parties through outsourcing programs. Product innovation and new product launches also included sustainability as a core element of decision-making in order to interlace sustainability dimensions in corporate growth and innovation efforts.

Schneider Electric (Masclans and Canals, 2019) offers an interesting perspective on the integration of purpose with strategy. In its quest for smart energy and reducing the environmental impact of energy generation and distribution, the firm made strategic investment decisions that clearly reflected its interest in connecting strategic decisions with purpose, including investments in software to reduce carbon emissions. This is very relevant since Schneider is not an energy producer, but an engineering company that designs and manufactures energy management and control systems to help other companies make better use of generation, distribution and consumption of energy.

Jean-Pascal Tricoire, CEO of Schneider Electric, and his top management team, realized the need to improve the quality and impact of their products and services to help customers reduce their energy consumption, while accelerating the company's digital transformation. They observed that software development could help Schneider Electric better monitor the performance of its systems, use data more effectively, offer additional data-driven services and develop a smarter energy-consumption monitoring process.

Schneider's 2017 acquisition of the British software company Aveva illustrates their conviction. It was a complex acquisition. The fit of Aveva's culture with Schneider's culture was a key issue. Although it was a complex acquisition, it was approved and executed with the belief it could expedite Schneider's shift to energy-management software, aimed at helping its customers optimize their energy usage and mitigating negative environmental impacts. This was not merely a business opportunity: It was a case where the sense of purpose shaped strategy and became an important driver of the decision-making process.

Striking the right balance between purpose and profit is essential. Under the leadership of CEO Indra Nooyi, PepsiCo adopted a notion of purpose ("Performance with Purpose") in 2006 to highlight the impact of its products on people's health and the environment, and its capacity to attract talent (Nooyi and Govindarajan, 2020). But the firm's strategy adapted slowly and its performance disappointed investors for a while. In mid-2013, Trian Partners, an activist investor, declared a 1 percent stake in PepsiCo's shares and started a campaign to force the board to restructure the company and split it into two firms (snacks and beverages).

PepsiCo's board and CEOs listened to the activist investor. They took these challenges more seriously, refined the company's strategy and made some key decisions. Its performance dramatically improved. In 2016, Trian Partners exited PepsiCo. The consistency between purpose, strategy and business model is indispensable in making purpose impactful. Nestlé is an excellent company that adopted the Creating Shared Value concept, a special notion of purpose. It confronted challenges in effectively integrating it into its strategy and business model for several years. During this transition, its economic performance fell short of expectations. But this specific notion of purpose made Nestlé a stronger company and in recent years its performance dramatically improved. Despite several challenges, both PepsiCo and Nestlé found a way to merge purpose with a profitable business model.

These cases offer some important questions for boards of directors to consider if they take corporate purpose seriously and want to integrate purpose into their strategic decisions (see Table 2.2). The first question is how strategy and strategic decisions are linked to corporate purpose. A second related question is how the firm's core activities and policies defined in its business model reflect and reinforce its purpose. This question affects numerous strategic decisions, since they provide opportunities for growth by increasing profitability or market share.

A third question is the degree to which purpose influences innovation, new projects and, eventually, strategic decisions. Companies'

Table 2.2. *Corporate purpose and strategy: Some questions*

- How is strategy linked with corporate purpose?
- Does the business model reflect the firm's purpose?
- How does purpose foster innovation?
- Does a strategic decision reinforce the sense of purpose?
- How does a strategic decision change the risk profile of an organization?

success not only requires consistent strategies executed in the short term but discovery processes to identify growth avenues for the future.

Innovation is an indispensable driver in any organization and the wellspring of new ideas for the firm's strategy. As the cases of Unilever and Schneider Electric highlight, a good purpose serves as a source of inspiration for companies in their exploration of new strategic ventures.

The fourth question for the board of directors is whether a specific strategic decision reinforces the sense of purpose. Do employees understand the decision within the context of the corporate purpose? Do they feel motivated or inspired by it? Once the strategic decision has been made and implemented, will the sense of purpose in the organization be higher or lower? Will the decision strengthen the firm's purpose? These are very relevant questions, particularly those that have implications for growth, scale and people's sense of engagement and commitment.

Just as a nonrelated diversification decision might not reinforce the firm's core capabilities, or even negatively affect its financial performance, strategic decisions detached from the firm's purpose might also wield a negative impact, particularly on customer and employee engagement. Consistency between purpose, strategy and implementation is essential.

The fifth question for the board of directors is how strategic decisions will change the risk profile of the company. This question involves both the financial risk of a specific decision and how it might imperil the very notion of its purpose. It might seem that the firm's purpose and risk profile are unrelated. In fact, they are related to one another. A higher risk profile may weaken the firm's purpose and its capacity to impact strategy, organization design and people development.

2.5.3   Purpose, Senior Management Development and Employees' Engagement

Companies with a purpose and rich culture need to hire professionals who are a good fit with the organization. Cultural fit is a necessity in recruitment. It is even more important with management hiring since managers coordinate people's work, engage employees and oversee their professional development. Ingka is a good example of a successful company with a highly competent management team that takes cultural fit into account in its hiring processes. Professional competence is indispensable but cultural fit is critical for companies with a clear purpose. As Ingka senior managers explain, hiring for fit is compatible with diversity and inclusiveness.

Unfortunately, hiring is frequently framed through the lens of capabilities that can boost productivity and performance, rather than in terms of cultural fit. In too many companies, senior-management recruiting decisions are biased toward the candidate's track record in reaching financial goals or increasing shareholder value or market share. This not to say that these performance indicators are bad. But companies that aspire to stand out through a special purpose also need to include other dimensions and attributes in their hiring processes (Pfeffer, 1997).

In particular, the board has a specific responsibility with CEO and senior management appointments. If the board truly considers purpose as a unique dimension of the company, board members should also ponder how they can assess candidates' capacity to absorb and renew the firm's purpose, translate it into strategyand make the firm's business model more sustainable.

CEO recruiting presents some special challenges. Different boards of directors follow different processes in appointing a new CEO (Bower, 2007). These take into account diverse approaches to internal or external candidates; the involvement of external executive search firms; and board members' personal knowledge of potential candidates. Whatever practices the board follows, the process should consider how the company's purpose is taken into account. The board is the final gatekeeper in the CEO selection process. It should control the entire process; even if it outsources some functions to external consultants, it should not delegate what is essentially its responsibility.

In the CEO selection process, the board usually starts with the company's current corporate challenges, required CEO capabilities to confront them and the recent experience of previous CEOs in the firm and in the wider industry. An in-depth examination of candidates' backgrounds is vital, including past performance, capabilities and attitudes, and major professional and personal achievements. Boards often prefer candidates with vast industry experience, a proven track record in economic performance and experience navigating some of the firm's existing challenges.

Only recently have specific indicators and processes around the candidate's cultural fit with the organization – such as tracking the person's experiences and fit in other companies – become relevant in the final decision. The same applies to the sense of purpose. Purpose is not associated with a single person, not even the CEO. But it is also clear that the moral and effective authority of the CEO can help a company accelerate the adoption of a wider notion of purpose and boost its relevance for the entire organization, its strategy and business model. Paul Polman and Jean-Pascal Tricoire are examples of the enormous energy that competent and decent CEOs bring to the discussion on purpose and its impact on their organizations.

Boards of directors should approve compensation packages for the CEO and senior management team that truly reflect the firm's commitment to purpose (Younger, Mayer and Eccles, 2020). Purpose-related indicators should also help define executive compensation. The combination of financial and nonfinancial factors is essential to performance-based pay for companies with a purpose.

Boards should also consider the controversy surrounding the sharp growth of executive compensation over the past two decades, which is higher in the United States than in other countries (Bebchuk and Fried, 2004). This trend stems from the widening pay gap in some organizations, as well as overall inequality in some countries. It is difficult to sustain a company with a high-level purpose if its mechanisms of executive compensation are unclear, regardless of performance, and contribute to expanding the firm's pay gap.

2.5.4 Purpose and Relations with Shareholders and Stakeholders

Shareholders are not accountable for the company's long-term development although they play a role by influencing the board of directors and the overall quality of the firm's corporate governance. They should also act as good stewards and serve their companies.

Board directors are elected by the firm's shareholders and should take their duties of care and loyalty seriously. They require reasonable, prudent and competent oversight of the company's business and operations to ensure it can develop for the long term and generate economic value sustainably. Board directors also need to avoid conflicts of interest with the company.

As part of their duty of care, board directors need to firmly understand their firm's purpose, articulate it and share it with shareholders. As share owners with basic rights, shareholders need to understand core questions about the company in which they have invested. These include why the company exists, what it is trying to achieve, how its strategy generates economic value, how it serves customers in a unique way, how it is organized to ensure strategy is effectively executed, how robust its leadership pipeline is and what elements define its culture. Any responsible shareholder should understand these dimensions well. Board directors need to be able to explain these attributes to investors. It is not a question of board members maintaining regular contact with shareholders. This is not their legal function. But in some circumstances, this might be the case, such as takeover attempts, transactions with a private equity firm or the entry of new shareholders who might exert control on the company with a relevant stake.

Both in large public companies like Unilever and family owned firms like the fragrance company Puig, board directors need to be able to clearly articulate the notion of purpose to shareholders, including its core attributes and links with the organization's strategy and business model. When this process is done effectively, shareholders will likely support the firm's purpose. On the contrary, when boards fail to do this job well, shareholders might not gain a strong grasp of purpose and, if performance deteriorates, might sell their shares or revolt against the board.

It is also the board's responsibility to find the best long-term shareholders for the company. Current shareholders might not be in the firm in the future. Investors might change their minds and have few constraints preventing them from selling their shares. Successful companies are supported by the right type of shareholders (Canals, 2010a; Mayer, 2018).

Boards should also identify and define some guidelines to engage critical stakeholders, with customers and employees as the first priority. The board should not manage the firm's relationships with these stakeholders. It is usually the function of senior managers. But they are so critical that the board should understand how the company interacts with them and decide on some basic criteria to develop them over the long term. Multi-stakeholder management is not an ideology: It is the outcome of the firm's diverse relationships with different parties with whom the firm can create value.

2.5.5 Assessing the Overall Impact of Purpose

The definition of purpose is complex and entails different perspectives. Its measurement is difficult. Purpose also helps define and unify the value the company aspires to bring to key stakeholders. This may include ESG factors, but stakeholder management encompasses more than these dimensions. The introduction of purpose that considers different stakeholder goals is complicated and requires the competence of board directors, who should help design and promote the firm's purpose and assess its real impact beyond a list of ESG factors. Assessing purpose also encourages managers to describe the firm's purpose and establish indicators that shed light on the company's progress toward achieving it. Financial performance remains very relevant. Nevertheless, organizational success and the achievement of purpose need to consider nonfinancial indicators. Every company should identify and share them with its key stakeholders.

The unbundling of purpose and identification of its core dimensions allow boards of directors and senior managers to lead their companies more effectively and better communicate with employees on the most relevant dimensions of purpose. Measuring indicators of purpose has become indispensable for boards of directors and CEOs in their interactions with shareholders and other stakeholders.

Companies need to develop their own unique reporting model. It will depend on the nature of each firm and the definition of purpose it adopts. In many cases, corporate purpose will include customer and employee well-being, as well as environmental and social goals.

ESG factors do not fully capture the purpose of many firms, although their relevance is growing as core dimensions of purpose. Their assessment and measurement are also very relevant. As Eccles and Klimenko (2019) point out, investors and corporate leaders increasingly understand that companies have a role to play in social challenges, such as climate change. Environmental, social and governance dimensions have become relevant questions for investors interested in companies' performance along these dimensions. Asset managers with trillions of dollars under management in many industries and countries have no hedge against the risks of the world economy. They cannot allow the economy or the planet to collapse. Investors also require additional metrics and performance indicators on key social or environmental dimensions, both to better understand the companies in which they invest and more professionally manage their investment portfolios. These dimensions can form an integral part of companies' corporate purpose if they so choose.

When Unilever approved the Unilever Sustainable Living Plan in 2010, it established which financial indicators it would track. It also created specific indicators in three core areas where Unilever hoped to make an impact. The first was environmental impact, including greenhouse emissions and water consumption, the effects of their sourcing in emerging countries and the sustainability of local agriculture production. The second was health and hygiene factors through personal care products in low-income countries, with the aim of enhancing the health of local residents, improving nutritional levels and preventing the spread of infections and diseases. The third was social impact, including employee development, inclusion and labor rights, particularly in emerging countries.

Although it seemed like a complex scorecard of goals and indicators, the USLP helped Unilever's managers develop a more holistic framework to lead a very large company. It also helped top management consider a broader range of dimensions and spurred creativity within the company to help improve its financial, environmental and social-impact performance. This wider perspective of organizational performance has been credited as an essential driver of leadership development within Unilever. It has also become a formidable magnet for talent attraction in recent years, especially among younger professionals. This capacity has enabled the company to compete with leading high-tech companies, known for their attractive work conditions and emphasis on "the next big thing" and solving complex societal problems.

Merging quantitative and qualitative indicators is complex because some areas – such as job satisfaction and employee engagement – cannot be measured exclusively with quantitative indicators. Based on the experience of many boards of directors and top management teams, unless the chair and some senior board members show a vested interest in nonfinancial dimensions, these may be overlooked and subordinated to financial, quantitative dimensions. The assessment of purpose and ESG factors requires deeper reflection and work.[13] Progress in this area entails a large coalition of audit firms,

---

[13] At the end of October 2021, there were some initiatives underway to create international sustainability standard frameworks, including the effort to coordinate the work by five leading voluntary standard architects: CDP, the Climate Disclosure Standards Board, the Global Reporting Initiative (GRI), the International Integrated Reporting Council (IIRC) and the Sustainability Accounting Standards Board (SASB).

asset managers, shareholders, scholars and regulators to devise new solutions to this new and significant challenge.

2.6   FINAL REFLECTIONS

This chapter reviews the notion and main dimensions of corporate purpose, its impact on corporate governance and the role of boards of directors in this area. It also summarizes complementary perspectives on the notion of purpose, its articulation to make it an effective resource for boards of directors and the reasons why purpose plays an important role in corporate governance and board of directors' functions.

A firm's purpose should include a clear reason for the company's raison d'être and the specific challenge or customer need it seeks to address. It should clarify how the notion of purpose connects with strategy, the business model and fundamental corporate policies, especially hiring, talent development and product innovation. There should be a clear understanding of how purpose is measured and which performance indicators the board of directors should consider. It should nourish a solid and healthy corporate culture.

Finally, I present a framework to help boards of directors approach corporate purpose. Boards of directors play an essential role in this respect and have a unique responsibility to ensure that the company has a well-defined purpose in place. This will have a positive impact on the firm's long-term development.

From its rather limited presence on boards of directors' agendas, purpose has emerged as an important area of interest for members and senior managers. It offers a new pathway for boards to reconnect companies with the larger society, a bond that was broken a few decades ago when a company's success began to be viewed only through the prism of financial performance. Purpose is a worthy effort for companies that aspire to become respected social institutions.

3 Boards of Directors in Corporate Strategy

From Maximizing Short-Term Shareholder Value to Creating Long-Term Value

3.1 THE BOARD OF DIRECTORS' ROLE IN STRATEGY

On February 10, 2017, Paul Polman, Unilever CEO, received a letter from Alexandre Behring, chairman of Kraft Heinz. It expressed Kraft Heinz's interest in launching an unsolicited bid for all Unilever shares, with the goal of merging both companies.

Unilever[1] had been spearheading a successful transformation process since 2009. Under Polman's leadership, the company adopted the Unilever Sustainable Living Plan (USLP) in 2010; this initiative brought about a fundamental shift in Unilever's approach to product development, raw-materials sourcing and their carbon footprint. With the explicit support of its board of directors, Unilever adopted very ambitious environmental, health, social and financial goals as part of its strategy, and they were consistently integrated into the firm's business model. Unilever had become a business champion of the multi-stakeholder strategy, while offering shareholders above average financial returns and guiding the company for the long term.

Unilever faced several challenges in 2017, including pressure to improve its efficiency and financial performance, as well as deliver on its environmental and social commitments. These included new-product developments targeted at younger consumers and a firm pledge to monitor the environmental impact of its operations. The

---

[1] A detailed description of Unilever's strategy since 2009 and the Kraft Heinz takeover bid is presented in Canals (2019). Polman and Winston (2021) also offer insightful perspectives on this event.

consideration of both financial and nonfinancial goals is a difficult balancing act for any company. Unilever's ambitions were broad by aiming at delivering in both areas. Kraft Heinz's attempted takeover came as a surprise, not only to Unilever's management and board of directors, but to the business community in general. In view of Unilever's solid performance and goal of driving positive social impact, what did the future hold for other firms embracing this dual approach?

The takeover proposal was a great opportunity for Kraft Heinz and its two main shareholders: 3G – the private equity group founded by some Brazilian investors and led by Jorge Paulo Lemann – and Warren Buffett. Buffett had already cooperated with 3G in other mega-deals, including the acquisition of Heinz and its subsequent merger with Kraft. For Kraft Heinz, there was logic behind a deal with Unilever. The acquisition would allow it to diversify geographically outside the United States, reinforce its position in emerging markets where Unilever was strong and create larger scale economies in purchasing, manufacturing, advertising, operations and technology.

The differences between Kraft Heinz and Unilever were significant. Unilever focused on product innovation. Kraft Heinz was centered on cost cutting and efficiency. Unilever was a global company, with a large presence in emerging markets. Kraft Heinz was strong in the US market. Unilever was making substantial efforts to reach a zero carbon footprint and integrate sustainability into its business strategy. Kraft Heinz was not known for its concern about the environmental impact of its operations. Nevertheless, a good company can create value by turning these differences into opportunities through a merger.

Unilever and Kraft Heinz had dissimilar business models. Although both had been performing well from a financial standpoint, many questions remained about the viability of combining two companies with such different cultures and strategic orientations. Unilever's long-term perspective and emphasis on product innovation, new-customer needs and social and environmental concerns, stood in sharp contrast with Kraft Heinz's focus on operational efficiency.

Unilever's board of directors, led by Martjin Dekkers, was in a tough position. Beyond their personal views, board members had the responsibility to accept or reject the Kraft Heinz offer based on its value for Unilever shareholders and other stakeholders. Unilever's directors had to seriously consider their duty of care. They recognized that, if a potential suitor offered an attractive price, they would face enormous pressure from certain shareholders and the financial community. Unilever's board was at a crossroads.

A week later, on February 17, the board opted not to hold conversations with Kraft Heinz and rejected its bid. It considered this decision to be in the best interests of Unilever shareholders and other stakeholders. In the judgment of Unilever's board of directors, the merger with Kraft Heinz was not a good option. A board of directors capable of making this type of decision must be very knowledgeable of the firm's strategy, value creation, corporate culture, talent attraction and retention strategies and customer engagement, as well as how its strategy is perceived by the financial community. Kraft Heinz and its main shareholders, 3G and Warren Buffett, accepted Unilever's response and kindly communicated their decision to not proceed further with the takeover bid.

This event sheds light on the relevant role of the board of directors in setting the firm's long-term orientation and corporate strategy. The CEO and senior managers' role in strategy has a long tradition in strategic management. Unfortunately, the role of the board of directors in this domain has received far less attention. Codes of corporate governance and other governance regulations may refer to the board directors' duties of care and loyalty, but their role in strategy is complex.

As underscored by digital transformation, decarbonization, trade wars, the recent pandemic and the new geo-political risks, companies need to reflect on their long-term development and strategy. This requires the board's involvement in debating and shaping the organization's strategy.

In this chapter, I discuss the role of the board of directors in the firm's strategy and present a framework to help address business strategy beyond financial analysis. In Section 3.2, I present different approaches on how boards should deal with strategy. In Section 3.3, I develop a strategy road map for boards, to help them cocreate the company's future by collaborating with the CEO and top management team. In Section 3.4, I offer guidelines on the strategy process – different from the concept of strategy itself – with a spotlight on how the board of directors can work with the CEO and senior managers on core strategic decisions. Finally, I present a typology of profiles of board of directors regarding their role in strategy.

3.2   THE BOARD'S ROLE IN STRATEGY: DIFFERENT APPROACHES

Relevant investors today, including institutional investors, family offices and private equity firms, expect boards of directors – not only CEOs or CFOs – to debate and promote the firm's strategy. They want to make sure that the board discusses and understands how the company creates value for the long term. Beyond legal duties or vague recommendations in corporate governance codes, investors expect board directors to become drivers of the company's strategy.

This view of the board of directors is coherent with the responsibilities of top management as they have been understood in strategic management.[2] In the next sections, I briefly outline the contributions to the board's role in the firm's strategy in the fields of corporate law, corporate finance and strategic management.

---

[2] The board of directors has not been considered explicitly as the final decision maker in strategy, with some notable exceptions. These include, among others, Pearce and Zahra (1991), McNulty and Pettigrew (1997, 1999), Carter and Lorsch (2004), Pye and Pettigrew (2005), Finkelstein, Hambrick and Cannella (2009) and Palepu (2012).

3.2.1   Strategy and Corporate Law

In Western countries, most corporate law systems highlight boards' main corporate governance functions, which stem from their legal duty to monitor the CEO and senior managers on behalf of shareholders. Shareholders as individuals do not get involved in the firm's governance. They appoint a board of directors to oversee the company's governance and monitor top managers' decisions and performance. They want to ensure that top managers adopt decisions that reflect shareholders' interests, but do not want to get involved in this role. There are some exceptions to this rule, such as in the cases of start-ups, venture capital firms, private equity firms and family owned businesses, where founders and investors have a major presence on the company's board of directors.

In the corporate law tradition, the focus of the board's functions is on monitoring top management and overseeing the firm's performance. The Cadbury Code in the United Kingdom (Cadbury et al., 1992) marked a departure from that approach. It signaled efforts to update the functions of boards of directors in coherence with the changing needs of companies and the specific value that good governance can create for the firm's long-term success. There was a new emphasis on the board's role in the firm's long-term development, beyond monitoring the management team. It inspired reflections on the rights of both shareholders and stakeholders. The board's collaboration with different stakeholders is critical for the firm's long-term development.

The board's function as the central governance institution and its mediating role between shareholders, top management and the rest of the organization (Blair and Stout, 1999) underscores one of its chief roles in corporate governance. Some corporate law authors (Lipton, 2017; Bainbridge, 2018; Gilson and Gordon, 2019; Fisch and Solomon, 2020; Rock, 2020) assume that boards should oversee the company's strategy in one capacity or another. However, the board's specific role in strategy and how this function is carried out is unclear. The board should lead the company with a long-term horizon and make decisions that promote its long-term value creation.[3]

This notion is gaining steam as companies and their boards of directors and shareholders are being accused of "short termism"[4] in their decision-making. Despite the ongoing academic debate about whether public companies are overly focused on short-term objectives, there seems to be a consensus that companies should create value for the long term. This is the specific dimension of strategy. The United Kingdom's unified Corporate Governance Code (2018) also took this approach. The debate on activist shareholders and the hypothesis that they create short-term value for investors[5] also underscore the need for companies to adopt long-term horizons. The mediating role of boards in this specific context is highly relevant.

3.2.2 Strategy and Corporate Finance

Corporate finance is another academic area that examines the role of boards of directors in strategy. In this field, most authors stress a common problem in public corporations: the separation of ownership (shareholders) and management and control. A vast stream of research highlights different incentives that principals can design to ensure agents' behavior maximizes the value of shareholder investments (see Jensen and Meckling, 1976).

In the corporate finance tradition, the role of strategy is mostly focused on capital allocation, diversification and merger-and-acquisition decisions. It is subsumed into the overall function of boards in

---

[3] See Barton and Wiseman (2014) and Charan, Carey and Useem (2014). Other initiatives also highlight this long-term orientation, such as Focus Capital for the Long-Term, created by the Canada Pension Plan Investment Board and McKinsey.

[4] There is heated debate about whether capital markets and boards of directors' decisions are dominated by short-termism. See Davies et al. (2014), Strine (2017) and Roe (2018).

[5] Bebchuck, Brav and Jiang (2015), and Becht, Franks, Grant and Wagner (2017), among others, observed value creation by activists' shareholders. See De Haan, Larcker and McClure (2019) for a more skeptical view on the role of activist shareholders in creating long-term shareholder value.

monitoring managerial decisions. It does not include any reference to the content or process of strategy or the firm's business model.

The dominant view in corporate finance is that a board's role in strategy and strategic decision-making should aim to maximize shareholder value (Ross, 1973; Jensen and Meckling, 1976). From a decision-making viewpoint, this perspective is clear, although, as some authors have noted (see, among others, Simon, 1976, 1991 and Hart and Zingales, 2017), maximizing shareholder value actually means may not be a good criterion. In a bounded rationality context (Simon, 1991), it is difficult to assert that each decision will maximize shareholder value. Moreover, shareholders are diverse and reflect different time perspectives and expectations. As a result, each will assign a different meaning to value maximization.

The diverse time horizons of shareholders is very relevant, because in order to continue creating long-term shareholder value, the company needs to invest in people, technology and product development, which may decrease short-term cash flows and dividends. As occurs with other complex managerial themes, the real world of business is not only finance, although it plays a significant role in the firm's governance. A case in point is a merger and acquisition, a realm where finance is highly relevant, but where execution, leadership and efficiently integrating people and cultures also play integral roles in the transaction's success. Corporate finance requires a strategic management outlook to understand the role of the board in corporate strategy.

3.2.3   A Broader Strategy Role for Boards of Directors: Contributions from Strategic Management

Corporate law and corporate finance provide a useful but incomplete approach to the board's role in strategy. They do not offer guidelines on how boards of directors should work effectively on strategy. The field of strategic management helps frame discussions on how a company creates sustainable value by considering its industry and how it defines an attractive customer value proposition, designs a business model and organizes its activities to serve customers in a unique way. A successful strategy requires crucial decisions that will help the company stand out in its industry. The strategic management field adds a diverse outlook to this debate. This includes contributions to better understand strategy, strategy dynamics, the interplay between resources and capabilities and sustainable competitive advantages and the specific role of top management teams in strategy.[6] These complementary perspectives describe the essence of strategy and its relevance to corporate governance.

A focus on shareholder value without the board's solid grasp on how economic value can be created may not be useful. The European banking industry provides some very interesting experiences. Deutsche Bank, Germany's largest bank and a leader in Europe, faced some of these strategic challenges following the financial crisis of 2008.

In the 1990s, Deutsche Bank had become the paradigm of a universal bank, competing both in the retail and investment banking industries. Over the past two decades, however, the bank invested primarily in people and assets to expand its investment banking business, efforts which were rendered practically irrelevant after the 2008 financial crisis and the shifting nature of banking activity. Deutsche Bank suffered a value deterioration of some assets, particularly those related to its investment banking and real estate businesses, with higher capital requirements and a substantial drop in profitability and equity value. It had a hard time adjusting to this

---

[6] See the contributions to understand industries and their effects on corporate performance (Porter, 1980, 1996; Ghemawat, 1991; Rumelt, 1991, 2011; McGahan and Porter, 1997); the dynamics of strategy over time (Ghemawat, 1993; Gavetti and Rivkin, 2007); the role of process in strategy (Bower, 1970; Andrews, 1971; Pfeffer, 1972; Donaldson and Lorsch, 1983; Mintzberg 2007); the resources and capabilities' view of strategy (Barney, 1991; Teece, Pisano and Shuen, 1997; Helfat and Peteraf, 2003); the business model perspective (Zott and Amit, 2010; Casadesús-Masanell and Ricart, 2011); and the role of the board of directors and top management teams in strategy (Finklestein and Hambrick, 1990; McNulty and Pettigrew, 1997; Hambrick, 2007; Finklestein, Hambrick and Canella, 2009; Wiersema, Nishimura and Suzuki, 2018 and Hambrick and Wowack, 2021).

unfamiliar landscape. Furthermore, the bank's retail business unit in Germany was not competitive. The retail bank business in other countries was in better shape, but too small to significantly affect the bank's overall performance.

Since 2010, Deutsche Bank's board of directors and top management team had been trying to bolster its investment bank business and become a European powerhouse capable of competing against US banks. Changes in the top leadership position – with three CEOs between 2014 and 2018 – made this transformation process more complex. After a failed merger attempt with Commerzbank in April 2019, the bank focused on divesting from most of its investment bank business and improving capital allocation. In the meantime, the complexity of the bank's challenges was a deterrent for some investors (Storbeck, Morris and Noonan, 2019).

Without a doubt, both the board and the top management team were trying to improve the bank's efficiency and profitability and increase shareholder value. Nonetheless, these goals were ineffectual without a well-defined and smoothly executed strategy. For boards of directors, a deeper reflection on strategy and the policies to drive long-term economic value are indispensable. A coherent strategy helps guide companies' long-term orientation and their potential for value creation, a core theme for boards of directors. This is why corporate strategy should serve as a central pillar in good corporate governance and a pivotal role of boards of directors. Boards of directors will be incapable of effectively monitoring the company's top management without a clear understanding of the firm's strategy, its resources and capabilities, and how the business model supports strategy.

Effectively dealing with strategy can be difficult for boards of directors for a variety of reasons. The first is that the board's role in strategy has not been clearly recognized by either regulators or investors. Until recently, the role of boards in most listed companies was to give a stamp of approval to management proposals. Second, there might be confusion regarding the strategic roles of senior management and the board. Strategy formulation is a key function of the CEO, who should understand the business well and make efforts to advance it, but the board should discuss it and approve it. The third reason relates to the difficulty in articulating decisions given the board's collegiality, the nature of its work and members' part-time dedication. That said, these factors can be overcome by a competent board.

The board of directors should help the firm create long-term value. As a result, the board of directors should understand, discuss and approve how the CEO and senior management approach the firm's strategy, business model and competitive advantages, and the sustainability of its value creation process. Since the board of directors is involved in the commitment of resources, strategic investments and other relevant management decisions, it should also take part in the reflection, discussion and approval of the firm's strategy.

In the following sections, I examine the role of the board and the strategy-related functions it should perform. The CEO and senior managers, as the original architects of this work, should discuss strategy with the board and execute it once it has been approved. I also present a framework to help boards address strategy while respecting the primary role of the CEO.

3.3   A FRAMEWORK FOR BOARDS OF DIRECTORS AND THEIR ROLE IN CORPORATE STRATEGY

High-quality strategic reflection and a solid grasp of the firm's business are essential capabilities for boards of directors to properly fulfill their responsibilities. An understanding of strategy and the firm's principal strategic challenges are fundamental for boards of directors to reflect on long-term value creation (Palepu, 2012). In the absence of proper work on strategy and strategic decisions, board members' fiduciary duties will not be met.

3.3.1   *The Board of Directors and CEOs' Collaboration on Strategy*

This section outlines the experiences of the boards of two international companies regarding strategy and strategic decisions. The

Cellnex experience offers the perspective of a spin-off from a larger company, Abertis, a global infrastructure management company, with relevant insights on boards of directors that should reflect on their company's future growth. The Amadeus case reflects the challenges faced by one of the largest European software companies in developing its US market and the board's concerns surrounding the acquisition. These cases also shed some light on the collaborative work between the board and the CEO on strategy.

3.3.1.1 Cellnex: A Growth Project

The 2015 launch of Cellnex,[7] a subsidiary of Abertis, the world's largest highway infrastructure management company, and the strategic insights developed by its chairman, CEO and board, offer useful lessons on what boards should and should not do regarding business strategy.

In 2015, Abertis was a leading company in highway infrastructure management, with stable cash flows, good profitability and a reputation for good management. CEO Francisco Reynés had refocused the company around highways since 2010, selling business units that were less interrelated with its core business. One of the business units that Albertis had developed since 1999 was Abertis Telecom, which mainly provided the emission of TV and radio signals via communications towers throughout Spain. It also had a network of telecommunications towers acquired from the Spanish multinational Telefónica in 2012.

Francisco Reynés, and Tobías Martínez, Abertis Telecom's CEO since 2000, were keen observers of the changes underway in the telecoms industry. They began discussing the potential of a new company centered on the management of telecommunications towers. As telecom operators became increasingly focused on content and attracting and retaining customers, they were placing less

---

[7] A discussion on the creation of Cellnex, its relationships with Abertis, corporate strategy, IPO and corporate governance can be found in Canals (2018).

emphasis on infrastructure management. This shift occurred in the United States in the late 1990s and early 2000s, when large telecom operators sold off their infrastructure subsidiaries. In their place emerged new companies specialized in managing this type of infrastructure, such as Tower Co. and American Tower. Reynés, Martínez and their teams spearheaded a thorough strategy process to reflect on the industry's evolution, customer needs, the firm's unique capabilities and those of its competitors, and market opportunities it could exploit. In Europe, this industry was still in its early stages, with no significant independent players.

They also had to discuss strategy with Abertis board members and work closely with them to ensure everyone was fully aware of the challenges and different alternatives in order to make an informed decision. In September and October 2014, several board meetings were held to discuss the firm's strategic guidelines and options to accelerate growth, design the IPO, define the type of shareholders the company would need and the role Albertis would play in it.

Cellnex was the name given to the new company. It went public in May 2015. The IPO was a tremendous success. Between May 2015 and December 2021, the share price was up by 350 percent, a testament to a well-defined strategy, excellent management, consistent delivery and fluid communication with shareholders, who truly valued the quality of the newly formed company's governance and management and the clarity of its strategy and execution.

Certainly, Cellnex's timing was opportune; the firm was able to effectually capture an emerging trend in the telecoms market. But it is worth noting that other European companies tried and failed to replicate its success. In discussions with Reynés, Martínez and board members, several dimensions of Cellnex's performance stood out. The first was the high quality of its corporate governance and board of directors: their expertise, diversity, engagement and ability to communicate efficiently with the shareholders and to deliver on their commitments. This relationship is always relevant, but even more so when the company needs to increase its equity and combine it with debt to fund new investments, as was the case with Cellnex between 2015 and 2020.

The second dimension was the relationships among the board, CEO and top management of the firm, and the quality of their debates on strategy issues. There was constant interaction between board members and the CEO, who worked together to develop a well-defined strategic framework and discuss fundamental principles and issues, always with a long-term horizon.

The third attribute was the clarity and uniqueness of Cellnex's strategy and its effectual implementation. The fourth dimension related to the professional qualities of the senior management team, led by the CEO, and their capacity to communicate with investors and deliver on their commitments. A clearly communicated strategy and consistent delivery generate a virtuous circle and serve as the strongest foundation of trust. This is the focus of Section 3.3.2, which delves into the building blocks of strategy discussions and strategic frameworks that boards of directors may find beneficial when working on strategy with the CEO.

3.3.1.2 Amadeus: Growth in the United States

Amadeus was the global leader in software for travel and hotel services in 2021. It was a well-respected, consistent company in terms of performance and delivery of software solutions for its customers.[8] Its experience serves as a good reference for boards and the practices they should cultivate to successfully collaborate with the CEO and management team. Amadeus was a spin-off of four European airlines – Air France, British Airways, Iberia and Lufthansa – which joined forces to create a software company to manage their reservation system. The company went public in 1991, was acquired by a private equity firm in 2005 and returned to public capital markets in 2010. Between 2010 and 2019, under the leadership of CEO Luis Maroto and

---

[8] For a deeper discussion on the company and its recent evolution, see Masclans and Canals (2020).

nonexecutive board chairman José A. Tazón, the company recorded outstanding economic performance, product innovation, talent development, growth and shareholder returns. Amadeus had combined internal innovation-driven growth, internal venturing and selective acquisitions to expand its current business and enter new markets.

Maroto and his team worked closely with the board in four core areas. The first was to speed up growth in their current portfolio of services by expanding specific offerings and geographies. The second was to continue improving operational effectiveness to ensure profitable and sustainable growth. The third was to invest in internal ventures that could accelerate growth in new areas, developed internally or in partnership with external start-ups. The fourth area was selective acquisitions that would allow Amadeus to quickly enter new segments and markets.

The board's deliberations of these transactions offer interesting insights on the collaborative work between the board and CEO, including the TravelClick acquisition in 2018 (Masclans and Canals, 2020). With the TravelClick deal, the board's discussions reveal that their primary concerns included not only financial performance but other qualitative areas of performance. For Amadeus' board of directors, the management team was wholly aware of the financial constraints and exercised prudence by offering a reasonable price for the target company. Their major concerns centered on the potential integration of TravelClick as the firm's first large acquisition in a segment of the hotel software industry.

Amadeus was already present in the hotel segment through R&D, software development and commercial teams. The threat of organizational overlap with its operations was real, and the board wanted to ensure the top management team had a solid plan to effectively address it to retain key talent in the acquired company. People make the difference in any organization, but particularly in software companies.

The board of Amadeus, by shifting its focus to the acquisition's implementation and the integration of both companies, not only signaled its concerns about the operation's risks; it also helped the CEO and his management team refine their plans regarding the merging of both firms and devise strategies to preserve key TravelClick employees. The board understood well the strategic and financial logic of the operation. The financial plans elaborated by the CEO and his team were reasonable. In board meetings on strategy issues, financial dimensions often dominate the conversation. Remarkably, the Amadeus board's concerns focused on other dimensions, too: people, culture, customer service and the assimilation of both organizations.

3.3.2 A Strategy Road Map for Boards of Directors

Strategy is the firm's set of guiding policies and decisions to address the firm's external and internal challenges, and coherently organize its resources and activities to meet its goals and achieve its purpose.

This definition is based on many previous scholarly contributions. In particular, it considers that strategy includes: a set of guiding policies and decisions (Chandler, 1962; Andrews, 1971); a diagnosis of the firm's challenges (Porter, 1980; Rumelt, 2011); the identification of trade-offs and decisions on key activities (Porter, 1985, 1996; Rumelt, 2011; Montgomery, 2012); the organization of resources, capabilities and activities to serve customers uniquely, innovate and create economic value sustainably (Barney, 1991; Ghemawat, 1991; Porter, 1996; Teece, Pisano and Shuen, 1997; Ghemawat and Cassiman, 2007; Cassiman and Valentini, 2018); business model, business activities and fit (Porter, 1996; Montgomery, 2012; Amit and Zott, 2021); and a purpose that explains why the firm is in business, its overriding ambition and the type of company it aspires to be (Bower, 1970; Andrews, 1971; Montgomery, 2012). The board of directors should govern strategy in collaboration with the CEO and senior management.

Strategy is a complex issue for boards of directors. Most research considers strategy to be the ultimate responsibility of the CEO and top management team. There is a need to broaden this focus to include

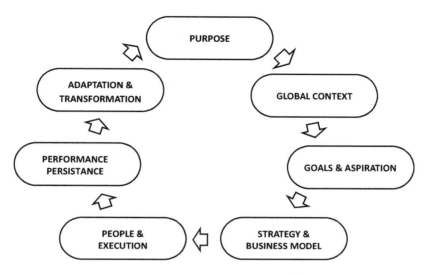

FIGURE 3.1 A strategy road map for boards of directors

the role of the board of directors. In many cases, board members have neither the time nor the expertise to work on the firm's competitive positioning and industry dynamics. It is important for board members to understand these issues since they directly impact the firm's long-term evolution. They should engage with senior management on these matters, without overstepping the role of management.

In this section, I present a strategy road map (see Figure 3.1) that boards of directors can use in their work on strategy with CEOs. It is based on relevant scholarly contributions to the field of strategy. I will review them in the following sections.

3.3.2.1 Purpose

The first element of the strategy road map for boards of directors is the firm's purpose (Mayer, 2018; Quinn and Thakor, 2019). As explored in Chapter 2, purpose may entail different dimensions and perspectives, but one element is indispensable: Purpose should explain why a specific company exists and what specific customer needs it aims to address. For this reason, purpose is at the heart of the strategy road map.

Unilever's purpose – "Making sustainable living common-place" – has shaped its strategy, business model, product innovation, culture and hiring and development over the last decade. In particular, its focus on sustainability and healthy products served as a catalyst for product innovation and strengthened its brands and customer loyalty. Moreover, purpose has also driven Unilever's standing as an employer of choice among young professionals.

The Cellnex management team expressed a sense of mission for the firm: to create a telecom infrastructure management company that would boost the effectiveness of telecom operators and better serve the connectivity needs of end consumers. There are many ways to express the purpose of a company and different perspectives to consider. Boards of directors and top management teams should make sure that their company has a purpose that explains why it is in business.

3.3.2.2   Understanding the Firm's Global Context and Opportunities

As Porter (1980) pointed out, industry structure determines the potential for profitability in an industry, as well as how the industry's economic value is distributed among different players (buyers, suppliers, customers or regulators). A competent board of directors should be aware of the firm's customers, suppliers and current and potential competitors. Since each party may impact the firm's economic performance in different ways, a holistic diagnosis of the industry is essential for any strategy discussion.

For the past four decades, corporate growth in Western countries has been closely tied to the process of international economic integration. Since the early 1980s, the globalization of markets offered an incredible growth opportunity for Western companies operating in emerging countries. Some firms successfully exploited this opportunity, while others failed in this endeavor. Boards of directors should also understand the potential fallout of decelerating globalization over the past few years, incited by trade wars and the COVID-19 pandemic, and its impact on specific industries and operations, since it may constrain corporate growth.

The same can be said of recent mega-trends: new geopolitical risk, digital disruption, the climate crisis, changing demographics, evolving consumer behaviors or new government regulations. Economic, financial, social and technology trends all have an impact on strategy and economic performance, especially in the long term. Boards of directors need to invest time to discuss these trends and assess their potential short- and long-term impact on the company and ensure that the senior management team works with some rigorous assumptions.

3.3.2.3 The Firm's Goals, Aspiration, Strategy and Business Model

As defined in the previous section, strategy is the firm's set of policies and decisions used to tackle its challenges and organize its activities to meet its goals and purpose. The board of directors should approve some corporate goals for the mid and long term, which are usually included in the firm's strategic guidelines. The board should also include in these guidelines a sense of aspiration, not only in terms of ambitious quantitative goals, but also in terms of what type of company they want for the future.

The CEO and the board itself should have the notion of purpose in mind, as well as these goals and aspiration, when they work on strategy. As a set of guiding policies and decisions, strategy entails a careful identification of the firm's challenges and trade-offs regarding how to serve customers, create value sustainably and achieve its goals.

Defining the firm's strategy requires the board of directors and senior managers to frame critical choices and make specific decisions. These decisions impact how the firm plans to create value and its ability to capture that value. These decisions involve choices about the firm's customer value proposition, its competitive positioning in the industry, its portfolio of activities and its geographical and business scope.

The implications of this view of strategy for boards of directors are diverse. Board members should understand the firm's major guiding policies, how it tries to serve customers, how its activities are organized and interrelated, whether the firm's positioning is unique and creates economic value and whether the firm has the resources and capabilities to sustain it.

Strategy is not only a rational process of establishing the means to reach explicit goals. It also involves a sense of aspiration connected to the firm's purpose and an entrepreneurial spirit to undertake new initiatives. The Cellnex experience sheds some light on this. Its top managers were keen observers of the changes underway in the telecom industry and realized they could design a value proposition for their customers that was different and unique. If they acted with speed and agility, Cellnex could become one of the leading firms in its industry in Europe in terms of quality of service and scale. Fostering this entrepreneurial mindset was a natural outcome of their renewed sense of aspiration to collectively achieve something greater than the initial business unit that operated under the Abertis umbrella. This sense of aspiration instilled the board and top management team with newfound energy to translate the purpose into action in a very entrepreneurial way.

The Cellnex board and top management needed to make some critical choices. They pondered the strategic choices for the new company, which revolved around some core concerns. One critical choice was whether Cellnex would operate as an end-to-end service provider of telecommunications infrastructure management – including the management of the towers and other sites – or only as a tower owner that would lease space to telecom operators. The latter was the option chosen by their US competitors. But Cellnex's top managers realized the company could offer a more sophisticated service that would better serve its customers. Its customers could reduce their needs for capital, investment and operational expenses by spinning off their towers of telecommunications.

These were frequent topics of discussions between senior managers and the board of directors. For Cellnex, achieving critical mass and arriving first were important because of the limited number of towers in the EU. Clarity and transparency, a candid approach debating the firm's different options, true interest in finding the best pathway for the company's long-term growth and the clear commitment of top managers were critical factors in convincing the board about the speed of growth, acquisitions and the equity and debt required to finance these operations.

The notion of business model has become a core element in the strategy debate. Strategy explains what the firm will do to meet its goals; the business model outlines how the company will operate to do so and create value (Zoot and Amit, 2010; Casadesus-Masanell and Ricart, 2011; Amit and Zott, 2020). The business model notion has some foundations in the earlier concepts of business activities and value chain (Andrews, 1971; Porter, 1985).

The election of the business model involves decisions on the firm's policies – from purchasing to pricing and sales – as well as the assets it plans to control, the activities to perform and the capabilities it needs to develop. While there are different definitions of the business model, this should always include the firm's customer value proposition, the activities to serve customers and its internal relations, the assets and capabilities it needs to operate and the management of these relationships and processes.[9] The customer value proposition is a critical choice that firms need to make and a core component of the business model. Once the value proposition for customers is clearly understood and perceived as valuable by customers, the company needs to ensure it can efficiently organize its related activities and operations, manage diverse internal and external

---

[9] Amit and Zott (2021) argued that a business model should include four elements that relate to its core activities: why, how, what and who. Johnson, Christensen and Kagermann (2008) suggested four dimensions for the business model: a customer value proposition, a profit logic, key resources necessary to operate and key processes.

relationships, sustainably offer its customer value proposition and create value for all parties through an effective implementation process.

The business model also elucidates how a company compares with its peers, not only in terms of product positioning, but across the entire value chain, including its degree of vertical integration. The business model is a relatively new concept but a common trait among long-standing, successful companies. Firms that are industry leaders, among them, Unilever, Nestlé, J. P. Morgan and Walmart, all developed very specific business models over the years that made their competitive positioning more sustainable. A strong business model is a source of numerous advantages, although may hinder the firm's evolution in times of flux. As the recent experiences of General Electric, Ford and Xerox reveal, the business model that helped them succeed in the past is not the model that will help them grow in the future.

In the current context of digital disruption, the risk of obsolescence is even more pronounced. With the emergence and growing dominance of big tech-based platforms like Amazon, Google, Microsoft and Alibaba, among others, the relevance of business models is even stronger. What sets these tech-based companies apart from their traditional competitors is not only technology, but the creation of new business models that leverage technology in a unique way to connect with end consumers.

An engaged board should understand the firm's business model and its connection with strategy, its core components and the elements required to be sustainable and serve customers in a unique way. By sharing their knowledge and capacity to debate and discuss business models, boards of directors add value to senior management teams and help them reflect and improve their own models.

3.3.2.4 *People and Execution*
Execution is a crucial pillar of the strategy road map. It includes specific policies to implement strategy and a comprehensive

monitoring and assessment system (Andrews, 1971; Simons, 2011). Strategy design is a rather analytical process, where logical dimensions supersede personal or emotional dimensions. In execution, the engagement of senior managers and the entire team is vital. A rational plan should be put in place, but the soft factors of engaging, motivating and uniting people around certain goals and objectives are truly important. For this reason, one of the board's primary functions is to thoroughly assess the quality of the management team and its ability to engage employees to implement strategy.

The experiences of Cellnex, Unilever and Amadeus also reveal that top managers lead by example by connecting emotionally with employees and engaging them to positively contribute to strategy execution. Planning, inspiration and engagement are indispensable for success. Paul Polman worked hard with his team at Unilever to improve organizational effectiveness. He understood that purpose was central to this effort, but that Unilever had to deliver economic results as well.

The inspiration that arose from the firm's purpose and values was critical for improving operational efficiency and boosting gross margins in lagging business units, which were slightly below the best-performing firms in their industries. Unilever derived 60 percent of its revenues from foods and beverages and 40 percent from personal care. Polman reorganized the company around four core business units in order to streamline the company and make it more functional: personal care, home care, foods and refreshment. He also moved away from regional structures and created eight major geographical areas.

The leaders of Unilever's business units and geographies reported directly to Polman. With the reorganization, Polman introduced changes in the values of managers, making them more accountable and entrepreneurial, with a stronger growth orientation. He also renewed the leadership development process by promoting younger employees to key positions, including more women and managers based in emerging countries. He also changed the management performance assessment and rewards system. He pushed for innovations to develop the company's leadership pipeline, including special educational and development programs for a large number of managers. These initiatives focused first and foremost on the leadership qualities the company would need in the future.

In order to speed up transformation, Unilever launched a new Connected 4 Growth (C4G) program in 2016. Its aim was to improve the organization and make it more agile, faster and more competitive, with an emphasis on four major areas: lowering costs through "Zero Based Budgeting"; simplifying structure and processes; stronger innovation by making products and brands more global and local; and engaging people. In particular, a core objective of C4G was to inspire Unilever employees to think and behave more like entrepreneurs and business owners, and give them greater leverage to experiment with new ideas and promote innovation.

In addressing strategy issues, the board should always remember that strategy implementation is above all a question of people working with people. The CEO and top management team have full responsibility for this function. The board should not replace the CEO in this crucial role, but should ask the CEO material questions to understand the management team's approach, which could make the difference between success or failure. The board should not dictate the CEOs' strategy execution, yet should collaborate with him or her to ensure that critical dimensions and risks are taken into account. Board members' expertise, wisdom and prudence in these areas are truly relevant for the success of strategy execution.

3.3.2.5 Strategy and the Persistence of Performance

A central question regarding the firm's strategy relates to how persistent the company's business model and financial performance are. The board needs to understand the competitive dynamics at play in the firm's industry and the sustainability of its positioning and financial performance. Multiple forces shape the dynamics of competition. Pricing is one of them. Yet the experience points out that the game-changers in any industry arise from strategic investments for new products or services, innovative business models or a combination thereof. Strategic investments with a degree of irreversibility define dramatic changes in industries (Ghemawat, 1991). The emergence of platforms that connect buyers and sellers of products and services, often without direct links to the assets being traded, perfectly illustrates the disruptive impact of some investments (Cusumano, Gower and Yoffie, 2019). Board members should be cognizant of the disruptive powers of new emerging companies and technologies.

Economic performance may deteriorate as a result of external or internal factors (Ghemawat, 1991). The external factors that negatively impact the dynamics of performance are: the threat of imitation and competitive dynamics – in terms of pricing, product quality or product variety – the threat of substitution by new entrants or incumbents that introduce disruptive new models, products or technology, and the holdup of cash flows by some suppliers or other partners. The internal factors that can decrease performance are related to operational inefficiencies or lower productivity.

A stress test on strategy should be carried out periodically and the board can play a very important role in it. The board of directors should ask the CEO and senior management team questions about the sustainability of the firm's current strategy and position, the risks of disruption, substitution and imitation and the potential deterioration of performance because of organizational ineffectiveness. The board's function in strategy is not limited to approving or supporting strategic decisions but to continuously and collaboratively engaging the management team to offer fresh perspectives, challenge assumptions and assess risks.

Mapping risks at the board level is also critical. The sustainability of a strategy may be jeopardized by operational, competitive, financial, strategic and external risks, as evidenced by recent trade wars and the global pandemic. Boards should consider and include them in their reflections on strategy.

3.3.2.6 *Adaptation and Transformation*

The firm's performance and its sustainability are vital issues for boards of directors and CEOs. The many forces shaping the business world today – digitalization, consumer behavior shifts, and slowing globalization among others – point to the urgent need for change and adaptation. It does not matter how successful the firm has been in the past. The future will probably require different business models and capabilities to serve customers well. The selection and design of a new business model is a mainstay of strategy. The CEO and senior management team are responsible for its design and development yet the board of directors also plays a critical role.

Modifying the business model to adapt to new realities is always complex. As Govindarajan and Trimble (2011) discuss, firms need to manage the present, forget the past and create the future. Cognitive capabilities tend to emphasize the past and the present and downplay the future. But good governance and professional boards of directors need to work with the senior managers to forge their company's future, as illustrated by the experiences of Amadeus, Cellnex and Unilever, among others.

An effective board of directors needs to articulate several important perspectives regarding the firm's transformation, a topic explored in greater detail in Chapter 4. The first relates to anticipating and understanding why the current business model may not be sustainable in the near future. In this instance, the sooner the board convinces the CEO, the better. The second is to work with the CEO to develop a shared perspective on the core components of the new business model and specific steps to move from the old to the new, with the requisite performance indicators to effectively monitor the transition. The board needs to ensure the proposed change is coherent with the firm's purpose. The third is the clarity of goals and actions to be taken. The fourth is managers' accountability with the execution of the strategy and its associated action plans. The fifth is consistent and coherent communication with shareholders, which should run in parallel with that of the senior management team in transmitting the firm's goals, strategy and decisions with employees, customers and other stakeholders.

The various building blocks of the strategy road map combine systematic observations of good boards of directors in action and theoretical notions from the field of strategy. This road map aims to help boards of directors become active decision makers in strategy issues, working in alliance with the CEO and top managers while leaving the company's management in the hands of the CEO.

3.4 THE STRATEGY PROCESS: THE ROLE OF THE BOARD OF DIRECTORS AND BOARD–CEO COLLABORATION

The role of the boards in strategy requires board members with high levels of competency and expertise, as well as a deep personal involvement and commitment to make it work. Unfortunately, these qualities are not enough for boards to effectively contribute to strategy. The board of directors should do its utmost to respect the functions entrusted to the CEO and senior management team in guiding the company's strategy. In view of their close contact with customers, competitors and suppliers, senior managers are better positioned to observe trends, challenges, opportunities and threats. The board would infringe upon the domain of top management if it did not allow the CEO to effectively carry out this role.

At the same time, the board should support the management team in other ways. The board of directors should make sure its perspective aligns with the company's reality; ensure top management can wisely and prudently define and execute the strategy; confirm that the assessment of the firm's capabilities is reasonable; verify that the firm is taking into account industry shifts and external changes; and assure that its projections and forecasts do not reflect an overestimation bias.

Beyond its monitoring duties, the board of directors serves as an expert advisor to the senior management team. It should pose the right questions to the CEO. It should challenge the assumptions made by top managers. This role requires the knowledge and expertise to effectively assess the quality of the management team. The board should act as a good steward of the firm's resources and capabilities. It should serve as an advisor to the CEO and senior managers, who find in the board not only supervisors but mentors willing to help them execute the company's strategy.

The next two sections underscore the collaborative relationships between the boards, CEOs and senior management teams that I observed at Amadeus and Unilever. The summaries of the extensive interviews conducted over the years with the CEOs and top managers of these companies are available in Masclans and Canals (2020) and Canals (2019), respectively.

3.4.1   The Collaboration between the Board and the CEO in the Strategy Process

The collaborative nature of the board of directors–CEO relationships at Unilever and Amadeus was particularly insightful. At Unilever, Paul Polman was convinced of the need to collaborate and work closely with the board on strategy and strategic issues. As he shared,

> [t]he long-term development of the company depends very much on a good strategy and its execution, so directors should spend a lot of time working on this area, understand the different issues well and provide useful insights and advice. In addition, board directors need to understand the company's overall objectives, its general direction, how well it is currently performing, and how it can win

Polman thought the CEO and the board of directors – not shareholders – should own the firm's strategy. They should understand it well, routinely discuss it in depth, be convinced about it, unite their people around it and sell it to shareholders. According to Polman,

> [s]ome CEOs have become too dependent on shareholders on deciding the firm's strategy. You need to pay attention to them, but strategy is a basic function of the CEO, who needs to work with the

board of directors. It is also important to remember that there is not one individual shareholder. Large companies have a diversity of shareholders, with different views and perspectives on strategy. Each may have different expectations and goals, not only about economic profitability. It is impossible to follow all their recommendations or to change strategy every time shareholders tell you to do so. You need to own your strategy and make sure that it is in sync with what reasonable investors who understand the company actually expect

During his first years as CEO, Polman spent considerable time with the board of directors to discuss Unilever's strategy and the Unilever Sustainable Living Plan (USLP). He and his team developed a business model that captured the core dimensions with an impact on stakeholders – customers, employees, shareholders, suppliers and society – and grounded it on a commitment to perform well. This was his way of convincing investors that people and sustainability should be put at the heart of the business model. He also traveled extensively to educate investors about Unilever's strategy, the Unilever Sustainable Living Plan and its intersection with customers, product innovation, sustainability and performance.

The boards of Amadeus and Unilever developed a series of procedures to address strategic issues (see Table 3.1). I present my own summary of these practices. The first is the board's commitment to dedicate time in every single board meeting to analyze and discuss and offer feedback on strategy and the strategic proposals of top management, including important strategic decisions. Boards often allocate an inordinate amount of time to compliance and simple information issues, to the detriment of strategy and strategic decisions. The second is to periodically review the strategic issues that board members should understand and judiciously share their views with the CEO. The third is the regular review of the firm's strategic plan. This is a very useful construct for framing deep conversations on

Table 3.1. *The strategy process: Some board practices*

- Each board meeting should include a review of strategy issues
- Regularly review trends and customers' concerns that may affect strategy
- Regularly review the company's strategy guidelines or plan
- Select and present in each board meeting a theme with an impact on the firm (e.g., innovation, talent development, climate change, technology disruption)
- Improve holistic reporting to the board, beyond financial issues and indicators
- Annual strategy retreat

strategy between the CEO and senior management team and board members. These conversations are vital to help board members genuinely understand the firm's challenges and strategy. Board members also help the CEO and senior managers challenge their assumptions and improve their models and proposals.

The fourth practice is to spotlight a horizontal issue – sustainability, globalization or technology, for instance – in every board meeting, even if the board is not yet ready to make any decision. Boards need to create a space for dialogue and reflection on these fundamental issues and their potential impact on the firm. In many cases, the board welcomes external experts to share their views on the chosen topic.

The fifth practice is providing the board with a holistic reporting system that comprises both financial and nonfinancial variables like the one Unilever developed for the Sustainable Living Plan. This is a critical facet of strategy. Just as in financial reporting, nonfinancial reporting should include key indicators – both qualitative and quantitative – that reflect the company's situation along core dimensions: people, leadership development, customer satisfaction, environmental impact and R&D.

The sixth practice is an annual strategy retreat with the board and senior management team to explore new strategic challenges.

This meeting offers the board additional time to better understand the firm's strategy, as well as the level of execution of its diverse actions and policies. It could also be combined with visits to the firm's subsidiaries, operations and customers in its core markets. These summits also give CEOs the opportunity to have lengthier conversations with board members to answer their questions and concerns, better understand their views and forge consensus on strategic decisions and future directions.

3.4.2 The Collaboration between the Board and the CEO in Strategic Decisions

As mentioned earlier, when the Amadeus board was debating whether to acquire TravelClick, its main concern related to the smooth integration of both firms, not the deal's financial aspects. In this way, the board underlined its concerns about the operation's risks and offered insights to hone the company's integration strategy. The board's emphasis on people, culture, customer service, organizational processes and team integration varies greatly from what typically occurs in board discussions on strategy decisions, when financial issues overshadow other facets.

The boards of Amadeus and Cellnex highlight interesting practices and reflections on the strategy process and the board's role in it (see Table 3.2). The first is to help the CEO and top management team evaluate and prepare a comprehensive analysis of the major decisions and present them to the board for a deep discussion with board members. Preparing for board meetings with high-quality and comprehensive information is the first step toward ensuring a good debate at the board level.

The second is to make sure that board members understand the nature of the decisions, their fit in the firm's strategy and the expected economic, organizational, competitive and human impact under different scenarios. The CEO and his or her team should help the board understand the potential implications of key decisions beyond financial performance. In particular, the board should understand the

Table 3.2. *The interaction between the board of directors and the CEO in strategy: A process*

- The CEO should prepare major strategic decisions and specific proposals to be discussed by the board
- Understand each strategic decision in the wider frame of the firm's purpose, strategy and capabilities
- The strategic decision should lead to a better customer experience
- Impact of the strategic decision on the firm's purpose, culture and values
- Check with and involve key shareholders in considering strategic decisions

---

effects of these decisions on the firm's capacity to grow and develop in the long term.

The third is the need to keep the firm's focus on customers when making major strategic decisions. Customer service is a clear source of competitive advantage for companies. It is too easy to compromise customer service via decisions that seem to improve efficiency but end up decreasing the customer experience. Good boards understand the firm's customers and their reasons for buying its products or services.

The fourth is to focus the discussion on the human, behavioral and organizational dimensions of the decisions, including their impact on retention, integration and motivation of key people. This is a fundamental shift from a purely financial analysis to a more comprehensive review of major strategic decisions and their execution. Amadeus' board, when acquiring a software company specialized in a customer niche different from its own, encouraged its CEO to devise a plan to effectively integrate and retain the team members of the acquired company in order to continue serving its clients.

The fifth aspect is to assess how a major strategic decision might affect the firm's purpose, culture and values. This reflection may be grounded more on qualitative dimensions than quantitative predictions and cause doubt among board members. Despite the uncertainty, board members' reflections on these dimensions and their careful consideration by senior management are strong indicators of their professionalism and commitment to the firm's purpose and long-term development.

The sixth aspect is the need to understand the expectations and reflections of key shareholders in this process. In the end, the board's behavior and attitudes show that board members took their responsibility of monitoring management and duty of care in their board functions very seriously, beyond financial performance and economic indicators. In this respect, the collaborative nature of the work between the board and CEO was essential to achieving this outcome and reveals a patently clear pathway on how boards of directors can boost their effectiveness in a highly uncertain world.

3.5   A TYPOLOGY OF BOARD OF DIRECTORS' APPROACHES TO STRATEGY: BOARD–CEO COLLABORATION

This section examines a typology of boards of directors in addressing strategy according to two essential criteria: the role of the board of directors and the role of the CEO and top management team in deciding the firm's strategy. The relative influence of each decision maker – the board of directors and the CEO – is also shaped by the level of collaboration between the board and the top management team. The relative influence of boards of directors and CEOs in shaping and determining the firm's strategy is not only indicative of the balance of power between these decision bodies; it also has a clear impact on the quality of corporate governance. This section uses the cases of Amadeus, Cellnex, Deutsche Bank and Unilever to explore this dimension.

The strategic decisions faced by Unilever's board in February 2017 in dealing with the Kraft Heinz bid shed light on the different degrees of involvement of boards in defining the firm's strategy. Under the leadership of its chairman, the Unilever board of directors had been deeply and proactively involved in the firm's strategic decisions over the years, as evidenced by their understanding and support of the Unilever Sustainable Living Plan. Although the plan originated from CEO Paul Polman and his management team, it was discussed, debated and approved by the board of directors.

The Amadeus and Cellnex experiences also point to the importance of the collaborative nature of work by the CEO and the board of directors in dealing with strategy issues. Through this collaboration, decision makers in both realms can work together to define and execute more innovative and successful strategies. The Deutsche Bank case points to the other end of the spectrum: powerful CEOs who controlled the strategy process for years and a board of directors – the supervisory board, according to German corporate law – unable to help define a credible strategy. This difficult collaboration between the bank's top management and board of directors also added complexity to strategic change.

Boards of directors and CEOs need to work together and interact effectively in strategy and strategic decisions. They serve as the company's highest governance decision makers. A solid understanding of their distinct roles is context specific, depending on the firm's country, industry, ownership structure and strategic challenges. The board and the CEO should fully understand the nature of the firm's challenges and realize that generic solutions to organize their collaboration do not exist. Each board needs to find its own solution.

This section presents a typology of boards of directors' involvement in strategy (Table 3.3). The emerging types of boards reflect the diverse degrees of commitment and engagement of board members and CEOs in the strategic decision-making process. The profiles of boards regarding their role in corporate strategy may be summarized as passive boards, interactive boards, strategy-shaper boards and collaborative boards.[10]

---

[10] McNulty and Pettigrew (1997) developed a model that describes the levels of part-time board members' involvement in strategy. They distinguished three levels of involvement: taking strategic decisions, shaping strategic decisions and shaping the context, content and conduct of strategy. The model I present here complements McNulty and Pettigrew's model with the board–CEO interaction perspective.

Table 3.3. *A typology of boards of directors' and CEOs' involvement in strategy*

		Strategy: CEO and Senior Management Engagement	
		Low	High
Strategy: Board of Directors' Engagement	**Low**	Passive	Informative/ Interactive
	High	Shaper	Collaborative

3.5.1 Passive Boards

The first board profile regarding strategy is the passive board. This profile presents low board engagement in strategy and limited initiative by the management team to explore strategy in depth with board members. It is a profile adopted by many boards when approving strategic plans, one of simple compliance. In this profile, the CEO develops the strategic plan with top management and presents it to the board, which eventually approves it following some discussion. But neither the work of the CEO nor that of the board in this area suffices to offer a sense of long-term orientation. The Deutsche Bank board after the 2008 financial crisis exemplifies this type of board.

Many boards still operate as passive boards. Passive boards may fulfill their essential functions and comply with laws and regulation. They may meet basic compliance issues, such as giving their approval to strategic decisions or strategic plans. They ensure processes are followed in different areas. Nevertheless, these boards are not very active in helping the CEO and top managers think about the broader questions that could impact the firm and its future. Their long-term horizons regarding shareholders and other stakeholders tend to be narrower in focus, perhaps because the firm has a dominant shareholder who makes all major decisions or because its ownership is so dispersed that no single shareholder wields enough power to improve the quality of decision-making.

Boards of directors with this profile are not overly engaged in discussions and debates on important strategic issues. The explicit reflection on the firm's long-term evolution is absent from board meetings. This is a critical weakness of this type of board, especially when companies face serious competitive challenges. Competent boards can play a vital role in exposing the top management team to new perspectives.

3.5.2   Informative/Interactive Boards

The second profile of boards regarding its involvement with strategy is the informative/interactive board. This type emerges in a context where the board is not particularly involved, and the top management team is more active and entrepreneurial about strategic initiatives. The board asks questions, suggests issues for the CEO to ponder and eventually approves the strategy.

This board profile emerged among companies that took governance seriously following the new corporate governance codes of the 1990s. In these boards, directors are doing a competent job but the atmosphere of board meetings and interaction between board members and the CEO do not foster deep engagement on strategic issues. This board profile occurs as well in companies where the CEO is also a key shareholder or closely aligned with one. In these cases, CEOs may consider themselves in complete alignment with shareholders and do not consider the board's role to be irrelevant beyond its legal obligations or advice on concrete business areas.

The interactive board is one step further in terms of board involvement. It requires competent board members who ask relevant questions and offer additional insights into top management's deliberations. In this case, either the board chairperson or the board's tradition and culture demarcate the limits on board members' involvement in strategy and the time delegated in board meetings to these discussions.

A good CEO can use an interactive board as a sounding board to gain new perspectives or deliberate long-term questions. The problem is that the board is not actively involved in reflections on strategy. In this profile, strategy is still essentially the responsibility of the top management and the board plays a limited role in forging the firm's long-term orientation.

3.5.3   Strategy-Shaper Boards

The third board profile is the strategy-shaper board. This board requires board members with relevant business experience, a competent chairperson capable of managing active board members and a forum that allows every issue to be discussed in an open, challenging way. This board tries to reinforce its involvement in strategy through its work with the CEO, and, in some cases, supplants the CEO in this role. Top management may have the right level of professional competence, but in this case, boards are more powerful for historical reasons, the presence of large shareholders in the firm's governance or the personalities of the chairperson and board members.

This is the case of companies whose dominant shareholders are private equity or venture capital firms (Garg and Eisenhardt, 2017). Entrepreneurs are helped and supported by a few experienced investors, who get involved in the firm's strategy. It is also the case of family owned firms when family members with deep company and industry knowledge relinquish their executive functions and adopt a significant supervisory and mentoring role as board members. Their experience and position as large shareholders may be particularly useful in a turnaround or transformation process. Finally, it is also the case of companies where one or several activist investors control part of the firm's equity and become important drivers of the firm's strategy by supporting the appointment of a new CEO or board members.

In some industries, business models should be designed, tested and implemented quickly. In this context, board directors' experience in other industries – such as technology or capital markets – can be useful in forging strategic decisions and cultivating positive inter-action with the top management team.

In these cases, the board takes a more active role, shapes the strategy and suggests specific strategic actions the CEO should follow to help the company excel in the long term. This profile requires deeply involved board members but runs the risk of senior managers playing a secondary role and an overdependence on the board for strategic decisions and orientation. The desired balance between the board of directors and the CEO may be broken here, and the board may overextend its reach if it does not sufficiently rely on the CEO and senior management team.

3.5.4   Collaborative Boards

The fourth profile is the board that actively collaborates with the CEO and senior management team on strategy issues. As in all good part-nerships, both the board of directors and the CEO and top managers bring different capabilities and experiences to help develop the com-pany in the long term. Each company needs to redefine this partner-ship over time, within the boundaries of the corporate legal system and company bylaws.

The collaborative profile involves intense and productive cooperation between the board and the top management team. This is the case observed in Unilever, Cellnex and Amadeus. There are several clear advantages of a collaborative partnership in strategy. The first is that it places the primary responsibility of strategy and stra-tegic decisions on the CEO and top management team.

The second is that it also fosters positive cooperation between the board and top management, with the shared understanding that both bring complementary capabilities and experiences to the firm's governance. If well managed, the depth and diversity of skills and capabilities are always opportunities, never obstacles.

The third is that the CEO and the senior management team have a partner – the board of directors – that is removed from the company's daily operations to discuss and reflect upon the firm's long-term strategy. If the board composition is diverse, with competent and committed board members, the outcome of these discussions will likely be even richer. The fourth is that its enables the board to better understand the company, its industry and its challenges. It also gives the board a deeper sense of ownership of the firm's strategy. Board members – not just the chairperson and the CEO – are able to better understand strategic issues and articulate a stronger response amid an unexpected crisis, such as Kraft Heinz's unsolicited takeover of Unilever. It is exceedingly difficult for board members to feel true ownership of the strategic decisions required in urgent situations, unless they are highly knowledgeable about the firm's strategy.

This approach also considers the principles of subsidiarity and delegation, which are crucial in any organization. Based on this tenet, the functions and tasks assigned to an individual or intermediate unit should not be carried out by individuals or units in higher positions within the organization. It is a principle of both organizational effectiveness and respect for the initiative and freedom of everyone working in the organization. It also ensures that organizational decision-making rights are allocated to people who are closer to the problems and challenges, and consequently better informed on them.

When the board of directors and the CEO work in a collaborative partnership, with mutual respect for their distinct professional duties, they help generate a culture of trust inside the company that gradually permeates the entire organization. And a positive, integrative culture also helps foster creativity, innovation and employee engagement. A positive culture promotes employee integration and cross-functional collaboration is a source of strength for any organization.

Finally, the collaborative model for boards of directors has implications for shareholders. It expresses the board's commitment to thoroughly understand the company, its business and its industry, as well as its people and core capabilities. It expresses the board of directors' intent to work with the CEO and the top management team. It also shows its willingness to share financial indicators and other relevant issues with shareholders, as well as engage them in the firm's purpose and aspirations. The model of the collaborative board better responds to the concerns of impact investors, who seek additional performance indicators and attributes in the companies they invest in beyond financial returns.

This model is particularly useful in times of organizational flux or industry transformation, when boards observe the approaching obsolescence of old paradigms and lack of clarity regarding new pathways of competition. A compelling strategy is necessary, both to provide managers and employees with a sense of direction, as well as to explain the company's new course to shareholders.

The collaborative model also offers boards a positive and constructive way to dissuade activist shareholders from attacking the company with proposals that may create short-term gains but whose long-term benefits are uncertain. For companies, one of the most effective ways to avoid problems with activist shareholders is to ensure they have a highly active and competent board of directors that understands the business well and works closely with top managers to steer the company toward long-term value creation. According to many targeted companies, activist investors found an entry to influence their strategic orientation simply because the board of directors was remiss in this responsibility.

It is easy to blame activist shareholders for the failure of these companies. However, in all probability, these activists would have never acted if the companies and their boards had a clearly defined strategy for sustainable value creation. Companies' mediocre economic performance and low share price reflected either lackluster strategies, deficient strategy execution or both. It is a firm's lack of strategic direction, passive board of directors and inability to explain strategic decisions to investors that eventually draws the attention of activist shareholders.

3.6   FINAL REFLECTIONS

Good corporate governance requires boards to deal effectively with strategy and enhance the quality of strategy discussions through holistic frameworks. The complex nature of strategy, coupled with the need for collaboration between the board and the CEO, poses a challenge for companies. The corporate law tradition and its focus on the duty of care and oversight of top management offer some useful reflections. Strategy fits well within the context of the board directors' duty of care, but offers few guidelines on its wider implications.

The corporate finance tradition offers evidence on the impact of major strategic decisions like corporate diversifications or M&As. The shareholder value maximization goal is a prevalent theoretical principle in finance but difficult to implement in the real world in view of top managers' bounded rationality, the need to define time horizons and the premise that not all shareholders are equal; they reflect different preferences and expectations. Even if shareholder value maximization was considered a good indicator in concrete circumstances, it would still not replace the strategy and strategic reflection process, essential to defining the firm's value proposition and ability to create sustainable long-term value.

With some exceptions, the strategic management tradition and complementary perspectives on business strategy fail to address strategy at the board level. Nonetheless, the research and practice of strategy offer useful perspectives on how boards of directors can approach strategy and strategic decisions and, more importantly, how a culture of collaboration can be nurtured between the board and the CEO and top management team.

In this chapter, I offer boards of directors a strategy road map to help them contend with strategy and strategic decisions. I also highlight dimensions of the strategy process for boards to consider. Several principles are useful in helping boards of directors work on strategy. The first is ensuring members have deep knowledge of the company's strategic challenges. The second is the reflection and discussion of these issues among board directors, the CEO and other members of the senior management team. The third is the quality of the issues raised, the questions posed and the reflections shared in these sessions. The fourth is a spirit of true collaboration between the board and the CEO.

Business strategy involves both content and process. The board's work on strategy requires professional competency in the deliberation and formulation of strategy. The board should also have knowledge of the strategy process, methodologies followed, involvement of senior managers and the sequence of events for execution. Robust strategies require effective implementation: The company needs a positive board culture and fluid collaboration between the board and CEO, who will execute the board-approved strategy and suggest adjustments if needed.

With an anchor in the strategic management tradition and clinical evidence of some companies that excelled through a combination of good governance, solid management and long-standing sustainable economic performance, I observed four basic profiles of boards of directors in dealing with strategy: the passive board, the informative/interactive board, the strategy-shaper board and the collaborative board. The categories are not clear-cut. In the real world, there are surely combinations of these four profiles.

Each board needs to adopt its own profile and define its role in strategy and strategy-making, as well as its relationship with the CEO and top management team. Today's global uncertainty and disruption have exerted a profound effect on companies worldwide, spotlighting the importance of the board of directors in the firm's strategy and long-term orientation.

4 The Role of the Board of Directors in Corporate Transformation

4.1 BOARDS OF DIRECTORS' DECISIONS THAT CHANGE THE FIRM'S FUTURE

In October 2017, Eloi Planes, chairman of Fluidra,[1] a leading manufacturer and distributor of pool products and solutions, was preparing for a meeting of the board of directors. A potential corporate deal with Zodiac, a US manufacturer, was on the agenda. Fluidra was listed on the Madrid Stock Exchange. At the time, the four founding families held around a 55 percent stake in the firm. How could Fluidra develop a growth strategy without destroying shareholder value?

Planes was mulling over new challenges in preparation for the board meeting: "We have achieved the strategic plan's objectives a year ahead of schedule and have much higher expectations and aspirations than we did two years ago. We can carry on with a plan with similar features and consolidate our position, or we can make a decision to transform the company and turn it into the industry leader." The decision was risky; 50 percent of the global pool market was in the United States and Fluidra's US sales accounted for only 5 percent of its total revenue.

Fluidra was founded in 1969 by the Corbera, Garrigós, Planes and Serra families under the trade name Astral. Headquartered in Sabadell, Spain, the company manufactured and marketed stainless steel ladders, drains and filters for swimming pools. By the end of the 1990s, its products were sold in Europe, Turkey, the Middle East, Oceania and the United States. It expanded globally by opening subsidiaries in each country with the support of local partners. The

---

[1] The description of Fluidra's challenges is based on Masclans, Tàpies and Canals (2020).

company developed a solid manufacturing platform and carried out acquisitions to broaden its product portfolio. Fluidra had a clear sense of mission: "Caring for people's wellness and health through the sustainable use of water in leisure, sports and therapeutic applications." The company designed, produced and distributed every component needed for building, upgrading and maintaining residential and commercial pools. It had a wide range of pool products on offer.

In 2002, the four founding families invited Banco Sabadell to acquire a 20 percent stake in the group in order to bolster the firm's financial structure and finance its international expansion. Between 2003 and 2006, Fluidra shareholders actively sought solutions to ensure the company's future, including the possibility of an M&A deal in the United States. The founding families wanted to continue to promote Fluidra's development.

In 2005, after ruling out a merger with the US firm Pentair, the board, with the support of shareholders, prepared the company for an IPO. Planes, a member of the second generation of the family, was named CEO in January 2006. The shareholders undertook further reorganization and created a single holding company to group the four existing companies in two business units: Pool and Water.

The board also approved a radical change in its composition. It would include nine members: five directors representing majority shareholders, one executive director (the CEO) and three independent directors. The independent directors, with diverse professional backgrounds, would complement the rest of the board.

On October 31, 2007, the company went public on the Madrid Stock Exchange at €6.50 a share, with a free float of 33.5 percent. The 2008 recession dealt a heavy blow to Fluidra. The 2009–2014 transformation plan focused on three aspects: improving operating efficiency, increasing cash flows and reducing debt. Between 2010 and 2014, the board changed the holding company structure and grouped all activities under a single organization, organized by functional divisions. The board of directors played a very important role in turning the company around during the 2008–2013 crisis and gave

Fluidra a different focus – balance sheet management and transformation.

Since 2015, Planes and the board had been deliberating on Fluidra's long-term project. They agreed the company needed to aim at a more holistic transformation after years of prioritizing efficiency and organic growth. In 2017, Fluidra was returning to pre-2008 cash-generation levels. Its share price was recovering: It had fallen from €6.50 in November 2007 to €2 by the end of 2010, then rebounded to €3 at the end of 2015, and €8.90 in September 2017. In 2017, Fluidra had a great innovation capacity, strong manufacturing structure and vertically integrated with an end-to-end model for the various activities in the value chain, ranging from innovation to production and marketing. In 2017, the board comprised four directors representing large shareholders, one executive (the CEO) and four independent directors. Some board members argued that only a large acquisition in the United States would be truly transformational.

In the United States, there were three major manufacturers with substantial market share: Pentair, Hayward and Zodiac. Zodiac was in an interesting position; it was smaller than Fluidra. Rhône Capital, a private equity firm, bought the company in 2016 and expected to exit in about six to seven years. Zodiac was strong in the United States but did not have distribution capabilities. Zodiac Pool's CEO and senior managers were competent professionals, but their compensation levels were high and closely linked to the future company value, whenever Rhône decided to sell its stake. Fluidra estimated Zodiac's valuation around 750 million. The terms of agreement would depend not only on synergies to be achieved but also on the corporate governance structure, the board of directors and senior management, and defining a new strategy to compete in the three major markets – the United States, Europe and Asia – as one company.

Planes wanted to keep Fluidra's purpose and the founding families together but knew a large corporate transaction would compromise the families' controlling stake. He was considering some key questions: how to devise a transaction between Fluidra and a US company? How to think about the future company's corporate governance. If Fluidra entered a transaction with a company owned by a private equity firm, should the new company still be listed? What type of board of directors should be established?

A possible transaction in the United States would also pose risks to its business model. Fluidra was a company that uniquely combined its capacity for innovation, manufacturing and distribution into a successful business model. Zodiac would complement Fluidra with a strong manufacturing capacity and solid innovation model in the United States. This would require a deep transformation of Fluidra and develop a new business model. The potential deal with Zodiac would be an opportunity to change but would also represent governance, ownership, strategic, financial and operational risks for Fluidra.

4.2   WHAT IS CORPORATE TRANSFORMATION? DOES IT MATTER FOR GOVERNANCE?

Fluidra's efforts to change over the past two decades illustrate some major features of corporate transformation (Table 4.1). The first is that transformation requires the development of new capabilities and intense learning at all levels in the organization. In the early 2000s, the different Fluidra business units were very entrepreneurial, yet without much coordination among them. This was positive in terms of agility and speed, but some units lacked the scale to compete and

Table 4.1. *Corporate transformation: Some attributes*

- Development of new capabilities and learning
- Investment and long-term time horizon
- Organization-wide change process
- Corporate purpose and employees
- Rethink strategy and business model
- A process with uncertainty: Focus on serving customers
- Leadership of the board of directors

were not reaping the benefits of synergies and other advantages of sharing resources.

Fluidra managers had to learn how to preserve this entrepreneurial spirit and, at the same time, coordinate actions and leverage the benefits of merging the resources of the different business units. In the transformation between 2008 and 2014, Fluidra managers learned how to survive and in a low-growth context. The Fluidra expansion in the 1980s and 1990s unfolded during growth years in most of the world economy. Fluidra managers had to develop new capabilities to work better with customers and boost product innovation in a time of slower GDP growth.

The second is that transformation involves developing new capabilities and additional investment. The execution of these decisions requires a long-term horizon. In fact, transformation aims to help answer the question of how the firm should look like in the next five or ten years. This is a key question for boards of directors. Capability development and changing an organization effectively require time and patience.

The third is that transformation encompasses the entire organization. A change related to a single department or business unit is not truly a corporate transformation. As Fluidra's story reflects so well, transformation involves the entire organization and should have a clear focus on serving customers better. The fourth attribute is keeping the sense of purpose alive and engaging employees. A shared purpose will help renew the reasons why the effort is worthy. Since transformation entails all organizational areas and employees, keeping purpose alive serves as a great pillar of the change process. Transformation requires a lot of energy and involves setbacks. Transformation is not only a rational exercise. It also includes behaviors that are indispensable for learning and developing new capabilities. Reminding people about the firm's purpose and why they do what they do is important to keeping them on board.

The fifth attribute is the strategy reflection. The company will need to adopt a new strategic road map under the leadership of the

CEO and the stewardship and approval of the board. In this road map, the customer value proposition is essential: How does the company plan to add value to customers? A new strategy involves a new business model, adopted by the company to deliver value to customers sustainably. As presented in Chapter 3, the business model includes a customer value proposition and involves the specific organization of the different functions and activities to create that customer value sustainably. By definition, the business model considers the company's relevant functions: sales, marketing, distribution, manufacturing, logistics, R&D and purchasing, and corporate functions such as talent development, finance and IT. Transformation is cross-functional, takes a holistic perspective and grounds its specific action plans on each business unit and department.

The sixth attribute is to reflect on how to tackle uncertainties and unknowns. In the transformation journey, some qualities are essential. The first is to keep the customer as the company's top priority. While transformation processes may be painful for companies, they should be painless for their customers. The second is that a transformation process will involve failures. It is important to foresee the mostly likely ones and, if possible, anticipate and hedge against them. Most importantly, top managers have to foster an attitude of learning from these failures. The third is that managers need to ask themselves what can go wrong in each step. In a transformation process, it is impossible to take into all account all the unknowns, but companies should consider different scenarios.

The last attribute is the need for leadership by the board of directors and the top management team. Many transformation processes are discussed from the top management perspective, but not from the board perspective. In this chapter, we will take this approach. As the Fluidra experience suggests, a talented group of senior executives would not have achieved the same results without the support and advice from the board of directors. Moreover, the board is ultimately the party responsible for the evolution of the firm and should govern this effort.

The experiences of Fluidra and other companies are very useful in pointing to corporate transformation as an organization-wide initiative inspired by a sense of purpose to shape how the firm will serve customers and other stakeholders in the long term, and how it will create value in a unique and sustainable manner. Transformation involves improving corporate performance but should be founded on a purpose that truly aspires to improve customers' lives. Efforts aimed solely to reduce costs, enhance revenues or restructure the corporate portfolio might be important steps, but alone do not constitute a transformation process.

As Ghoshal and Bartlett (1997) explained in their breakthrough study of transformations, many companies in recent decades tried to reinvent themselves, often when facing notable crises. An important observation is that transformation seems to deliver better results when companies adopt it in times of success, instead of waiting for a crisis. The high number of failures in corporate transformation suggests that specific issues and challenges on transformation should be put into perspective.

The first is related to the scale of transformation. Some authors claim that transformations should be big (Faeste and Hemerling, 2016). Since transformations are organization-wide, they require substantial effort. The bigger the goals, these authors suggest, the deeper the commitment the challenge may generate among managers and employees. At the same time, transformation should include specific steps and goals that define the journey's ambitious destination. Hamel and Prahalad (1994) suggest that firms should aspire to change by taking concrete and well-prepared steps, even if some of them are considered small. Ghoshal and Bartlett (1997) also suggest a similar reflection in their phased perspective of transformation, a process that allows breaking down the different stages of the journey and defining the specific milestones and goals in each step.

The second issue is about speed. Some authors suggest that transformations should be ambitious and fast to remove obstacles as quickly as possible (Miles, 2010). This is one side of the story. The other side is that transformations do not happen in a vacuum. Companies need to continue serving customers and delivering good financial performance. Top managers need to balance the need to adequately serve current customers while transitioning to a new model. This is one of the key challenges in most companies that undertake a digital transformation process in order to serve customer with online sales. The transition to online sales does not happen overnight. As many banks and retailers have experienced over the past ten years, companies need to create a new business model, while retaining more traditional customers. Managing both realities is complex.

The third is that successful transformations usually involve changes in individual behaviors. These take time. The depth of the transformation's impact will depend on how the organizational structure changes, but also on how individual behavior evolves as a result of the process. In today's asset-light capitalism, the impact of individuals is more important than in the past. For this reason, ensuring that people stay aligned and engaged with the company is probably more important than other criteria, such as the speed of change.

The notions of scale and speed in corporate transformation underline some major obstacles that may derail organizational change efforts. Learning from mistakes is extremely important. Boards of directors should be aware of these experiences. The empirical evidence on change (Kotter, 1990; Johnson, Hoskisson and Hitt, 1992; Hoskisson and Johnson, 1993) suggests that the major obstacles in change processes are related to mediocre strategic orientation. The first major reason for failure is a mediocre strategy, with unclear goals, a narrow focus on customers' service, obsolete capabilities and lack of consistent policies and action plans.

The second reason is related to poor execution and the lack of coordination among the different departments and business units involved in the change process. Very often, this is also the direct consequence of a lack of proper communication, which is an indispensable success factor in any major initiative, and even more important in the case of transformation.

The third reason for failure is the pretense of changing an organization without relevant changes in the culture and individual behavior. A transformation process should involve both the hard and soft dimensions of change. Boards of directors should not get involved in this process but should be aware of its complexities and advise CEOs and senior executives about them.

4.3   TRANSFORMATION DRIVERS AND DILEMMAS: INGKA'S SUSTAINABILITY STRATEGY[2]

The nature of corporate transformation may change dramatically, depending on two starting conditions. The first is the strategic, organizational and financial strength of the firm. A firm that starts a transformation process in good shape is more likely to transition successfully to a new organizational and business model. The second is the origin of change: It could be external – technology disruption or radical changes in consumer behavior – or internal, such as pressure to innovate and improve. Ingka's recent story of transformation highlights some of these key dimensions and helps define core typologies of transformations.

As examined in Chapter 2, in June 2020 Jesper Brodin and Juvencio Maeztu, CEO and deputy CEO, respectively, of Ikea's retail arm Ingka, were preparing a discussion on the company's future for the board. Ingka had embarked on an important transformation effort in 2017, driven by the need to revitalize its traditional retail business, develop new products and services for customers, boost digital transformation and advance its sustainability efforts. They had been working on this project for several years as CEOs and wanted to accelerate change by creating a clear framework on transformation for the firm's supervisory board. Ingka's board was very supportive of

---

[2] This section is based on Masclans and Canals (2021) and complements the discussion on Ingka in Chapter 2.

the new initiatives. At the same time, its members were concerned about new business models, as well as financial profitability in order to strengthen Ingka's capital base and guarantee its independence and support key social causes.

4.3.1   First Steps in Transformation: The Role of Purpose (2018–2019)

In 2017, Ingka was facing several challenges that were impacting the retail industry. Sales and profitability had been slowing down over the past few years. Urbanization and digitalization, as well as social concerns such as sustainability, were changing the way people lived and impacting consumer behavior. Additionally, online retailers and large platforms such as Amazon and Alibaba threatened Ikea's market share in some countries. To tackle these challenges, the company began an important transformation in 2018, establishing three strategic goals aligned with IKEA's vision: to become more affordable, accessible and sustainable.

The vision of Ikea's founder permeated the firm's culture and values, serving as a guide for managers and employees and their decision-making processes. The CEOs believed that purpose had to play a key role in Ingka's transformation. As Maeztu observed, "Kamprad had a big vision that helped inspire thousands of people at IKEA. It created an emotional link between the company and the brand. The challenge was how to grow the company based on that purpose. Are we investing enough in the type of products that are consistent with our purpose? Are we making enough efforts in making Ingka more sustainable?"

They developed questions to articulate Ingka's purpose around Kamprad's sense of mission, three of which were particularly important: Is the notion of purpose well articulated and understood? Does this notion of purpose inspire our people? Is purpose integrated into Ingka's strategy, decision-making and operations?

In September 2019, digital transformation and sustainability were two key initiatives that the board decided to emphasize.

Chapter 2 explores the company's digital transformation. In this section, the focus will be on Ingka's sustainability strategy.

4.3.2 Purpose and Sustainability: Strategic Choices

In 2018, the company launched the Ikea Sustainability Strategy: People and Planet Positive. Its aim was not only to reduce its carbon footprint but also to create a positive impact on climate and people. In this new strategic framework, Inter Ikea described the sustainability agenda for all Ikea businesses, franchises and value chain. The Sustainability Strategy was reviewed annually by the Ikea Strategic Sustainability Council, a body that included representatives from the main Ikea companies and franchisees. The council focused on strategic questions affecting the wider franchise system for the people and planet agenda.

The Strategic Sustainability Council identified three major sustainability challenges with a relevant impact on the firm's business model: climate change, unsustainable consumption and inequality. To address these challenges, three areas were chosen, with specific goals: healthy and sustainable living, circular and climate positive and fair and equal.

The first area, healthy and sustainable living, was key. According to estimates, households consume one third of the world's global energy and 10 percent of global water consumption. Enabling as many people as possible to generate renewable energy and reduce their home energy and water consumption would have a great impact. Water, food and air quality were also major concerns for people around the world. Ingka offered new, affordable solutions designed with circular principles in order to prolong the life of its products and thereby promote a sharing and circular economy, such as furniture leasing. Additionally, Ikea would offer affordable products aimed at being water and energy efficient, and generating renewable energy, such as solar panels. This would enable people to optimize their water and energy use, reduce waste and adapt their homes to help mitigate the impact of climate change.

The initiative on circular and climate positive was also relevant. Preserving ecosystems was one of Ingka's major concerns. Pressure on forests, fisheries and agriculture, loss of biodiversity and wildlife, ocean pollution, soil erosion and increasing levels of air and fresh-water pollution were affecting the lives and livelihoods of millions of people around the world. Ikea had an impact on some of these dimensions by sourcing raw materials and its manufacturing and logistics operations. It started to develop responsible sourcing programs, improving resource utilization and reducing greenhouse gases in order to confront these issues.

By 2030, Ingka's ambition was to reduce the greenhouse gas emissions throughout the value chain in absolute terms compared to 2016 levels. It also committed to regenerating resources while growing the Ikea business by becoming a circular business built on clean, renewable energy and regenerative resources, with all products produced from renewable and recycled materials. As an example, in 2019 Ingka owned about 210,000 hectares of responsibly managed forests. That year, Ingka began several small-scale tests to explore the feasibility, viability and desirability of different furniture subscription models. Customers leased the furniture and Ingka was responsible for maintenance and repairs upon return. Then, Ingka cleaned, refurbished and made the furniture ready for its next home. When the furniture had been reused as many times as possible, Ingka recycled the materials and components to produce new products.

4.3.3   Dilemmas in Transformation and Sustainability

As Brodin pointed out, corporate purpose inspired Ingka's innovation and long-term perspective:

> As a big brand with a purpose, we have a unique opportunity to really make a positive impact on people and the planet. Actions speak louder than words, and we keep pushing forward to reach the Ingka ambition for 2030: to become a circular and climate-positive

business and offer healthier and more sustainable solutions at scale that more and more people can afford.

Brodin and Maeztu were thinking about bolder steps regarding strategy and capital allocation. Their reflections and debates touched on several dilemmas. The first dilemma was the balance between the old and the new retail business model. The old retail business model involved vertical integration, from sourcing and manufacturing to retail centers and the final consumer. The new business model involved a de-integration of the value chain and closer attention to evolving customer needs. The focus on digital and online sales was driven by market share and growth – not by profitability – and led by digital savvy people. Managing people in the retail business with a more digital focus was also a challenge.

The second dilemma involved a balance between profitability and sustainability. The policies and decisions required by Ingka's strategy of decarbonization would not deliver short-term results. Was the company prepared for longer paybacks?

The third dilemma was the balance between current financial performance and transformation of the business. Improving current performance would require additional optimization of operations, lower costs, additional investments in traditional stores and better margins. Transformation was uncertain; would require technology, big data and customer service investments; generate higher costs and lower margins; and would not deliver results in the short term.

The fourth dilemma was how to preserve Ikea's culture and values as they were conceived by the founder while undergoing a transformation and moving out of the company's comfort zone through the addition of new businesses, employees, capabilities, formats and sales channels.

The fifth dilemma was how to incorporate new metrics to guide decision-making and how to better engage managers and employees. The metrics traditionally used by Ingka to report to the board provided some benchmarks, which had been useful for many years. Ingka needed to introduce new criteria and metrics to assess the business of the future in a more comprehensive way. In 2020, Kasper and Maetzu developed a new value creation map along four dimensions: Customers, People, Planet and Company. Within each dimension, Ingka management established new value creation goals.

Likewise, Ingka defined new indicators to assess corporate goals. The first set of metrics defined how accessible the company was to customers. Some indicators in this area would include global market share, local market share and quality of service as perceived by customers. The second set of metrics was related to affordability. In some segments of the retail industry, there were companies with great market access but higher prices. Ingka wanted to remain more affordable to its customers. This issue involved relative affordability: how affordable products were today in relation to the past. It also considered product affordability in relation to the average customer's income over time. Finally, it considered the customer's willingness to pay for a better, longer lasting product, and how this attribute changed over time.

The third set of indicators concerned carbon footprint and sustainability issues. The fourth set included indicators to assess how well the company treated its people, suppliers, partners and society. There also was a set of criteria involving financial and operational performance, with the traditional indicators to evaluate the success of a retail firm.

In May 2020, amid the COVID-19 disruption, business leaders across the organization started a process to review all priorities and place them into different categories: what to stop; what to pause; what to modify; what to continue; what to accelerate; and what to add. While COVID-19 represented a challenge, it also offered an opportunity to sharpen their decision-making and concentrate resources to both navigate the crisis and enhance their competitive position.

Brodin and Maeztu had discussions with the board about how to adapt strategic decisions and which criteria should be used to measure performance and financial strength. They were very conscious of the difficult pathway they had to walk, aimed at transformation while ensuring consistency with Ikea's culture and values, as well as prudent financial policies. Defining the key areas of performance was critical to speeding up the transformation and building on Ingka's uniqueness.

4.4 DIFFERENT PERSPECTIVES OF CORPORATE TRANSFORMATION

Puig, an international fragrances and fashion company, has grown very quickly over the past twenty years. At the time of writing, it is among the largest global players in the fragrance industry. It was founded in Barcelona, Spain, in 1914.[3] In 2021, it was a third-generation family business with a very professional board of directors and top management team. Family members were acting as responsible shareholders. Starting in the 1970s, Puig grew internationally by buying domestic brands in large markets, such as Carolina Herrera in the United States, and Nina Ricci and Jean Paul Gaultier in France. Its strategy consisted of launching perfumes associated with luxury brands.

Over the past years, the board of directors has considered ways to diversify into related areas. Cosmetics was one of them. The opportunity came in May 2020. Marc Puig – the chairman of Puig and a member of the family's third generation – had been in conversation with the owners of Charlotte Tilbury, a high–growth UK cosmetics firm with a very strong digital presence. The global pandemic was not an obstacle, and Puig was able to conclude the deal and acquire the British company in May 2020, outbidding other larger cosmetics firms.

The price of the deal was considered high by some industry peers, but Puig had the advantage of playing for the long term and framing its strategic decisions and acquisitions in terms of generations. Moreover, this acquisition helped consolidate a

---

[3] Palepu and Nueno (2014) offer a description of Puig's strategic opportunities.

transformation process at Puig at a time when some traditional sales channels for fragrances, such as airport duty-free shops, had dramatically decreased their sales. This acquisition allowed the firm to invest in the fast-growing cosmetics business. It also helped Puig strengthen its presence in online business. Puig also got a notable boost in presence in China, where Charlotte Tilbury was very strong.

Puig's acquisition of Charlotte Tilbury offers an example of an entrepreneurial company whose board and senior management team were exploring new growth opportunities. Puig's reaction to the COVID-19 crisis and the fall in perfume consumption was not one of retrenchment and restructuring. The board thought it was the right time to do a deal that could transform the company, expand its business and ultimately make the whole firm more competitive. This type of transformation requires not only financial strength, but, more importantly, a good understanding of industry dynamics and trends and the board of directors' willingness to work with the top management team to explore opportunities and eventually close a good deal.

The experiences of Fluidra, Ingka and Puig discussed in this chapter, as well as those of Amadeus, Cellnex, Unilever and Schneider explored in previous chapters, shed some light on the context and drivers of corporate transformation. Table 4.2 describes the main external and internal drivers of change identified in the companies discussed in this book (see Table 4.2). Boards of directors and top managers need to solidly grasp the context in which their firm's transformation is taking place. The success of transformation will depend on the firm's adaptation to a specific context.

The experiences of Fluidra, Ingka and Puig highlight that transformation may encompass different types of actions and activities. The first is transformation aimed at cutting costs. In 2017, Ingka needed to become more agile, develop its online business and streamline operations to make sure that its model could survive in an era of online commerce. Improving cost effectiveness and streamlining operations are always useful to improve performance, especially when there is a transformation process underway.

Table 4.2. *Drivers of corporate change*

Internal	External
• Boards of directors	• Shareholders' pressure
• Employees	• Product market competition
• A new CEO	• Climate change
• Need to boost performance	• Capital markets' pressure
• Talent attractiveness	• Technology disruption
• Corporate venturing	• Customers' pressure
	• New low–cost competitors
	• Regulators
	• Public opinion

Those companies' experiences also suggest that transformation, in order to be successful, needs to develop new activities with new clients and generate additional revenue – not only reduce costs (Canals, 2000). The first avenue for progress in this area is improving the effectiveness of traditional sales channels. This is what Fluidra did during the years following the 2008 crisis, by encouraging entrepreneurial initiatives across the organization and supporting good sales practices that could increase revenues, from one area of the organization to the rest. Sales effectiveness is an important metric that should be monitored.

The second avenue for revenue growth is product innovation or market penetration. This may take longer to make an impact, but is indispensable for any company to foster growth. This is one of the engines that Ingka used to speed up growth: the development of new products and categories, and new circular economy business models capable of adapting quickly to changing market conditions and consumer behavior.

The third avenue is inorganic growth, which may come from joint ventures or acquisitions of other companies. Fluidra also recognized the need to use this pathway to grow, even in the middle of the

2008 financial crisis. With financial prudence, it bought some local firms in promising markets, creating platforms of future growth. Acquisition decisions may lead to growth in the same products or markets, or in different businesses, increasing the level of diversification and expanding the business portfolio.

A transformation process that only involves cost cutting is likely to fail. Boards of directors and CEOs need to think of ways to reinvent the firm with new sources of revenue, or rejuvenation of traditional products or services. Growth is not an end unto itself, but organizations that do not think about growth may lack entrepreneurial spirit. This examination of drivers of transformation leads to the topic of specific typologies of change.

Using the experience of Fluidra, Ingka and Puig as references, I will discuss different perspectives and potential pathways of transformation depending on drivers of change. They can be useful in helping boards of directors think about transformation. The nature of these drivers varies across industries and countries.

The first typology of transformation comes from the combination of two factors: the origin of drivers of change – external or internal factors – and the overall strategic health of the firm: strong or weak. These two factors help define both the direction of change and the sense of urgency that top managers should apply to the process. They define four pathways of transformation: reinvention, restructuring, renewal and adaptation. Table 4.3 summarizes the outcomes.

Table 4.3. *Drivers of change and organizational health: Some pathways*

		Organizational Health	
		Strong	**Weak**
Driver of Change	**External**	Reinvention	Restructuring/survival
	Internal	Renewal	Adaptation

When the main driver of change is external – for instance, technology disruption – a company's reaction depends on its specific strengths and capabilities. Companies in good organizational health – with solid capabilities, competent and committed employees, and deep customer engagement – are better equipped than others to react to these changes. This was the case of Fluidra in navigating market changes after the 2008 financial crisis. The driver of change was external, the company was in good shape and it decided to reinvent itself.

This was also the case of Ingka in addressing the challenge of sustainability and key social issues in 2019–2021 in a more proactive way, far beyond what regulation requires. The driver of the change was essentially internal and Ingka's board and top management decided to set very ambitious goals aimed at increasing the use of clean energy, reducing energy consumption and promoting the circular economy. It was an impressive case of transformation, with demanding requirements established by the board of directors and senior managers.

Organizational health is not a static concept. The Nokia experience highlights this point. When Apple unveiled its iPhone in 2007, Nokia was the leading company in mobile phones and enjoyed a very strong technology lead in many of its products as well as a strong financial position. Nokia's late reaction to the new generation of smartphones deteriorated its competitive and financial position (Siilasmaa, 2018) and when the board undertook a major restructuring in 2012, its organizational health was considerably weaker.

In facing external changes, the reaction of firms should be agile, but companies in a weaker position should reflect on the steps necessary for its survival with an increased sense of urgency. This is a similar situation as one that may unfold with a radical restructuring forced by some investors. The health of the organization will have a different impact on companies: Some will have the time and resources to execute the restructuring process; others may lack the resources and time to adjust and change.

When the strength of the organization is weaker, its capacity to positively address the forces of change is more complex. This was the

Table 4.4. *Transformation objectives and their impact on business units and the corporate group*

		Business Units	**Corporate Group**
Objectives	**Efficiency**	• Restructuring	• Divestment
	Revenue Growth	• Product innovation • Sales channels efficiency • Acquisitions that boost revenue	• Investment • Entry into new business

case of large retailers such as Marks and Spencer, or large bookshop chains like Borders or Barnes and Noble, with the rise of e-commerce. These companies had to accelerate a restructuring process to cut costs as traditional sources of revenues were dwindling and the revenues generated by the new business model were still small. Before long, these companies had to fight, not only to advance transformation, but for their own survival. They exemplify why it is important to tackle transformation when the company is in good shape, rather than waiting and starting from a position of weakness.

Table 4.4 presents the second typology of strategic decisions related to transformation. They are the outcome of the combination of the objectives of change – organizational efficiency or growth – and the type of change that they create in individual business units and the corporate group. The nature of transformation depends on whether a company is a single business or a business group with several business units. Transformation of single business units requires concrete initiatives to ensure the business unit can learn the new capabilities necessary to compete in the new context and become more sustainable in the long term. When a business unit seeks better efficiency, the transformation actions center on restructuring. When a business unit seeks additional growth, the focus should be on product development, market penetration and acquisitions.

Transformation of a corporate group is conceptually simpler: It involves a reconsideration of the companies where the group wants to invest or own a higher stake, the business units or companies that the group wants to exit and new companies where the group wants to enter as a shareholder. Any of these decisions is complex; involves enormous resources; affects other investors, employees and other stakeholders; and requires the attention of top management. But it is conceptually simpler and easier to achieve than the transformation effort of a single business unit, where the development of new capabilities, investment in new assets, employee motivation and customer trust remain key success factors and require careful management.

4.5   BOARDS OF DIRECTORS: GOVERNING CORPORATE TRANSFORMATION

The sheer scale and impact of corporate transformation suggest that the board of directors – as the company's ultimate decision maker – should understand, discuss, approve and eventually monitor the transformation process, as in the cases of Ingka, Fluidra and Puig. It is also worth noting that this idea has not been reflected in most studies on corporate transformation, where the effort seems to start and finish with the CEO and top management team. The role of senior managers is essential in understanding the firm's challenges and competitive landscape' assessing the firm's performance vis-à-vis other players; providing a sense of long-term orientation; articulating a phased process with specific milestones, goals and deadlines; and building a team that will closely follow this journey and support the entire organization. Since transformation is so relevant for the future of any company, the board should also get involved and work with the CEO and senior management team.

The aforementioned experiences of Ingka, Fluidra, Puig and Unilever are very useful in this respect. They offer steps to help boards of directors reflect, debate and decide on transformation (Figure 4.1). These steps include, among others, understanding the firm's context, developing purpose as a pillar of transformation, defining strategy, establishing indicators to monitor progress, engaging employees and

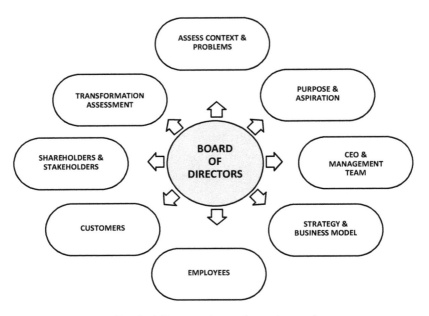

FIGURE 4.1 Board of directors: A transformation road map

customers and communicating with shareholders and other key stakeholders.

4.5.1   Understanding the Context, Diagnosing Problems

Almirall is an international pharmaceutical company based in Spain. Founded in 1943 by the Gallardo family, in 2021 it was a third-generation family business listed on the Madrid stock market, with a free float of around 35 percent of its capital. Almirall went public in 2007. At that time, it was organized around five therapeutic areas and had a strong presence in Western Europe, Latin America and the United States.[4]

Almirall had been very successful since its foundation, but its scale was small in comparison with pharma industry leaders. This had an impact on its financial capacity to invest in R&D. Since the late

---

[4] See Caldart and Canals (2018) for a discussion of the main strategic challenges that the board of directors of Almirall faced.

2000s, the board of directors, led by Jorge Gallardo, a second-generation family member, had been working with the top management team to help the company develop critical mass in specialized segments in the pharma industry. The company gradually divested from some therapeutical areas. A major decision came in 2014, when Almirall decided to sell its respiratory division to AstraZeneca, including a successful patented product.

The board of directors had thought a lot about the firm's future and decided to become a specialized pharma company in dermatology. Almirall already had a good portfolio of products in this area; notable international presence in the United States, Germany and Spain; and the internal R&D capabilities to become a relevant player in this market segment.

Transforming a company when it is still performing reasonably well – in particular, when it is a family business with highly committed shareholders – is a complex process. It requires a board of directors that behaves very professionally; possesses an in-depth understanding of the industry, threats and opportunities; promotes an entrepreneurial mindset; and collaborates with the top management team to explore opportunities and discuss potential decisions.

Almirall's experience offers a good framework to understand how boards of directors can help senior management teams approach transformation and focus the process on creating a better company for the future. The first step in this process is fully understanding the industry and the firm's context, recent performance and threats and opportunities.

Board directors do not have a full-time job at the company. Board directors may not know in detail the changing expectations of customers, or competitive threats that the firm may face. Senior executives do. Directors may not have enough details about the company to organize a comprehensive transformation plan. Senior executives do.

But board directors can provide a very useful, external and independent perspective on transformation, which complements the senior executives' inside knowledge and expertise. They can also build bridges between the firm's senior management and shareholders. The first step is to build a common understanding of the context between the board and the CEO. Defining the type of change that the company is aiming at will help. As discussed in Chapter 3, regarding the role of boards of directors in strategy, the ability to ask the CEO the right questions is one of the most important competencies of board directors.

In the process of understanding the context and rethinking the firm's strategy, the framework presented in Chapter 3 (Figure 3.1) can be useful. Understanding the context is relevant because the board of directors, the CEO and the top management team should make a shared diagnosis of the situation. This should include both an understanding of the business context and the reason the company needs to change.

Very often, these reasons will relate to the firm's underperformance in revenues, costs, innovation or customer service. A good diagnosis should include a full description of the situation, as well as a thorough explanation of why it is happening and why the board was unable to foresee or act on these factors earlier. Asking these questions may be embarrassing, but sincerity and candor are vital in these conversations if boards aspire to move beyond compliance and become effective drivers of positive change in companies.

A good diagnosis should not only be internal. It should include an external perspective, in particular, with some indicators on how the company is performing in comparison with other firms in the same industry, both in financial and nonfinancial terms. Some challenges that companies face can only be seen when they see how they similarly affect other companies and how other firms react.

4.5.2 Purpose and Aspiration

Any transformation process should start with a clear "why." The answer to this question should include the root of the firm's underperformance, but if change is to be implemented effectively, it should also connect with the firm's purpose and values, as the Ingka case highlights so clearly. When purpose and values are integrated, they provide a source of engagement and a unifying message for the entire organization. In the end, purpose is important – including when the company needs to change – an aspect that the board should understand and promote.

The transformation process should also include a sense of aspiration or stretch (Hamel and Prahalad, 1994), a perspective that helps participants see beyond the short term and visualize the company's end ambition and how things might look like in some years' time. The effort that transformation entails also requires guidance by a sense of purpose and an aspiration to create a better company for all.

The board should also work with the top management in defining the priorities, aspiration and goals of the transformation process. It has the final responsibility for the firm's long-term orientation and should actively participate in this as well. The CEO and senior managers will work on goals, strategic plans, policies and milestones. The board needs to make sure that the goals are consistent with long-term company needs, aligned with investor expectations and coherent with different stakeholder aspirations regarding the change process. In this journey, establishing criteria to govern the process is essential and the board should define them. In any change process, the uncertainty is high and new unknowns will appear along the way. Defining useful criteria to better explain the goals the firm aspires to achieve will help fine-tune the process.

All transformation processes involve important changes. Different individuals in the company have different views on which aspects need to change and the decisions to invest in new units and divest from others. These changes take a toll on people. It is important to establish clear priorities in this process to facilitate the communication and implementation of the different policies and action plans. Both the transformation plan and its implementation should follow a logic that is easily understood by all key parties. In particular, among these priorities, employee engagement and a focus on customer service and satisfaction are key. If the change process does not lead to better customer satisfaction, the process will fail at some point.

Criteria and priorities are also important in defining key milestones and the sequence of actions – in particular, those related to customers and employees. Some transformation plans are overly focused on shareholders and increasing financial returns in the short term. This is especially true when an activist investor pushes for a potential divestment of specific business units to increase shareholders' return in the short term. Making a company smaller and its shareholders richer by selling off divisions and paying out substantial dividends is an option for activist investors but the goal of a sound transformation process should be to help the company become more competitive in the long term. It is for this reason that the board and the CEO should define a set of criteria that will shape the different policies and action plans, as well as the speed of the process itself.

4.5.3   The CEO and the Management Team

There has been some debate on the need to change the CEO or management team in times of transformation. This decision should be based on the company's specific circumstances and the credibility of the current CEO to bring about change. This discussion is also related to the drivers of change in each company. When the driver is essentially external – unhappy shareholders, customer churn, or activist investors – the pressure to change the CEO and the top management team is more intense. When the pressure is more internally driven, as part of the ongoing renewal that all organizations require, the current CEO and top management may be the right people to lead the effort.

The insight offered by effective boards of directors is that the board can greatly contribute to the company by working effectively with the CEO and top management to achieve the goals established. In particular, the board should give the CEO its support to ensure the effort's success. This support is even more vital in a transformation process because of the uncertain nature of what is at stake.

Collaboration does not mean that the board becomes lenient with top managers. But it does mean becoming more aware of the company's challenges and problems and the professional and personal hurdles that the top management team needs to overcome. Without this spirit of cooperation – which requires considerable time and personal commitment – corporate boards may not fulfill the duty of care expected from them.

A particular dimension of this support is helping the CEO make sure that the company has the right team of individuals for this effort. One of the common mistakes in change processes is entrusting the same individuals to manage both the regular operations of the firm and the change process. The normal outcome in this case is that regular operations and sales suffer, and that the change process advances slowly and ineffectively. In these instances, the experience of board members in other companies or industries that have already undergone a transformation is very beneficial. The board should not replace the CEO in managing the company, but can help by asking the right questions and bringing complementary perspectives to the discussion.

4.5.4 *Strategy and Business Model*

The strategy road map for boards of directors presented in Chapter 3 continues to be useful in a transformation process. In particular, when debating transformation, three dimensions of the strategy reflection require special attention from board members.

The first is a solid understanding of the firm's resources and capabilities needed to survive, and the business model necessary to compete for the future. Too often, strategy discussions focus on market positioning and evolution, which are important. But board directors should also understand which resources and capabilities sustain the firm's potential advantages in its different markets of operation. Eventually, resources and capabilities define what the company is good at. For this reason, an assessment of which capabilities will be necessary in the future is critical. This is even more important in times of higher uncertainty or transformation processes shaped by digital disruption. The capabilities and initiative of the firm's individuals are indispensable for the success of the transformation process.

The second is a holistic discussion of strategic decisions such as investments, divestments and joint ventures. In crises driven by financial distress, boards of directors may feel pressured to generate cash from transactions. This may be a necessary step in some cases, but the consideration of investments or divestments should be more holistic by contemplating their impact on the firm's strategic positioning, the capabilities of the business units involved and the wider organization and employee motivation. Strategic decisions require careful deliberation beyond their obvious financial dimensions. In a transformation process, the board of directors should pay even more attention to it.

The third factor is the performance indicators that the board will use. A board of directors that governs for the long term needs to consider not only financial indicators, but also other nonfinancial indicators that are key for the firm's long-term development. They should include, among others, customer satisfaction, growth of the customer base, innovation, sales of new versus established products, employee engagement and environmental and social impacts. A good transformation process needs to clearly define what the firm wants to achieve, the commitments of the board of directors and top management team and how they will track the evolution of these dimensions.

Since inertia is an important stumbling block in many organizations, potential obstacles to change should be carefully assessed by the board. In any change process, there are some key obstacles that need to be removed. The board is not the final responsible body to eliminate these obstacles, but should be aware of them and help the top management team in this endeavor. The first obstacle is the lack of clarity or focus on what needs to be done. Agreeing on a multidimensional journey requires a good planning process, including the definition of specific goals, milestones, policies, people in charge and clear communication and transparency in reporting the results.

The second is the potential disengagement of employees when faced with a complex change process – in particular, when this decision involves downsizing. In any change process, the motivation of people in dealing with customers and colleagues is key to making the process successful. The board should make sure that the top management team understands this need and makes prudent policies to maintain employee engagement.

The third is the complexity of the process itself. Companies are organized to produce and sell goods and services. Managing both the regular attention to customers and normal activities may not be compatible with managing an important change process. The outcome in some organizations is a decline in the quality of customer service and other regular activities because of the decreasing attention paid by employees. On the other hand, the change process never achieves total momentum because it is understaffed. The experience of change processes is that normal activities should continue unless they require immediate change, and their key people should remain in their positions. A new team that speeds up transformation should lead this effort in parallel, making sure that normal activities continue and that the adaptation process to the new reality gradually takes place. There is no perfect balance in this process and the board does not need to be especially knowledgeable about it. But it should be aware of these trade-offs and make sure that the CEO and top managers are organizing plans and activities accordingly.

The fourth is to clearly assess the pace of progress and the success in achieving its goals and milestones. A core element of the change road map are the indicators that the company will use to ensure that the process' orientation and speed of progress meet the expectations of the board and key stakeholders.

4.5.5 Engaging Employees and Improving Customer Satisfaction

A successful change process requires engaged employees willing to tackle the challenge of change, acquire new capabilities and adapt to the new context. The empirical evidence shows that change will not deliver good results unless the people involved assume and engage in the process to make it happen. This is also very relevant because, in many transformation processes, the focus is placed on the organizational redesign required to drive change. Without a doubt, if there is a change process and new strategy in place, the old organization may be not be effective enough in order to achieve the expected results.

Nevertheless, the true emphasis should be placed on employee motivation and engagement. Employees are the agents of change and the drivers of better performance. Organizational change should not only reflect the new strategy and orientation of the firm but also how people will work in the new context. Organizational design and reward systems should aim at both fostering change and delivering the good results expected from that change. In this respect, boards of directors need to encourage the CEO and top management team to focus on employee engagement and commitment to continue serving customers.

Boards should also pay attention to customers, their satisfaction and how they will be affected by the process of change. Without customers, there is no company. They should be at the center of the process, and better customer service should become the true objective of any organizational change. This is easier said than done. In particular, customer service may suffer when transformation processes are driven by the need to boost efficiency and streamline operations. If this process aspires to be effective, it needs to safeguard customers and customer service.

4.5.6 Engaging Shareholders and Other Key Stakeholders

The CEO and senior managers should keep the organization's focus on customers and the team updated on the situation, the progress made, challenges and action plans to overcome them. The board also needs to work with the CEO and top management to set clear goals, expectations and policies, and offer managers useful feedback. The board also needs to take responsibility for shareholder communications. Even when the responsibility of direct communications with shareholders is in the hands of the CEO, CFO or director of investors' relations, the board should monitor it closely and offer its best advice to the CEO.

Any transformation process may put the company in a context of high uncertainty. Shareholders might be concerned about the future of the company and the value of their investment. This a shared view both among investors in listed companies and family firms alike. Their board of directors should be aware of this and work with a long-term orientation, while bearing in mind that investors might have different expectations and time horizons. The board should try to keep investors aligned and supportive of the transformation process. This is what Fluidra did in 2008–2014 during the recession, and once again in 2017 when deciding whether to merge with Zodiac.

These decisions involve a continuous dialogue with the firm's shareholders. They have a significant stake in the company and want to stay informed, and the company needs them for its long-term projects. How the board engages with shareholders in this specific context is very important. The quality of this engagement will shape and determine the quality of stewardship that investors display toward the companies they invest in.

The CEO and senior managers should concern themselves with the communication process with employees, customers, suppliers and other stakeholders. A simple reflection is that any stakeholder should receive regularly a good explanation of the transformation effort and its motives from the firm's management. Winning the battle of communication is key to making transformation successful, since it will help engage relevant stakeholders in the process.

4.5.7 *Assessing Transformation Results*

The transformation road map also needs a regular and comprehensive assessment. This requires a set of indicators to track performance, follow the implementation of the different initiatives and offer a clear description of the state of the firm. Selecting the right indicators is more important in a change process than in normal times. These indicators will also show the underlying goals and targets that the board aspires to achieve. Performance indicators are powerful tools to clarify messages, unify efforts and focus the energy of the organization.

They should be fully aligned with the company's purpose, aspiration and strategy, and reflect the major concerns and expectations around the change process of the different parties involved. Over time, a good set of indicators helps the board and senior managers reflect on the evolution of the change process, highlight which factors are working and which need adjustment, confirm the orientation of the process and change direction when necessary.

4.6 FINAL REFLECTIONS

Transformation processes are important inflection points in corporate life. They define how the company may look like in a few years' time. More importantly, the process will impact its reputation, credibility in the eyes of customers and attractiveness for employees and investors.

Transformation has been studied in management and strategy from the perspective of top and middle management, but has rarely been discussed from the boards of directors perspective. This discussion is necessary for two reasons. The first is legal and functional: Boards of directors have the responsibility to protect the company and support its long-term value creation. Corporate transformation may impact this capacity. The second reason is that corporate transformation involves complex strategic and organizational decisions that affect not only performance but also organizational capabilities, employee engagement, customer perceptions of service and overall firm reputation.

This chapter presented a road map on transformation for corporate boards. This framework includes critical steps: renewing the sense of purpose, understanding the firm's context, fostering a sense of aspiration, confirming trust in the CEO and management team, redefining strategy and the business model, maintaining employee engagement, improving customer service, ensuring stakeholder and shareholder engagement and defining indicators to assess change.

At the same time, the CEO and top management team are the key agents in this process. Their collaboration is critical. They should reflect deeply on it, understand the challenges well, design the process and think carefully about its implementation, while keeping a focus on customer service and employee engagement. For its part, the board should understand and approve the project, help the CEO with major questions and warnings on potential risks not considered in depth and support the CEO and senior management team, while paying particular attention to communication and engagement with shareholders and key external stakeholders. Collaboration between the board of directors and CEO is extremely relevant in corporate governance and, in particular, in a corporate transformation process.

The Board in CEO and Senior Management Selection, Development and Succession

5.1 THE CHALLENGE OF LEADERSHIP DEVELOPMENT

One can hardly find a more consequential board of directors' decision than the appointment of the company's CEO. In 2008, the board of Unilever was aware of the company's challenges, its underperformance since the late 1990s and its organizational complexity. The board of Unilever was wise enough to realize that the firm lacked a good leadership pipeline and that the next CEO should come from the outside. After a careful search process, the board appointed Paul Polman as Unilever's new CEO, who assumed the role on January 1, 2009.

Unilever's strategy and transformation under Polman's leadership was explored in Chapter 3 It is clear that the company changed significantly over his ten years at the helm. The experience of Unilever – and those of other companies profiled in this book such as Schneider Electric, Ingka, Fluidra or Amadeus – underscores the deep impact that a CEO can have on a company.

During his tenure at Unilever, Polman placed great importance on sustainability and innovation around healthy and sustainable products (Canals, 2019). The Unilever Sustainable Living Plan became the gold standard in the consumer products, food and beverages industry, and served as a bright beacon for other companies. A less known but deeply important initiative was the tremendous effort Polman and his team dedicated to leadership and people development. They had clear convictions about the importance of hiring, developing and retaining an exceptional team of people in order to sustain Unilever's transformation and growth.

The preparation of the company's next-generation leaders was a priority for Polman from the very beginning. The board was also keenly interested in this initiative. Unilever launched a range of educational initiatives for managers and young professionals via highly structured programs, some delivered in collaboration with international universities. These programs addressed specific business issues – like digital business and sustainability – as well as managerial competencies and leadership development. Thousands of Unilever employees took part. Particular emphasis was placed on developing female leadership and preparing women for managerial positions, and promoting cultural diversity in management teams.

In November 2018, Polman, in coordination with the board of directors, announced he would step down in May 2019, completing a ten-year tenure as Unilever's CEO. His leadership received very high marks from employees, customers, competitors and investors. During his tenure, the firm's financial returns had been above industry average and its sustainability strategy was a reference in the business world. But the most important legacy that a CEO may leave behind is an outstanding team of individuals equipped with the capabilities and motivation to take the company to the next level and build on the firm's success. Unfortunately, this issue does not always get the attention it deserves in discussions about CEO performance.

It is interesting to observe that Unilever's efforts to promote the next generation of managers, were not always considered by most investors and analysts, who were more focused on the formal dimensions of ESG factors. Unilever made very important advances in emerging countries, ensuring people were treated with respect and fighting against gender discrimination and child labor in countries where laws were still lax. Unilever also respected workers' rights and paid employees above the minimum wage. From this viewpoint, institutional investors considered Unilever a great company in terms of social dimensions – the "S" in the ESG acronym.

But most investors disregarded one of Unilever's most important initiatives: preparing the next generation of leaders, one that would include as many women as men, a better age distribution and better cultural balance. Unilever offered training and education to its entire talent pool, not just future leaders, as part of its efforts to make workers more employable in a fast-changing industry that required digitalization, marketing, operations and sales capabilities. The company's tremendous impact on people's employability was very relevant for its future competitiveness, as well as for shareholders. Sadly, most investors rarely asked about it. They were vastly more interested in Unilever's financial performance and sustainability initiative. As with sustainability, Unilever was also spearheading new initiatives in talent development and its leadership pipeline, which were key drivers for the firm's long-term performance. Unfortunately, the formal list of ESG factors does not always take these areas into account. But investors should pay close attention to them. Employees' quality makes a true difference in corporate performance, as many family businesses and private equity and venture capital firms can attest.

This chapter will explore the role of the board of directors in leadership development and people management. In the next section, I offer a brief overview of the role of the boards in CEO development and succession planning, which is a duty of the board. In Section 5.3, I discuss why many boards have not been up to the challenge of governing people's policies and talent development. In Section 5.4, I discuss the role of the board of directors in people's development.

5.2   BOARDS IN CEO DEVELOPMENT AND SUCCESSION PLANNING

A firm is much more than the CEO at the top of the pyramid. In organizations, both success and failure belong to the team. Nevertheless, the empirical evidence of many companies suggests the CEO's significant capacity to push the firm to the brink of collapse, as recently witnessed in WeWork, Wirecard and Uber, among others. This is especially true when the board does not do a good job in monitoring and working with the CEO. The opposite is also true. The CEO's influence in building trust with employees and customers, developing the firm's long-term strategy and engaging shareholders and other stakeholders can make a difference. Moreover, the CEO also sets the tone in terms of values and leadership by example, and acts as the driving force of people development.

5.2.1 Human Dimensions of CEO Succession Planning

CEO succession planning is the first step in naming the next CEO. The process of evaluating the current CEO, defining a succession pathway, clarifying the professional competences and personal attributes the company needs for the future, assessing candidates, ensuring a smooth exit of the current CEO and eventually appointing the new CEO, is long and complex. It involves analytical capabilities and empathy, data and wisdom and a comprehensive diagnostic of the firm's challenges. The current CEO may have been working with the board of directors for several years. Her strengths and weaknesses may be clear, but her personal bonds and trust with board members – or lack thereof – will influence the exit process. While the CEO profile needed for the future may be clear, the process of defining the current CEO's exit pathway can incite huge controversy.

This is even more evident in companies where the founder is also the CEO. In July 2017, Uber's board of directors announced that Travis Kalanick, its CEO, largest shareholder and founder, would step down and that Dara Khosrowshahi would lead the firm (Wong, 2017). This pronouncement was driven by some Kalanick's decisions and behaviour revealing certain elements of his behavior that put the company's reputation at risk, sparking a potential crisis with investors and customers. Kalanick had been a creative entrepreneur who helped grow a company and an industry that was nonexistent before Uber. At the same time, his management style, treatment of drivers and other employees, the culture he encouraged and his contempt for regulators, were all serious threats to the firm's reputation and long-term development.

For boards of directors, these conflicts become even starker when dealing with founders or large shareholders who also happen to serve as the firm's CEO. A strategic decision can be approved or postponed, new market entries can be accelerated or delayed and resource allocation to fund new projects can gradually increase or decrease. These strategic decisions are extremely complex, and in many cases, the level of irreversibility also may be high. In the case of a CEO exit, succession planning is a complicated issue, compounded by board directors' personal relationships with the current CEO, the role of values in evaluating candidates and the need to reach a consensus.

Board members' capabilities in navigating complex human and interpersonal relationships are also important. The best time to design a solid CEO succession plan is when the company is performing well. The interplay between the firm's strategic situation, recent performance, challenges, reputation and ability to attract good people and stable shareholders, offers a picture that boards should have in sharp focus when considering the next CEO and the succession process.

This combination of factors makes CEO succession one of the board of directors' most significant decisions, yet it is one that few organizations manage successfully. Even companies that have done it well for years may, at some point, falter in this critical area. One such example is General Electric, admired for decades for its ability to develop outstanding business leaders. After a long tenure that began in 2001, Jeff Immelt stepped down as CEO on June 12, 2017 (Colvin, 2019), as discussed in the Introduction.

The board had been working on Immelt's eventual succession for some time, but in the end, the pressure from capital markets and the growing doubts about some candidates limited its scope of choices. Immelt was replaced by John Flannery, a GE veteran and head of the health-care business. The succession's circumstances were not well planned by the GE board. The fact that in October 2018 Flannery was replaced by GE board member Larry Culp also reinforced the view that GE's succession planning had failed. The decision itself – appointing a board member to replace a CEO – was quite unusual, particularly in a listed company. The GE board gave the impression that it was lagging behind events in this relevant area.

In recent years, other well-known companies such as Boeing, Deutsche Bank, HP, HSBC and McDonald's have experienced similar problems in CEO succession planning: departing CEOs without a well-designed succession planning process. This is a very complex topic for boards. Some board members with years of experience point to CEO succession as the toughest board decision they ever had to make. It is a decision that combines hard choices, sometimes accompanied by financial constraints, with soft dimensions, which are interwoven into interpersonal issues and the personality traits and qualities that will influence the new CEO's performance. It is possible to apply a data-driven approach for this decision, but not with the type of data typically used in other strategic decisions. The experience of some companies, large and small, that have managed this process smoothly – including Ingka and Unilever, as discussed in this book – underline core areas that deserve the board's careful attention and the detailed preparation by the board's nominating committee, that is in charge of leadership appointments and compensation.

5.2.2 Different Approaches to the CEO Succession Process

There are three broad approaches to CEO succession (Bower, 2007). The first is to look mainly for internal candidates. This option is particularly compelling when the company has shown solid performance over the past years and has strong leadership, particularly, if it underwent a recent transformation. The new CEO may have to face one in the future and the critical capabilities required to lead this process need to have been put to test.

In this case, the board can adopt two action plans. The first is that the board is aware of potential candidates and does not make its views public. In the second plan, an internal process is opened formally; candidates know they are on the short list and a horse race is set into motion. This approach seems to guarantee transparency to the process but generates considerable pressure, not only on potential candidates and their business areas – which need to continue to perform well during the race – but also on their teams. It is a process with a clear delineation of winners and losers that leaves behind scars, including talented people who decide to leave after their boss has lost the race.

The second approach is to look outside and opt for external candidates, particularly if an important corporate change is needed. By looking outside, the board can compare the profiles of internal candidates with external ones. This approach may be necessary when the company faces an important change and the internal pipeline of candidates is narrow. This situation may also reflect a failure on behalf of the current CEO and the board of directors in nourishing leadership development within the firm.

The third approach is to have inside–outside candidates (Bower, 2007). These are candidates whose careers have been largely outside of the firm, but who joined recently to help promote change and are performing reasonably well. They are expected to offer both an external approach and a strong grasp of the firm's internal perspective.

Any of these approaches may need to consider another important dimension: the decision to separate the roles of the chair and CEO – a tradition followed in most Western European countries – or have the same person occupy both roles, as in many US firms. The separation of these roles enables a greater diversity of candidates for the CEO position, since the new CEO will lead the company, but not the board of directors. This leaves some complexities of governance and board leadership outside the realm of the CEO search.

The board of directors and, in particular, its nominating committee, should discuss these issues in depth. They are critical. This committee should play a central role in defining the boundary conditions of the decision, ensuring a rich and diverse CEO candidate pipeline, defining a process and gaining a deep knowledge of the candidates.

5.2.3   The Board's Nominating Committee and the Board

The most complex task for the board's nominating committee is agreeing on the definition of the required competencies, skills and personal attitudes that the future CEO should espouse, as well as assessing candidates' overall fit with the company's culture and strategy.[1] Boards should hire senior managers for competencies, attitudes and personal fit. Many boards of directors tend to outsource a great deal of this complex challenge to search firms. External professional services firms can be of great help but should not replace the role of the board in understanding what type of CEO profile the firm needs, getting to know the candidates well and adequately judging their fit with the company. External firms can help, but the board should lead the process and assume its responsibilities.

The debate on whether the next CEO should be internal or external is legitimate, as discussed earlier. The board of directors should work with the current CEO and other senior executives on the firm's leadership pipeline. A thorough assessment and personal knowledge of these candidates is indispensable. Sequential assessment may lead the board to suggest different assignments for potential candidates in order to broaden their expertise and competencies. Search firms can also provide external benchmarks to compare the firm's leadership pipeline with that of other firms, and offer insights on which competencies need a boost. Based on these analyses, the board might consider the need to explore external candidates.

The board's nominating committee should have a leading role in this process, dedicating time to work on the best solutions. There is a question of how much time and effort the board should allocate to CEO assessment and succession issues in board meetings and nominating committee sessions. Many boards have good practices for strategic investments and capital allocation decisions. On the contrary, board members might see only one CEO succession process during their years on the board. This makes this process more exceptional.

---

[1] Adams, Keloharju and Knupfer (2018) and Kaplan and Sorensen (2020) highlight critical issues in CEOs' traits, competencies and performance. See Canals (2012) for a broader framework on senior leadership competencies.

Board members should offset the infrequency of CEO appointments with careful analyses and planning.

The nominating committee should report to the entire board on their deliberations and progress. It is very important that this committee reaches a shared diagnosis of the situation: the current CEO's assessment, the time frame of his tenure, the new CEO's competencies and attitudes and the current pipeline of candidates.

For board members, this decision-making process requires professional expertise, wisdom, and prudence: It is very easy to make mistakes in this complex process. By assuring a healthy and informed debate among board directors, with all doubts and concerns clearly communicated, the pathway to a shared diagnosis becomes easier, and the ongoing reviews and ultimate decision will be more effective.

5.2.4 The Succession Plan's Timeframe

The board and the current CEO should share a specific time horizon to plan an orderly transition when the firm requires it. This may change as the company's context evolves or due to unexpected events – such as a CEO's health crisis or a severe misstep with bad reputational effects – leading to an early CEO departure. It is important to note the upsurge in CEO turnover in listed firms during the last two decades, particularly in the United States, resulting in shorter CEO tenures.

The board of directors has the final responsibility for hiring and firing the CEO. It should do a good job in assessing the current CEO and offering advice on how to improve his leadership. It also needs to prudently plan the succession process, even if the CEO has been recently appointed. Boards should avoid the embarrassing situation of having to name a transitory CEO because the former CEO left and the new one has not yet joined the company. Firms waste precious time and de-motivate their people when senior managers' transition processes are not managed professionally.

The board's nominating committee should work regularly on this matter and define a time horizon. It should know all the internal candidates well and have a current map of the professional competencies the job requires. The nominating committee should ask the current CEO for her views on the process.

Once the board of directors has made the decision to appoint the new CEO, clear communication is essential as a sign of respect for all individuals involved in the decision – the departing CEO, her close colleagues and the new CEO – and to ensure the decision is relayed through official channels. For this reason, it is recommended that, whenever possible, the board considers a group of candidates until the very end, without making a formal decision too far ahead of its planned communication. Among other things, this option gives the board some additional freedom on when and how to announce the decision. It is also important for the board to establish a clear schedule for the CEO transition and departure process.

5.3   THE BOARD IN PEOPLE POLICIES AND DEVELOPMENT: A MISSING FUNCTION?

The board's responsibilities in appointing and developing a CEO seem clear. Its duties are less clear-cut in the wider realm of people development. The experience of the companies analyzed in this book is relevant: Their boards pay attention to people's development. This effort is very impactful on the firm's culture and the quality of the leadership pipeline. Over the past few decades, the role of boards of directors in overseeing people-management issues has been marginal. This is one corporate function that boards have largely delegated to the CEO and senior managers. Only more recently, as cases of gender and racial discrimination in the workplace have become more evident and social activism on these issues has grown, have some companies and their boards of directors reacted by adopting new policies to address them. Institutional investors have recently started to ask companies to report on them.

The experience of Amazon offers an important lesson. The technology giant experienced a heavy reputational blow in August 2015, when *The New York Times* reported particular aspects of its personnel policy (Kantor and Streitfeld, 2015; Taylor, 2018). Employee complaints had emerged in some of Amazon's warehouses, especially in the United States, citing grueling working conditions and substandard safety measures.

Employees leveled serious accusations at Amazon. Its policies stood in sharp contrast with its reputation as one of the world's leading tech companies. Amazon reacted to these criticisms by improving some practices and acknowledging employees' freedom to defend their rights and safety. In 2018, for the first time, US-listed companies had to disclose compensation figures for their CEOs, as well as median employee compensation. The pay gap at Amazon was revealed to be much higher than in other tech companies. Public opinion and politicians reacted angrily to Amazon's labor policy and pressured the company to change tack. In October 2018, Amazon announced its decision to raise its minimum wage in the United States to $15, a substantial increase for the lowest-paid employees. The company also increased the minimum wage in the United Kingdom.

In his final letter before stepping down as CEO on April 15, 2021, Bezos regretted not placing more attention on people policies during his leadership. In this context, the board of directors faced some relevant questions. Was Amazon's board of directors knowledgeable of the firm's people policies? Were these policies appropriate for a company that had an aspiration for excellence and uniqueness? Was the board cognizant of the reputational risk associated with those policies? If talent development and employee engagement are key for any company, why was the board of directors not paying more attention to them?

The Amazon case highlights critical dimensions of the role of boards of directors regarding people management and development. The board of directors should oversee how the company is hiring, developing and retaining talent. It should also thoroughly assess the effect of company practices on the firm's reputation and market value. Unfortunately, not too many boards of directors look at people development in this way. An excessive focus on economic efficiency seems to be the name of the game for many boards.

5.3.1 People Management: The Search for Efficiency

An organization should be efficient and create economic value. A company cannot increase its payroll inefficiently: It would create artificial jobs that may put the firm's survival at risk. But there is a need to recognize the recent shift in the corporate world to the other extreme of the pendulum toward cost efficiency: an increase in job outsourcing, wage arbitrage and investment in robots in order to reduce labor costs. The dominant paradigm of treating people as resources – human resources – has led companies to reduce people's contributions to a wage and shrink labor costs as much as possible in order to increase efficiency. If this trend gains traction, in many countries unemployment may rise structurally and more people will become dependent on social welfare. Some deeper questions follow: Can companies and individuals find prosperity in a society where the right to work and contribute through personal work disappears? Will society have responsible citizens if meaningful work is scarce? These are complex questions that should not be sidestepped – not even by boards of directors – because they impact a firm's long-term survival.

An efficiency-based approach to people management has dominated both theory and practice for the past few decades, with some notable exceptions (Pfeffer, 1997; Ulrich and Brockband, 2005; Cappelli 2013; Cappelli and Keller, 2014). In the 1990s, once digital technology allowed for offshoring, and globalization expanding its scope, employees' contributions began to be considered merchandise that could be exchanged at market prices. Companies should be managed effectively. The challenge is to find the right balance between achieving efficiency and motivating and treating people with respect, an indispensable dimension of a positive corporate culture.

Companies today rely more on subcontracted work than in the past and it might be more efficient. The question is the impact of subcontracting on employee engagement and other indicators like customer satisfaction and innovation.

By placing efficiency as the dominant goal in people management, companies have generated some risks. The first is a disengaged workforce and a mediocre culture, which will make it more difficult to attract and hire the right people. The effects are diverse. Until recently, boards did not pay attention to pay disparity, discrimination or harassment. Overlooking the human side of organizations is not only risky from a financial viewpoint; it is morally questionable. Will a company that does not respect its own people respect its customers or suppliers?

The second risk is the firm's contribution to a wider societal problem of disengaged workers, whose pay in many industries and countries is being squeezed by the rising use of technology and the higher returns on capital in its diverse forms (Piketty, 2014; Eeckhout, 2021). The shrinking middle class and the emergence of populism in the United States and other countries offer a cautionary tale on the ascending risk of disengagement among a growing percentage of citizens who feel that the game is unfair.

Boards in advanced countries have lagged behind in managing those risks: pay gap, employee engagement, harassment and working conditions. Amazon is just one example of a relevant company whose employee policies are not up to speed. Boards should avoid risk factors related to workers' rights: pay, working hours, working conditions, safety and discrimination, among others. This is a growing area in compliance, and boards of directors should make sure the company has the right policies in place.

In some high-profile companies, corporate crises around people policies have sparked a negative reaction among regulators, lawmakers and large asset managers. The upswing in minimum wages in some countries, broader employee protection during COVID-19 lockdowns and harsher punishments for certain behaviors (harassment and discrimination, among others) all reveal a trend toward stricter regulations.

Capital markets regulators are also stepping in. On August 26, 2019, the US Securities and Exchange Commission decided that listed companies would have to provide a description of their human capital resources in cases where this disclosure would be material to and have an impact on the company's business. This rule is principles-based, not prescriptive, and does not include a framework to define the main standards.[2] This makes comparison among companies more complex. This is a step that is been adopted by other national regulators as well.

Large institutional investors such as BlackRock, State Street and Vanguard, among others, are also expanding their approach to people policies in their investee companies, by providing guidelines on core areas and principles for companies' reporting. These recommendations touch on relevant topics but omit others that are also material to the company's business and performance. Asset managers and other international institutions have recently launched their own frameworks to assess people policies in corporate reporting. It is interesting to note the compliance-oriented approach of these benchmarks. Regulators establish rules and frameworks, and companies comply. Investors feel that they are in safer hands because companies behave within the established framework. The question is: Is this risk management and control approach enough to govern people policies and have a world-class team of employees?

5.3.2   People: Beyond Risk Management

Companies should hire great people and develop them. The shift from risk control to a more positive and innovative oversight of people management is indispensable for boards of directors. Unfortunately,

---

[2] The SEC rule proposes that firms offer "a description of the registrants' human capital resources, including the number of persons employed by the registrant, and any human capital measures or objectives that the registrant focuses on in managing the business." By the end of 2021, the EU Commission was also working on a new directive regarding human rights across the firm's supply chain.

experience suggests that regulation or frameworks motivated by compliance are not overly effective. Rules and regulatory frameworks – even voluntary ones – may be reasonably good for financial information, yet they only reflect a small portion of reality. The situation is even worse for nonfinancial information, where rules and frameworks lack the informational advantages present in other contexts and industries. Moreover, this information should not only be useful for investors: It should essentially be useful for the firm's governance. New rules and regulations like the one proposed by the SEC seem to be designed to help investors understand the companies they invest in. But equally important as helping investors is encouraging boards of directors to consider the relevant, material factors that drive the firm's long-term development.

In 2020, the World Economic Forum, in collaboration with the big four accounting firms, defined a proposal to tackle this challenge. It offered a more integrated framework for ESG factors (World Economic Forum, 2020). It is organized around four major themes – purpose, planet, people and prosperity – each defined with its own indicators.

This framework suggested three basic areas for reporting on people: (1) dignity and equality; (2) health and safety; and (3) skills for the future. It goes a step forward and tries to measure central aspects of people management. Unfortunately, it does not cover some key areas in people management. It does not assess whether the level of people's skills and capabilities is adequate to lead the firm in the long term. It does not consider whether the company is good enough at generating and developing talent internally, and whether essential positions have a good succession plan. It does not refer to the culture of the organization nor to employee engagement. Finally, a reflection on what makes the company attractive for current employees and future hires is not clear. In a nutshell, the framework proposed is useful to disclose specific indicators of human capital, but falls short in its response to these essential questions.

These themes have a tremendous impact on the way boards of directors and investors consider the reality of the firm's employees. In particular, the critical question for boards is how a deeper engagement of the board in people policies and practices can help the senior management team do a better job of hiring, developing and engaging people, transform a company into an employer of choice and enhance the firm's overall reputation.

Boards of directors should use a holistic portfolio of indicators to assess people's contribution and development. These indicators should relate to performance but also competencies, skills, capabilities and engagement. Many chief people officers in premier companies are doing a good job in this respect, but need to highlight better the impact of their work and their influence on the CEO and the board of directors. This influence should be intellectual, emotional and moral. It is intellectual because it needs to be founded on facts and arguments. It is emotional because chief people officers need to convey the sense of urgency to develop employees with at least the same persuasion and intensity with which CEOs and chief technology officers (CTOs) support digital transformation. It is moral because we are dealing with persons who possess an intrinsic dignity.

People management and people policies have not developed a reputation for effectiveness, state-of-the-art practices and relevance, as other business areas – such as finance and technology – have, over the last decades. CFOs have become more relevant because investors and capital markets want to better understand the firm's financial models. CTOs have grown in importance with mounting computing power and digital transformation. Despite the many references to people as strategic assets, some boards of directors still consider employees to be a generic resource, readily available when the company needs it. Over the years, I have met some CEOs in international companies who did not believe in the value of developing their own people. They simply trusted the job market and its supposed efficiency to provide their firms with the right candidates at the right time. The implicit assumptions in this reasoning are that the firm's culture and values do not matter, and that employee turnover is not a relevant indicator of the quality of the firm's management.

In some companies, senior managers in charge of people or HR receives less recognition and lower pay than the CFO or the CTO. There is a call for CEOs to count on the chief people officer (CPO) more for company leadership. These complaints carry real weight. But there is also a need to devise better frameworks to manage people in contemporary organizations. This step needs to go hand in hand with the CEO's greater recognition and reliance on the chief people officer for the firm's long-term growth. The board of directors should play a role in helping the firm better manage employees and their development. When the board does not consider or understand these policies, the potential for undervaluing people policies and mismanagement is high.

An additional reflection on the words that are used to refer to persons as employees is important: In this book I chose to speak about persons, people and people development, not about human resources or human capital. People are not resources. People are not capital. Each person has an irreplaceable and unique dignity. I speak about persons who have rights and duties, and can make a difference in organizations through their work and attitude in a variety of ways. I speak about the people department, a unit that designs policies to support employees' development in their unique professional roles to help the company grow. I also speak about the chief people officer, the senior manager in charge of this unit. Words are important in shaping minds and perspectives, including those of the board of directors. For these reasons, I use the notions of person, people management and people's development to refer to employee policies.

In the next section, I define some principles for developing people in organizations for the long term. These principles can help boards of directors and CEOs place people on top of the governance agenda.

Table 5.1. *Key themes on people and leadership development for boards of directors*

- Principles of people's development and governance
- The board of directors in governing people development
- Leadership capabilities, CEO's development and succession
- Diversity
- People's development
- Chairman, CEO and board directors' assessment
- Assessing the professional value of the firm's people

5.4 THE ROLE OF THE BOARD IN PEOPLE DEVELOPMENT AND GOVERNANCE: HOW CAN THE BOARD OF DIRECTORS ADD VALUE?

The Unilever experience in people development and the Amadeus acquisition of TravelClick (see Chapter 3) highlight how boards should consider people and harness their competencies in strategic decisions. In this section, I refer to the role of board of directors, although within the board of directors, the board's nominating and compensation committee should debate first these issues, in preparation for future board meetings. Table 5.1 summarizes the major themes and areas related to people and leadership development that the board of directors should address.

5.4.1 Principles on People Development and Governance

In the 1980s, as companies began placing more importance on finance, other corporate functions such as sales, marketing and people management needed to rediscover their role in corporate leadership. In the case of people management, scholars and consultants designed new frameworks to help senior managers develop people more effectively and make this function more strategic. Some of these efforts had great intrinsic value, while others were a PR effort. Buzz phrases like "the

Table 5.2. *Some principles on people's management and development*

- Consider each individual person
- People have their own motivations and expectations: Connect them with the corporate purpose
- Companies need a spirit of collaboration
- Collaboration requires trust
- The firm's long-term value is determined by the quality of its people
- People can improve through assessment, mentoring, learning and development
- The chief people officer should be a strategic partner of the CEO
- The board of directors should supervise and give fair advice on people's management and development policies

---

war for talent," "talent-first organizations" and "creating a magnet for talent" became part of the corporate lexicon.

Unfortunately, many of these frameworks lacked a solid foundation. The analogy of financial reporting is useful. Finance and financial accounting have become critical fields because they offer robust frameworks to understand companies' financial flows and stocks and how financial value is created. These frameworks may not reflect the whole reality and may be more backward-looking than future-oriented, but with some caveats, they have well-defined criteria and are helpful to better understand the firm's value. Frameworks that try to assess the firm's people or the company's environmental effects still need to make progress.

This challenge has no easy answer, but before considering how the board should assess and govern the firm's people, it is useful for board directors and CEOs to reflect on some fundamental people-management principles and notions (see Table 5.2). Most of them come from the companies studied in this book.

The first principle is that CEOs and boards should view employees as persons, individual human beings with not only talent but values and aspirations. Persons have intellectual capacity, emotional power and free will, and CEOs should respect and appreciate each person's contribution. Recognizing only their functional talent and not seeing them as unique human beings is a huge mistake. Moreover, some people may not feel fairly assessed when their bosses do not fully appreciate the value they bring to the organization. But the disappointment runs deeper to beyond repair when employees realize their bosses do not respect them as human beings. A company that aspires to be talent-driven needs to put the wholeness of each person's humanity first.

Each person has intrinsic dignity and deserves respect. Respect is an important, indispensable quality. When someone provides a service to another person, even in a transaction, a sense of humanity brings the relationship to a higher level for both the recipient of this expression of humanity and the one who offers it. In the case of employees, who dedicate their professional work and a good deal of their daily life to an organization, paying a fair wage is a matter of justice, but justice may not be enough. Gratitude is also a signal of respect. If the board of directors aspires to set the tone for what working in a company genuinely means, its members should display a level of humanity toward the company's employees, expressed in both small things and in more relevant policies and decisions. Only companies with this level of humanity will be able to fully engage their employees and inspire them to be creative and service-oriented in their dealings with customers.

The second principle is that most people want to work for something larger than what they alone can do. Firms with an authentic sense of purpose offer a guidepost to individuals who aspire to make a professional contribution and serve customers, colleagues, communities and other stakeholders, and make a positive impact on society at large. Gartenberg, Prat and Serafeim (2019) presented evidence that some notions of purpose help employees find meaning in their work.

The third principle is that organizations succeed when their senior management helps individuals work with other individuals. Organizations thrive on collaboration and cooperation. The need for coordination, even in the digital age, is truly relevant. Unless people learn to work with each other collaboratively, it is difficult to advance the firm's performance.

The fourth principle is that collaboration requires trust. Developing trust within an organization is complex. One can recognize its existence when it is there, but must address specific factors in order to make trust flourish. Trust is indispensable: Without it there is no cooperation, and without cooperation, individual performance will not translate into corporate performance. Outstanding individuals may create some nice solos, but respected companies require more than excellent solos scattered about the organization. Trust requires the combination of three ingredients: professional excellence, which establishes standards of professional conduct and stable performance expectations; personal values, which ensure fair and consistent behavior, irrespective of external pressures; and the willingness to promote the common good of the organization.

The fifth principle is that what makes companies great is not capital, not even technology. As seen so often in entrepreneurial firms, capital is available to most of them and technology is frequently developed as a recombination of existing ones. In successful start-ups, the quality of the entrepreneurs and the team they assemble is what drives growth. Products come and go, technologies thrive and after a while, become obsolete. People make the difference when it comes to customers and colleagues, and capital and technology are there to serve them. This is important for boards of directors to remember.

The sixth principle is related to people's assessment. Ensuring that employees' assessment is done in a professional way is a primary task of the board of directors. It is also clear that this job cannot be done simply by aggregating data on people. Boards need to make sure that the data they get is relevant for their essential function: getting to know the people who work in the company, in particular, current and future leaders. The board should also make sure that the senior management team has a system to continuously improve the pipeline of people in key positions and offers specific development programs, such as mentoring and learning opportunities, to help them magnify their contribution to the company.

Data on pay gap, safety and discrimination are very useful to identify and resolve problems the company may have. Unfortunately, this is only a defensive solution. Companies that want to excel need to think proactively about developing their people and helping them reach their fullest potential, regardless of race, gender or nationality, with a fair and professional approach. When this happens, discrimination tends to disappear.

This reflection is an urgent call for action. The metrics designed to date to assess people and people policies focus on some areas that mainly try to avoid potential abuses and discrimination, but disregard the critical role people play and their capacity to contribute to the firm's long-term development. Boards that do not understand this are missing a crucial pillar in governance. This is a reason why I advocate that people-related factors should be a category by itself (P, the people factors), different from S (social) factors in ESG dimensions (Strine, 2019). When ESG factors were designed, investors described S factors with the intention of highlighting risks related to the firm's employees, including issues of discrimination, fairness and safety, among others. These factors are important. But effective boards and senior managers should consider how to engage and develop people – the driving engine of any company – and make their organization a magnet for outstanding professionals. People should be the first of the nonfinancial factors to be considered in reporting. From ESG factors, companies should move to consider PESG dimensions, starting with people (P).

The seventh principle is that the chief people officer becomes a strategic partner of the CEO in leading the firm. The evidence from many companies that had the potential to grow highlights a common weakness: the lack of enough competent people to manage the transition from one step to the next and meet customer expectations when operating at a much larger scale. This is a time in which the scarcity of people with the right competences at managerial and leadership levels is truly relevant. The current uncertainty in the global economic context makes these leadership capabilities even more important than in times of greater stability. Chief people officers and their teams are part of the solution: They should be up to the challenge by operating with the same level of effectiveness as other members of the senior management team.

The eighth principle is that boards of directors should not manage the people division but should make sure that its policies align with the firm's purpose, culture strategy and business model. People's selection and hiring, assessment and rewards and development fall to the CEO and chief people officer. In the same way that the board gains knowledge, understands and approves the firm's financial statements and strategic decisions, it should also understand and approve relevant people decisions. In particular, the board of directors has the duty to ensure the company has a good pipeline of people with the leadership capabilities needed in the future. They should also assess whether recruitment, development and reward systems are consistent with the firm's purpose and strategy, and that succession plans for key positions are clearly defined.

The board should foster accountability as it relates to people management. Just as financial and commercial goals are shared across the organization, key indicators designed by the people division should also be conveyed, using a level of transparency respectful of each person and their privacy. The chief people officer should ensure that the people division defines high-level standards and accountability. It is also the duty of the executive committee to establish accountability in people decisions, including appointments, development initiatives and compensation policies. Finally, the board needs to be accountable in governing people: its work with the CEO and CPO, the strategic areas chosen, the major policies approved or reviewed, capabilities to be developed, chief appointments and other decisions such as compensation. Reporting in these areas is complex, but the board should make a concerted effort to do so.

The final principle is that the board should get to know senior managers and potential candidates for leadership succession. Only by developing personal knowledge of the firm's individuals and their capabilities can the board gain a strong grasp of their leadership competencies and suitability for the firm's future leadership opportunities. Boards of directors and especially the board's nominating committee have a special responsibility to get to know key people well and evaluate their potential for leadership. The board's nominating committee should try to gain a deep awareness of their professional competencies and how they can help develop the company for the long term.

These reflections set the tone for the contributions that a highly professional people division should make in companies that truly believe in the power of individuals. CEOs should deepen and broaden the role of the chief people officer in the company's strategic challenges. Chief people officers should work in close collaboration with other senior managers to create the solutions that the company needs.

The board of directors should also take the lead on how a company views its employees and their professional contribution. It is not only a matter of treating employees according to legal rules. It is showing professionalism and respect in its decisions. It is understanding that the company very much depends on the leadership capabilities and the contribution of every single employee. It is also about the type of company that the board and senior management team aspire to lead and develop (Kochan, 2015). In addition, there are key positions that require special competencies. The board should make sure that the team in charge has them and that a proper succession plan is in place in the event that it is needed. People development is at the heart of the firm's long-term growth and boards have a duty to understand and take an interest in it.

5.4.2 The Board of Directors in Governing People Policies

The board of directors provides the long-term orientation for major corporate policies, in collaboration with the CEO. It should also play this role in people policies. Specific areas can be considered. The first is that the board should draw a bridge between the firm's strategic challenges and the strategic initiatives it will undertake to address them, and the professional competencies[3] that its people will require to succeed in this endeavor.

Let us consider the case of a digital transformation initiative. The board may set up some clear goals, approve some initiatives and bring in external experts to speed up the process. But this decision may prove unproductive in the long term unless the board ensures that a plan is in place to internally develop the needed competencies, and that a core team is able to lead and execute this transition. The same reasoning applies to all levels of the organization: People's capabilities today are different from the capabilities required in the future. The board should make sure that the CEO and the CPO have an updated map of current capabilities, those required in the future and a plan to develop those the firm does not have today and should have tomorrow. This capability gap and the plan to tackle it should be reviewed and known by the board of directors. It is even more critical than having the right technology in place. Technology can be bought. People's capabilities need to be developed within the company's specific context and they take time. Board directors should understand and act upon them.

The competencies map and the identification of competency gaps lead to the search effort for specific capabilities. Finding, recruiting and onboarding people with the necessary capabilities becomes a priority for the board and the senior management team. As the board would do with other areas of great strategic impact, it should assess progress in this area. When the board of directors shows interest in

---

[3] I use the notion of competences, which includes knowledge, capabilities, interpersonal skills and attitudes (Canals, 2012).

people and their development, it is reflected in the atmosphere of the organization.

5.4.3 Leadership Capabilities

The next theme relates to leadership and managerial capabilities. The board should get to know the professional competencies of the CEO and senior managers. The CEO oversees the executive committee and should make decisions on hiring, developing executive committee members and creating a team. The board should know these individuals and by working with them the board will be able to assess senior managers better, plan effectively the CEO and senior managers' succession and help them develop important people-management competencies.

Digital transformation, disruptive innovation and customer focus are important initiatives for which some specific capabilities are needed. Nevertheless, the competences that companies need most for the long term – and which tend to be scarce – are leadership competencies (Cappeli, 2007): people with the capabilities to understand the context; diagnose the company's situation and challenges; define goals and set a sense of orientation; coordinate the entire organization; motivate and engage people; and define realistic plans that can be executed. In a world of increasing specialization, leadership competencies are truly in short supply. Even in high-tech contexts, it is leadership – not technology – that truly makes the difference.

Leadership also requires a good understanding of people's values and motivations, and their capacity to lead others by example. When boards assess senior managers or CEOs, they should consider these dimensions and their ability to lead an organization successfully and take it to a new level. In this respect, boards do an especially good job when they delve deeper into what makes a CEO or a senior manager unique, what motivates them, what makes them effective or what makes them weaker. This is a difficult conversation to hold between board members because among other things, there is not a lot of hard data. Developing leaders is so critical for the long-term health of organizations that board directors need to refine the capability to truly understand other people, gather the relevant information about their professional strengths and weaknesses and make prudent judgments about them and their capacity to assume new roles. The board should also engage the CEO in a constructive and collaborative conversation on these topics.

The board has a special role in CEO and senior management development, as discussed earlier in this chapter. The development of future leaders is an essential function that the board should monitor. As the cases of GE and Wells Fargo highlight, the failure to appoint a competent CEO or the abrupt exit of a CEO reveals the company's lack of preparation in grooming potential successors. This is also an indicator of the mediocre judgment of some boards regarding the strategic priorities that their firms are facing.

This interaction between the board and the CEO also includes the formal assessment and feedback that the CEO shares with members of the executive committee team. It is good practice for the CEO to formally write their assessment so that the facts, their consequent judgments, goals and aims are all clearly formulated and defined. The CEO can share the basic information contained in these written reports with the board to deepen its knowledge on how senior managers perform in different areas, the CEO's assessment, the definition of their areas for improvement and the collective capabilities the senior management team needs to develop as a team.

5.4.4 Diversity

Around the world, the evidence of the lack of gender diversity among senior management teams in listed companies is overwhelming. Boards of directors have traditionally prioritized corporate growth and opportunities ahead of leadership development and diversity. Most listed companies are predominantly led by white males in CEO and senior leadership positions. In its 2021 Fortune Global 500 List, *Fortune* reported that women were running 23 of the

500 companies included in the ranking; in 2020, there were only 14 (Hinchliffe, 2021). Six women of color were serving as Global 500 CEOs. These figures represented an all-time high. This situation is improving due to pressure from regulators to establish quotas and demands from institutional investors, pressing for diversity. The empirical case for gender parity seems to be positive on corporate performance, in particular, by improving accountability, collegiality and the quality of risk-taking (Adams and Ferreira, 2009; Post and Byron, 2015; Adams, 2016; Kirsch, 2017).

The case for gender diversity is firmly grounded on the principle of fairness and the effects of diversity on the quality of decision-making. This attribute helps improve the quality of debate and decision-making in any group, and diminishes group-thinking biases. Nevertheless, the fact today is that senior management teams should have far more diversity, in particular gender diversity, and far more women in leadership positions. The experience of many companies is that grooming women for leadership positions may take senior manager dedication, and require flexible work policies. The effort is both fair and worthy because companies need this leadership diversity. Moreover, future qualified women on boards will very much depend on the number of women in senior leadership positions today. Developing female leadership in companies is indispensable to have more diverse and better boards in the future.

5.4.5 People Development

The board should review people development policies: how the firm helps every person grow personally and professionally in the company, especially senior managers. It should be coherent with the firm's competencies map. A person's effort and commitment are essential, but the corporate context and opportunities for formal learning, mentoring and coaching, as well as new challenges, widen the possibilities for development. This is extremely important since the value and impact that the firm's employees have today might not be useful tomorrow. What facilitates the transition from one set of capabilities to another is a bridge with three pillars: the employee's willingness to learn, professional challenges that provide on-the-job learning and formal opportunities for learning, such as programs and mentoring, among others.

People's development is an area under the responsibility of the CEO and the CPO. The board needs to make sure that people goals and policies support the firm's purpose and strategic goals. The board should become familiar with them and discuss the impact of the company's different policies that promote employee development.

Creativity in developing learning opportunities is always welcome, but evidence and experience are also important in guiding people's development. The board should review and understand the evidence and the impact of past programs in the company, what worked and why, as well as what did not work. There are three areas where the board can have a productive conversation with the CEO and the CPO on people's development. The first is the scope and frequency of new professional opportunities and challenges offered to employees, with opportunities for competency growth. A better understanding of how these initiatives work, what makes them effective, the number of people they benefit and their impact for both the company and the individual, are relevant questions for the board.

The second area is mentoring. People grow as much by individual learning as with the help of others. Companies that excel at producing leaders are organizations with top-quality mentoring systems. Mentors provide not only valuable experiences but also concrete pathways to manage conflicts, improve performance, navigate challenges and develop professionally. A good review of how mentoring is structured, how employees benefit and how mentees can at some point become mentors are among the dimensions to consider when assessing the quality and scope of mentoring.

The third area is formal learning in specific development programs. In some programs, the focus is more technical on specific business knowledge. Other programs may focus on capabilities development. As with other investments, the CEO and CPO should clearly explain how these programs connect with the firm's goals and strategic initiatives, their specific objectives, how they address these goals and their relationship with corporate projects that can immediately benefit from the program's learning. An assessment of the programs and their impact on the company is indispensable. In particular, the board should understand what makes these programs truly transformational for people and for the company as an organization.

5.4.6 Assessing the CEO, Chairperson and Board Members

The board should formally assess the CEO on a regular basis, at least once a year. The CEO usually works with the board on many issues and interacts with board members. The formal assessment of the CEO should be led by the chair of the board or the chair of the nominating committee, who relies on committee members for this process. It should include the suggestions of every single board member. A regular CEO assessment is good policy, consistent with what companies should do with all of their employees. In the case of the CEO, however, its impact is even greater since it affects the entire organization. CEO compensation should be clearly linked to the CEO's performance and assessment.

The board should also lead an annual assessment of the chair of the board and board members. This assessment can be undertaken by an external board member – perhaps the chairperson of the nomination committee – and should include the formal views of all board members. The board may count on the support of an external consultant, who interviews board members individually and develops a formal assessment report. Even when an external consultant is involved, it is important to involve the chairperson and some members of the nominating committee to complement and contextualize the consultant's assessment.

The dynamics among board members may affect their conduct and contribution. In the end, the board needs to develop a unique quality as a team, where the collective decisions taken and initiatives adopted have a deeper and more transformational impact than the astute insights of individual board members. Understanding and assessing a board director's ability to contribute to a team is very different from evaluating their individual capabilities. A board director will be useful to the board and the company if her capabilities can be leveraged within the context of a board of directors as a team.

The assessment of board members should also include specific areas for improvement, both at individual and board levels. The quality of governance is not only defined by a set of indicators; it is also the outcome of directors' commitment to improving the quality of the board as a team.

5.4.7 Assessing the Professional Value of the Firm's People: A Framework

The big four auditing firms and large investors recently developed a series of frameworks and metrics to assess people policies, including pay gaps, discrimination, inclusion and safety. While they offer some useful ideas, the consensus is that they do not adequately capture the principles of people development for the twenty-first century.

As discussed in Section 5.4.1, people engagement and development is a unique area where the board should place great attention, beyond compliance. It is a complex challenge but one that needs to be addressed for both reporting purposes and to help the board of directors and executive committee effectively develop the firm's people. An essential concept in people policies is not to measure people but rather to assess their professional and personal qualities, and performance. Measurement involves quantitative indicators. Assessment involves both quantitative and qualitative indicators.

In Table 5.3, I present a holistic framework that boards of directors and senior managers can use to assess people's contribution to the company – beyond compliance – with a special focus on what makes companies a unique professional context for people. The framework is organized around the principles of people management and development discussed in previous sections of this chapter, including the board's core responsibility in this function.

Table 5.3. *A framework to assess people's policy: A board perspective*

1. Demographics and Diversity
- Employees' composition by business units and departments, describing age, gender, nationality, education and number of years in the company

2. Professional Competencies
- People's competencies by business units and geographies: knowledge, capabilities, soft skills and attitudes
- Required competencies in five years by business units and geographies
- Indicators of major competencies' gaps

3. Employees' Dynamics
- Employee turnover by business units, functions, gender and age
- Voluntary turnover by business units, functions, gender and age
- Employee hiring, landing, promoting and firing

4. Leadership Development
- Leadership pipeline in the top management team and 1 and 2 levels below
- Succession plans for the top management team and 1 and 2 levels below
- Job opportunities and internal promotions

5. Development and Learning
- Investment in learning and development: number of annual hours of learning and spending
- Mentoring opportunities (number of people and hours)
- Development and learning: on-the-job opportunities (number)

6. Corporate Culture and Values
- Engagement: identity, meaning, commitment, team work, opportunities
- Culture and values: collaboration, identity, satisfaction, meaning
- Work climate
- Flexible working, family-friendly policies

7. Compensation and Other Economic Indicators
- Compensation indicators; variable compensation, disclosed by functions, gender and race
- Entry level wage and pay growth, by units and gender
- Pay gap in relation with the top 5 percent earners

Table 5.3. (*cont.*)

8. Human rights, Health and Compliance
• Human rights
• Health and safety indicators, across the value chain
• Unions and collective bargaining

This framework includes some of the most significant themes that boards of directors can consider in people governance and people development – the P (people) factor mentioned in Section 5.4.1 in this chapter. It is structured in eight categories and can be adapted to the needs of specific companies. The first is employee demographics and diversity, to offer a good description of the firm's people by professional categories, gender, education, age, countries, business units and professional trajectory. The second is people's professional competences and education, by business units and geographies. The board should have a clear idea of the professional competencies that the firm's people have and the ones that they do not have and will need to have in the next few years. Competencies and skills gaps are issues of great importance for any company in times of change.

The third area is employees' dynamics, including voluntary turnover, hiring, development, promotions and dismissals. The fourth is leadership development, including leadership pipeline, succession plans and internal promotions. The fifth is development and learning, including learning projects across the board, mentoring and other development initiatives, and on-the-job learning. The sixth is corporate culture and values, including key factors such as engagement, culture, values, family-friendly policies and flexible working opportunities. The seventh is compensation and other economic indicators, including executive compensations, schemes of variable compensation by professional categories and pay gaps. The final area is human rights, health and compliance. Each one of these themes can be expanded or broken down into sub-themes, with an indicator for each.

This framework also addresses the overarching challenges in people's decisions and contribution to the firm's long-term development. It can be expanded or condensed, adapted to companies of all sizes in a variety of industries. Each company can develop its own set of specific indicators around these basic concepts. For the board of directors, this framework can offer a broader perspective of the quality of people, people policies and employee engagement and development, beyond mere compliance. A board of directors can use this framework – or an adaptation – to diagnose, understand, assess and eventually change some people's policies. In the same way as the board regularly discusses financial or sales activities, the board should also have an overall view of people policies and reflect on how to improve the quality of governance in this critical area.

5.5 FINAL REFLECTIONS

As companies confront increasingly complex strategic challenges, it is more critical than ever that they secure the best pool of people with the right competencies and attitudes to address their core challenges. The experience also shows that managing people and people development continue to pose a significant challenge for most companies. While senior managers may have learned to work more effectively on financial and technology issues, their ability to develop people and nourish the talent pipeline is not an easy task.

At the firm governance level, this challenge looms even larger. Traditionally, very few boards of directors have adopted the assessment of the firm's people competencies as one of their duties or functions. The upswing in corporate crises around people (gender and race discrimination, sexual harassment and poor working conditions, among others) has increased the material effects of these factors on financial performance. This effect has consequently attracted the interest and attention of regulators, institutional investors and proxy advisory firms. Some institutional investors are pushing companies to disclose these people-related dimensions. The gap between what boards of directors should know about people, on the one hand, and the complexity of managing and developing people in an organization, on the other, is widening.

In this chapter, I review how boards of directors can contribute to an effective governance of people's development. Specifically, I present a framework with a more holistic picture of how people management and development can be designed and assessed at the board level.

The role of the board of directors in people management and development is critical. In particular, the board should assess and monitor the professional competencies needed for top management positions; define specific people-management and development principles; approve employee assessment and compensation models; and provide related performance indicators for investors and other stakeholders. In particular, the board has the exclusive responsibility to assess and make succession plans for the CEO and other senior managers. As a truly transformational function in any company, the board cannot pass the responsibility of these decisions to anyone else. The evidence points to too many failures in succession planning, which is why boards of directors need to work on this area with a very professional approach, allocate time and energy to it, develop a solid pipeline of candidates and proactively manage the process and timing ahead of unplanned events.

6 From Board Structure to Boards as Effective Teams

6.1 IS THE BOARD OF DIRECTORS A TEAM?

On May 15, 2017, Atlantia, the largest Italian highway infrastructure company, made a bid to acquire all Abertis shares, with a total market price of €16.3 billion. Abertis was Cellnex's largest individual shareholder, owning 34 percent of its shares. Other relevant institutional investors had shareholdings of less than 5 percent each. Following its IPO in May 2015 (see Chapter 3), Cellnex continued to expand its reach by acquiring telecommunications towers throughout Europe from major telecom companies. Investors found this entrepreneurial company very attractive. Its management team sought opportunities to manage telecom infrastructures, had a highly effective management model and executed deals efficiently.[1]

The Cellnex board was focused on helping the top management team with M&A deals, including their financial structure, investor relationships and other governance issues. Abertis had four members on the Cellnex board. With Atlantia's takeover offer, the stability of Cellnex's largest shareholder was at stake.

Suddenly, potential ownership changes forced the board of Cellnex to think about newly relevant shareholders. Some institutional shareholders appreciated Abertis' role as a long-term, large shareholder in Cellnex. But the board would need to rethink the company's future ownership structure. The Cellnex board did not know what Atlantia would do with Cellnex's shares if the takeover of Abertis was successful.

Atlantia's takeover offer took an unexpected turn on October 16, 2017, when ACS, the largest construction company in Spain,

---

[1] See Canals (2018) for a description of Cellnex's strategic challenges.

launched a competing offer of €18 billion for Abertis through its German subsidiary, Hochtief. Abertis was in play and, as a result, Cellnex entered a more uncertain ownership stage, with potentially negative effects on its ability to conclude new acquisition deals..

The Cellnex board of directors met frequently to discuss the impact of changes in the ownership structure of the company. Since its IPO, Cellnex had an effective corporate governance model, which also depended on Abertis' role as a reference shareholder in Cellnex. The other shareholders were institutional investors that did not have enough weight in the company to define its future course. The board began to explore alternatives that could safeguard the Cellnex growth project.

The board of Cellnex was created when the company went public in May 2015 and was relatively new. Half of its board members were independent directors with deep expertise in corporate finance and telecoms. They had been doing a good job, but the prospect of Abertis leaving Cellnex triggered a shift in the board dynamics. After this unexpected event, the board became a stronger team. Their members were committed to the company's success and further promoting its growth by exploring options in the company ownership.

On April 12, 2018, ACS, Atlantia and Hochtief agreed on a joint takeover of Abertis for a total value of €18.1 billion. They also announced that Abertis would divest from Cellnex. The good news for Cellnex was that Editione, an Italian family office, liked Cellnex and its team, and expressed its intention of becoming a shareholder of reference. The board of Cellnex worked hard, not only to find solutions to Abertis' exit, but to support the company and its management team in the various acquisitions over that period. In the middle of an uncertain context, the board worked as an engaged team and an effective driver of the firm's long-term development.

When a shareholder of reference announces its decision to divest from a company, it is not uncommon for board members and senior managers to abandon the company and the project. New shareholders might bring in new ideas and capital, but these transition processes are complex for any company, its governance and its management. The Cellnex board became an even stronger team and more engaged with the company's future.

How does a board of directors become a team? Should it function as such? Which qualities help it operate as an effective team? Corporate law does not mandate that boards of directors operate as a team. Institutional investors tend to inquire about numerous structural dimensions of a company's board of directors, but very few ask about the board's dynamics and effectiveness as a team (Cheng et al., 2021). Nevertheless, in many jurisdictions, corporate law assumes the board to be a collegial institution under the leadership of its chairperson. Investors also expect boards to make good decisions to support the company's future and protect their investment. This requires the ability of the board to work as an effective team, with clear goals and specific ways of operating and making decisions.

This is the theme of this chapter. In the next section, I introduce the definition of an effective team. This discussion examines whether the board of directors can be considered a team and which attributes it should embody to behave as a functional team. I then discuss specific dimensions that help turn the board into an effective team, including members' interpersonal relationships.

6.2   CORE ATTRIBUTES OF EFFECTIVE TEAMS

The evidence from the experience of Cellnex and other boards of directors shows that the quality and depth of board decisions depends on how the board approaches problems as a decision-making body. Moreover, the collaboration between the board and the CEO depends to a great degree on the diverse perspectives that board members bring to the discussion, which complement the internal perspectives of the CEO and senior managers.

This is also the case with top management teams (Hambrick, 1987; Finklestein, 1992). The CEO and management team work together based on their own experience, as well as input from their colleagues in different business functions and units. Many business problems and challenges are unstructured, characterized by limited information and great uncertainty. Problem solving requires the energy and power of teams made up of distinct personalities and backgrounds to diagnose, shape and provide structured solutions to their most pressing problems.

The literature on teams in the strategic management field has flourished over the past two decades (see, among others, Hackman, 2002; Edmonson, 2012; Katzenbach and Smith, 2015). Unfortunately, the corporate governance literature on boards of directors has not explicitly considered this team perspective in boards, with notable exceptions such as Blair and Stout (1999), Huse (2007, 2009), Pick and Merchant (2012), Winters (2018) and Bratton (2021), among others. This vantage point is increasingly relevant for boards. The current strategic uncertainty makes the work of boards of directors even more demanding and complex, requiring the collaborative work of board directors as a team, as evidenced by the Cellnex case.

Hackman (2002) summarized many years of research on what makes a successful team. He described the core dimensions that promote team effectiveness: stability, a clear and engaging direction, an enabling team structure, a supportive organizational context and the availability of competent coaching for team members. High-performance teams also share other attributes. The first is that they satisfy internal and external clients. The second feature is that they develop capabilities to find effective solutions to problems. The third is that their members find meaning in their job. Hackman (2002) and Edmonson (2012) help identify the overriding qualities of good teams. These findings are summarized in two main factors: the architecture of the team and the team personality (see Table 6.1).

6.6.1 The Team Architecture

The architecture of the team defines its basic structure, composition and diversity. It also includes a definition of the team's goals and the specific way in which members will combine their efforts, in particular, when members hold other roles in the organization. Hackman

Table 6.1. *Team: Architecture and personality*

Team Architecture: Key Factors	Team Personality: Key Factors
• Structure	• Purpose
• Composition	• Values
• Goals	• Shared mindset
• Diversity	• Psychological safety
	• Accountability

(2002) emphasizes that teams should have clear goals and composition: People know who the team members are, the team has clear boundaries, team membership is stable and the team's goals are known. In particular, the clarity about the composition of the team, its goals, resources to carry out its mission and the functions it is expected to perform are essential elements for their functionality. These attributes that define the basic structure of a team are very relevant: They might provide an excellent context for collaboration among team members, or, on the contrary, they might make it more difficult.

6.6.2 The Team Personality

The team personality defines how the team actually works. It explains the team's specific goals, how the team sets its strategy and action plans, how its members coordinate the different activities to be developed and how they assess performance and learn from experience. In the team personality, some basic elements can be identified.

The first element is the sense of purpose of the team: why it exists, what it is supposed to do, which goals it has, which values will orient its work and the sense of direction to achieve these goals. The leadership and membership of the team are essential, both to understand the team's mission, as well as to ensure the team has a clear sense of what needs to be done. A team's members should possess sets of complementary skills necessary to work on the projects, make decisions, and develop and implement the different projects.

The second is the shared mindset of the team (Haas and Mortensen, 2016), which encompasses the goals, assumptions, aspirations and tactics that the team will use and follow to make its work effective. In particular, goals will help shape a successful team if they are specific, measurable, attainable, relevant and time specific (SMART).

The third element is the team's development of psychological safety. Edmonson (2018) defines this as the shared belief among team members that the team is in the right context to assume risks and is not being punished to do so.

Psychological safety develops and grows in the presence of several crucial factors. The first is the respect that team members have for each other and their contributions. This atmosphere is essential not only to assume risks, but to engage in meaningful collaboration with other team members. Respect needs to dovetail with the capacity to ask questions and respectfully disagree with others. "Agreeing to disagree" to ultimately reach an accord is a complex process that leads some teams to the verge of collapse. But decision-making in contemporary organizations requires competence in managing these conversations and the capacity to respect others despite disagreements.

The second factor that contributes to psychological safety is the trust built inside the team. Trust relates not only to an individual's behavior – being loyal, truthful or committed – but also extends to the professionalism that team members display in their work. It is a necessary condition for success that every individual does the right things. Without this level of professionalism, trust will disappear very quickly.

The third factor is the team's clear focus on the goals it is expected to reach within a concrete timeframe. Team members should have the energy and resolution to achieve them in order to have a positive impact on the entire organization. Since goals may be difficult to reach and sometimes even elusive, teams need to combine energy with resilience to deal with failures and unexpected obstacles in their pathways.

The final personality factor is the shared notion of accountability. Transparency regarding the information used, the decisions taken and the results achieved is absolutely critical to the success of any team. A team should be accountable to team members and the entire organization.

6.3   THE BOARD OF DIRECTORS AS A TEAM

Top management teams have generated a rich literature in strategic management (Pfeffer, 1972; Hambrick and Mason, 1984; Hambrick, 1987; Finklestein, 1992; Daily and Schwenk, 1996; Edmonson, 2012). Unfortunately, with some exceptions, the notion of boards of directors as teams has not attracted much attention.

The concept of the board of directors as a team, or the expectations that it functions as such, is neither formally defined in corporate law nor in the mainstream literature on corporate governance. Notable exceptions include Blair and Stout (1999), Huse (2007, 2018), Westphal and Zajac (2013) and Winter (2018), among others. Huse (2007) and Ees, Gabrielsson and Huse (2009) have developed a model of the behavioral theory of boards, based on the team production theory (Blair, 1995; Blair and Stout, 1999). Their contribution is important because the human dimensions in boards of directors and team dynamics both impact the board decision-making process.

The experience of the boards of directors discussed in this book highlights the importance of the board working as a team, beyond the individual personalities of its members. A team creates the context in which different board members debate and interact. It may be an enabling mechanism for deep discussions or a stumbling block. Moreover, a good team of individuals may never achieve substantial results if the team context does not enable their individual contributions. This is also the experience in boards of directors with outstanding individuals, where the structure and dynamics of the team does not make the group effective.

The configuration of boards of directors as teams is complex. A brief review of core attributes of boards of directors explains the reasons behind this complexity. The first feature is that boards of directors do not have explicit goals for the board as a team, except for those explicitly defined by corporate law or the firm's bylaws, such as approving annual accounts, adopting specific decisions, compliance and supervising the CEO and senior management team. Board members work with information prepared by the CEO and the senior management team. They do not have firsthand knowledge of most of the company's issues but rather approach them through the frame prepared by top managers or experts (auditors or consultants). Even in the case of a CEO replacement, the information that the board can gather on potential candidates relies, more often than not, on the information provided by a search firm. Finally, in most cases board members do not work full time at the company.

The second attribute is that the role of board directors is not an executive job, but a combination of a supervisory, advisory and decision-making role. It does not involve a full-time commitment to the company. The supervisory nature of the board's job, its part-time dedication and the ambiguity regarding its goals makes the board work complex. Board directors do not have clear indicators of performance since their activity falls in a supervisory/advisory role. This is especially true in monitoring and working with the CEO.

The third feature is that this supervisory role can greatly benefit from the perspectives and views of other board members. Here, the diversity of experiences and backgrounds can help reach a clearer diagnosis of the company's problems and frame decisions better. This advantage can only be nourished if the board works as a real team, where different personalities learn to contribute to the team debates, interact positively with other board members and accept their own limitations. It also requires that the chairperson does a good job and poses questions, listens, synthesizes and creates a culture of respect and professionalism when offering advice and supervising, and, when necessary, makes the appropriate decisions.

The fourth feature is diversity among board directors, which is important for several reasons such as fairness, inclusiveness and gathering a variety of perspectives and views. Boards need to develop shared frameworks to deliberate the company strategy, work with the top management team, interact with shareholders and key stakeholders and nourish and grow the top management team. Too much cultural diversity – for instance, many board directors living in different geographies and time zones – may also create new problems, in particular, when a board confronts a crisis. Videoconferences can be good to discuss specific problems and make decisions, but they may not offer the best context for creating the conditions of trust that boards of directors need when faced with complex decisions, such as replacing the CEO. Choosing the right level of cultural diversity is extremely important to avoid boards turning into dysfunctional decision-making bodies.

The fifth dimension is that, even in high-level board decisions, such as approving a strategic plan or an acquisition or defining executive compensation for top managers, board members need to implement decisions through other people. Boards have the power to make some decisions and frame others, but senior managers execute them. This makes the work of board directors and their accountability more difficult to define and more ambiguous to assess. Top managers have more control over the decision's implementation and its associated financial or nonfinancial indicators than the board of directors.

6.4   THE TEAM ARCHITECTURE: BOARD STRUCTURE

Board structure is one dimension in corporate governance that has attracted considerable attention among scholars and regulators (see Adams, Hermalin and Weisbach, 2010; Adams, 2018; Daems, 2020).

Companies that start from scratch or undergo a profound change process have an ideal opportunity to redefine their board and design it so that it can work as a team. When Cellnex was preparing its IPO, its chairman and CEO thought that it should adopt the best standards of corporate governance in Europe to become a trusted company by shareholders and other stakeholders. They made a

Table 6.2. *The board architecture: Some features*

- Separation of the roles of the chair person and the CEO
- Board composition and size
- Board committees
- Board diversity
- One-tier versus two-tier board of directors
- The rules of the board

number of important decisions regarding the new board: a majority of external, independent directors with strong credibility in the telecoms industry; strong international diversity; separate the roles of chairperson and CEO; and have a small board in size, to allow board members to actively contribute and easily interact with one another. The new board quickly developed into a very effective team, helping to lead the company and its phenomenal growth since 2015. These decisions on the board architecture were central in creating an effective board. The next section outlines some dimensions that are critical in shaping board structure (see Table 6.2).

6.4.1 Separation of the Roles of the Chairperson and the CEO

In the United Kingdom, the rule of separating the roles of chairperson and CEO is clear. In certain continental European countries, this separation is not required, although it may be advisable, and is always left to the discretion of shareholders. In the United States, in most listed companies, the same person holds the dual role of chair of the board and CEO.

The academic literature highlights some advantages regarding the separation of both roles in terms of its impact on economic performance, such as its ability to help avoid conflicts of interest, prevent an abuse of power and improve the quality of the CEO succession processes. Nevertheless, the aggregate empirical evidence in this respect is thin. Boyd (1995) and Dey, Engel and Liu (2011) found minimal effects between CEO and chairperson separation and corporate performance. The practical evidence is that the role of leading the company belongs to the CEO. Since leading the board to govern the company is a different role, it might be advisable to have two different people to perform these functions (Cadbury, 2002). In countries where no legal norm exists, the final decision belongs to the firm's shareholders; large shareholders, in particular, play an important role in defining these functions. The importance of having two different people for these two functions is even clearer when the company is facing conflicts among different shareholders. Disputes among shareholders should not interfere with the good management of the company, and an independent board chair may be a guarantee for the firm's governance.

6.4.2   Board Composition and Size of the Board

The number of board members also impacts board effectiveness. Numerous board directors may impede the processes of debate, sharing perspectives and decision-making (Coles, Daniel and Naveen, 2000). On the other hand, a small board may offer certain advantages in terms of functionality, but have less expertise and lack enough directors to do a good job on the board committees. It is not only the size of the board that matters but also the firm's complexity and the profiles of different board members.

Board members may have different backgrounds. Some board directors may be relevant shareholders or may represent a shareholder, which is a typical scenario in the cases of family businesses and private equity–controlled firms. Other board members could be external, independent directors chosen by the board's nominating committee and appointed by shareholders. Finally, a board member may also serve as a senior executive in the company, such as the CEO or CFO. The identity of board members is one of the most important factors highlighted in the literature on the board's effectiveness. It is known that a board dominated by senior executives may not provide enough oversight to these same executives in their managerial roles.

This was one of the reasons behind the failure of managerialism in the 1970s and 1980s and one of the drivers of change in corporate governance afterward.

It is also known that a board controlled by large shareholders may facilitate a better alignment of incentives between the board, the senior management team and shareholders. But in some cases – for instance, when the dominant shareholder is a family or different branches of a family – this option may generate personal conflicts that the absence of external board members would not help mitigate. A shareholder-controlled board may also have a narrower business perspective and lose the diversity advantage.

6.4.3   Board Committees

Recent corporate governance codes have established specific board committees that listed companies and other significant companies should have. This set of committees usually includes the audit committee, the nomination and compensation committee and the governance committee, among others, depending on the jurisdiction. Beyond the legal requirements, committees play a very important role in corporate governance. They allow board directors to work more actively and intensively with the CEO and senior management team on fundamental issues such as financial reporting, compensation and succession plans. They prepare the future discussions by the board of directors on relevant issues that require directors' special attention. The composition of these committees, their leadership and the support they receive from the entire board are all indispensable attributes needed for the board to work effectively on these issues. Committees do not replace the board of directors but work with the entire board to make its contribution more effective in crucial areas.

6.4.4   Board Diversity

The notion of diversity associated with boards of directors has evolved somewhat slowly, lagging behind calls for diversity in management teams. Codes of corporate governance have reluctantly accepted the need for board members' diversity, particularly gender diversity. As reported in Chapter 5, only twenty-three women served as the CEO of a Global 500 Fortune company in 2021 (Hinchliffe, 2021). The empirical evidence on the role of women on boards and their impact on performance is positive (Adams and Ferreira, 2009; Post and Byron, 2015; Adams, 2016a; 2016b). The need to include more women as board directors is a challenge for the corporate world, both in terms of the lack of decision-making effectiveness in a male-dominated world and an unfair playing field.

This trend is not only driven by a pursuit of greater gender or race equality but the perception that board diversity can contribute to a healthier and deeper debate at the board level on strategic decisions such as CEO hiring, development and succession and compensation plans. It is important to consider both dimensions. In the end, investors and workers expect companies to be well managed. Employees, customers and investors place their faith in the quality of the management of the companies they work for or invest in. Issues of competence and fairness should be considered when focusing on how boards can promote diversity.

In parallel, the complexity of the work of boards of directors and the growing global scope of many firms call for diversity in other very important dimensions. Diversity aims to counteract groupthink and help minimize self-overconfidence bias, which leads individuals to think they can separate personal from professional interests (Kahneman, 2011). It is useful to comment on two relevant forms of diversity and their effects. The first is cultural diversity. In companies with customers, operations and people throughout the world, it makes sense for the top governance body to have members who understand both the business and the firm's different countries of operation.

The lack of cultural and geographical intelligence at the board level explains numerous failures of international companies entering foreign markets. The 1998 Daimler–Chrysler merger failed due to the lack of cultural awareness of the top management teams and boards of directors in understanding the other party. Some of the challenges that European and US companies have encountered in China in recent years emerged not because of strategic issues or Chinese governmental pressure, but from a lack of understanding of the local employees and customers. The board of directors should not be the final protection wall to save a deal. A good board of directors should have competent board members whose cultural background and experience in certain countries can help the company navigate the troubled waters of globalization. The experience on some boards reveals that too much cultural diversity may hinder board effectiveness due to a lack of shared principles (O'Reilly, Williams and Barsade, 1999; O'Reilly and Williams, 2003).

Diversity of expertise is also a dimension expected from boards of directors. The increasing strategic uncertainty that companies face requires a deep awareness of issues that transcend traditional business functions like finance, marketing, technology or sales. Efforts to reduce the firm's carbon footprint, accelerate digital transformation, understand geopolitics, develop a value proposition that makes sense for next-generation customers and foster relations with governments are some of the new challenges that companies face today. Not all board members need to be experts on all of these issues, but boards should gather members with concrete expertise. The board's governance function may be undermined if these issues are not taken seriously or if they are approached with the same perspective and biases in board discussions.

6.4.5   One-Tier versus Two-Tier Boards

The board of directors as the top governance body is the dominant model in most countries today. Its function is clear: to govern the company for the long term and supervise the CEO and top management team. The board governs the firm and delegates the day-to-day management to the CEO and senior managers. This defines the one-tier board. There are a few notable exceptions to this model. The most significant deviations in the EU are found in Austria, Germany, the Netherlands and Poland, where the two-tier board is the normal board structure. In Germany, the supervisory board ("Aufsichsrat") comprises shareholders' appointees, independent board members and employee representatives (up to 50 percent of board members for companies with more than 2,000 employees). Their legal functions are more limited than in US and UK boards and focus mainly on supervising the board of management ("Vorstand"), which has both governance and executive powers.

The Dutch corporate law system has similar institutions: the supervisory board ("raad van commissarissen") and the management board ("het bestuur"). The supervisory board's main duty is to monitor and advise the board of management. The duty of the latter is to manage the company. The board of management is exclusively comprised of senior executives and the CEO, oversees the top management of the company and also assumes key functions in other areas, such as approving the strategy and strategic decisions and overseeing the firm's compliance. The German and Dutch cases underline the importance of institutional factors and legal traditions in different countries in understanding the effectiveness of boards.

6.4.6 The Explicit and Implicit Rules of the Board

Boards of directors are subject to both corporate law in the jurisdictions where the company operates and specific company statutes, which usually include the firm's purpose, the structure of the board of directors, the rules of the board and other governance issues. Company statutes also need to define what shareholders and other stakeholders expect from the board of directors beyond compliance.

Some company statutes may approve a company's purpose, corporate values and brief statements on how the company should deal with employees and different stakeholders. There is a high diversity of particular company statutes within the rules of corporate law. Companies should be more explicit about purpose and shareholders should have a say in this. At the same time, boards of directors should take the firm's purpose into account and ensure that strategy, CEOs hiring and development, compensation and other corporate policies are consistent with that purpose.

Corporate statutes may not be very explicit about these details but can offer boards of directors a good frame to take their purpose seriously and organize the work of the board so that it can govern the firm effectively. Boards may also define explicit rules on how they will address certain issues, which issues will be discussed regularly, how the CEO will present issues to the board, and guidelines concerning the regular interaction between the board and senior managers.

6.5   THE PERSONALITY OF THE BOARD OF DIRECTORS AND THE TONE AT THE TOP

On September 8, 2014, Hertz's board of directors announced the departure of CEO Mark Frissora following mounting pressure from shareholders after a series of accounting errors were revealed. He was replaced on an interim basis by Brian MacDonald, a senior executive with expertise in turnarounds. On November 21, 2014, MacDonald was replaced by John Tague, another external executive who was brought in by Carl Icahn, an activist investor. In an August 2014 filing to the Securities and Exchange Commission (SEC), Icahn said that his investment company had acquired an 8.48 percent stake in the company. Three weeks later, he convinced the board of Hertz to accept his own three nominees to the Hertz board (Wright, 2014; Stempel, 2020).

Hertz was one of the leading global vehicle rental companies. CEO turnover was preceded by a relevant company announcement in May 2014, when Hertz declared that it would be unable to fill its Form 10-Q for the first quarter of 2014, mentioning some mistakes in reporting revenues in previous years. In July 2015, the Hertz board explained that it would need to restate its financial reporting between 2011 and 2013. In its announcement, the firm disclosed some material effects of dubious decisions that had been adopted by the top management in previous years. These decisions reduced some expenses and increased certain revenues, resulting in an overstatement of its pretax profit of about $87 million. In 2016, the US Securities and Exchange Commission sanctioned Hertz for negligent violations of the securities law, but Hertz senior executives and board members were not penalized.

In March 2019, the Hertz Corporation filed a complaint against its former CEO Mark Frissora, and other senior managers. Hertz was seeking to recover $70 million in compensation payments and $200 million in damages derived from Hertz's decision to restate its financial statements in 2015. In particular, Hertz's allegations claimed that the CEOs' management style and temperament fostered extreme pressure on the firm's environment and compelled his management team to contrive dubious ideas to boost growth.

Hertz's claims were based on the assumption that the CEO, CFO and general counsel had committed accounting fraud (Cleary Gotlieb Steen Hamilton, 2019). Hertz's assertions also described incidences in which the CEO and senior executives showed an aggressive leadership style, the failure of the board of directors to appropriately monitor the CEO and the inability of the board and the CEO to set the right tone for the company. The Hertz complaint specifically referred to "the right tone at the top." A positive tone at the top reflects board behavior that is exemplary and evidence of an effective internal governance model grounded in ethical values.

The Hertz case offers an opportunity to reflect on the principles and ethical rules that board directors espouse and how they shape the board as a team, as well as the understanding of the tone at the top. The Hertz experience also helps frame important questions about the board as a team. The first is how the board and the CEO interact regarding strategic decisions and their implementation. Beyond the formal process of approving decisions, a question that arises naturally is how boards of directors work effectively to help and guide CEOs in their responsibility of developing the company for the long term. In this respect, the relationship between Frissora and the Hertz board was a decisive factor in the events that ensued.

A related question concerns the board's role in defining aggressive strategic goals and pressuring the CEO and management team to achieve them. In these cases, how does the board's decision-making process take into account the firm's resources and capabilities? Are some goals too ambitious or perhaps even greedy?

A third question pertains to how the board interacts with the CEO in between board meetings, for instance, at the end of each quarter when the board is reviewing formal financial reports. The frequency and quality of information flows between the board and the CEO determines the board's basic knowledge on the company, the CEO and her management style.

A final question pertains to the regular performance assessment of the CEO, the CFO and other senior executives by the board of directors and, in particular, its nominating committee. A serious breach in ethical behavior may happen at any time, but its likelihood is higher when there is a lack of professionalism, fairness and trust in the assessment process of senior executives. Moreover, a good assessment process helps board members get to know senior executives and their strengths, weaknesses and pressure points. While it is not an automatic process, the board can introduce and use many levers of monitoring and control, formal and informal processes, which can help prevent future ethical crises. In light of this crisis, how much responsibility did board of directors bear in the executives misbehavior? This issue is not limited to simply legal duties; it also includes moral obligations that arise from the professionalism and integrity that board members are expected to exercise.

The Hertz case is also a prime example that shows there is more to board effectiveness than board structure and composition. Many corporate crises start at the board level. They are related to an array of situations and decisions that arise in the middle of a crisis. Firing a CEO, a major strategic mistake, reporting some unexpected economic losses, restating previous financial reporting or admitting unethical practices, are all major upheavals in the life of a company and, in particular, of its board of directors. Understanding and shaping the personality of the board is an indispensable step in making the board a more effective team.

In particular, boards of directors, in their role as the top collegial decision-making institution in any organization, may suffer from a number of weaknesses or biases, such as groupthink (Kahneman, 2011) or ignorance about the major issues at stake when the CEO brings them to the board. This ignorance might stem from the unexpected nature of the events, the lack of elaboration of these issues by the CEO or top managers in reporting to the board or the lack of preparation and experience of board directors. A clear example is the lack of global experience among board members in international companies. Strategic ignorance is a major board weakness, which can lead to very poor board decisions.

The second weakness is the excessive level of adhesion to the CEO's proposals. Diversity of perspectives in the board of directors is indispensable to more clearly diagnose the company's problems and eventually make better decisions. Unanimity in the final decisions is the output of a successful and rich discussion. A shared mindset is a condition of high-performance teams, but a shared framework should not be translated into instantaneous unanimity in the decision-making process unless the right questions have been posed and properly discussed.

A third weakness of boards of directors is board politicking or in-fighting among board directors (Pick and Merchant, 2012). This scenario emerges when different groups of shareholders through their board representatives promote their individual preferences or interests and fight for them at the board level. This may happen in a family business context, when different branches of the family have different aspirations for the company's future and advocate for them, sometimes in a very dysfunctional manner. This situation also arises when two or more groups of relevant shareholders hold opposing views on the best path forward. Finally, it also occurs when activist investors fight a board of directors and try to secure seats on the board to change the firm's strategy and advance their own agenda. In these cases, the interests of individual shareholders supersede the firm's interests, the point of creating enormous pressure on the company itself.

A fourth weakness relates to the level of confrontation between the board of directors and the CEO. The board may think that it should monitor the CEO. The CEO may think that he has the final say on most company decisions and that the board is more of a burden than a genuine source of help. CEO dismissals or failed CEO succession plans suggest that this is a real and serious problem that boards currently face.

A related weakness in some boards of directors is the distance between the board and the top management team, or between the board and the rest of the organization and its customers. Agency theory has placed so much emphasis on the board's duty to monitor and exercise effective management oversight that many supervisory board mechanisms end up isolating the board from the reality of the company. The need for a fair, fresh and objective diagnosis and valuation of alternatives, reasonably distanced from the pressures of the top management team, is necessary. Board meetings with only external board directors may also be beneficial. The challenge with external board directors is their part-time dedication and lack of deep awareness of the company and its business. They need many hours of contact with senior managers and other key people to fully appreciate the firm's strengths and weaknesses.

Some of these crises also emerge in boards of directors with a solid structure and composition: a board with the right size, a fair number of external directors and a high level of diversity. The failure of these companies and their boards' inability to prevent a crisis is more related to the culture of the board, and formal and informal relationships among board members. The next sections explore the core dimensions needed to create a board positive personality and identity to help it to successfully govern the company, especially in times of crisis (see Table 6.3).

Table 6.3. *The board's personality: Some features*

- The board's purpose and culture
- The board's values
- The board's agenda
- The chair person
- The board as a human group

6.5.1 Board's Purpose and Culture

In recent years, institutional investors and major asset managers, in their effort to increase the level and quality of their stewardship, have stressed the need for boards to nourish the right tone at the top. As the Hertz crisis illustrates, defining it is not easy. What this concept aims to communicate is the combination of professionalism, dedication and ethical values that board directors should embody in their service to companies.

This set of factors is relevant, yet a previous step needs to be taken. What is the role of the board in a specific company? What specific purpose should the board have?

The ability to effectively respond to these questions is relevant for several reasons. As discussed in Chapter 1, in many countries, corporate law establishes a few functions of the board, including monitoring the CEO. Corporate law also establishes the personal responsibilities of board directors in the case of breaches of trust in the company's or their own behavior. But corporate law gives boards of directors a broad margin to organize their work. With this notion in mind, boards should reflect deeply on their mission in the companies they serve for a couple of reasons. First, the company's purpose may include implicitly some expectations regarding the board of directors. The firm's purpose is a positive reference to improving both the structure and composition of the board, and its identity and dynamics. Second, a well-defined purpose highlights the main qualities the company seeks in its board members and in turn, defines their fit to be on a specific board.

A comprehensive set of personal attitudes and qualities is critical in any board of directors. The board should understand, review and help to gradually renew the firm's culture and values, as we will explore in Chapter 7. It is also an implicit understanding that board members should behave accordingly, leading by example and serving as positive role models of professionalism and integrity for the entire organization. In the same way as people cooperate across the firm's business units, the board and the CEO also need to develop a positive working relationship based upon respect, trust and accountability.

A board of directors should adopt the firm's purpose, nourish it and update it when necessary, as discussed in Chapter 2. At the same time, the board should be a good steward for the long-term development of the firm. This purpose encompasses financial performance, social outcomes and environmental impact. A good purpose does not fully define the tone at the top yet creates a context to think about it and serves as a foundation for basic criteria, that the board should define.

6.5.2   *Board of Directors: Key Values*

As discussed in Chapter 5, Puig is a Spanish third-generation family-owned business and one of the world's largest fragrance companies. Since its founding in 1914, it has grown into a truly successful global firm. Its international expansion began in the late 1960s. Antonio, Mariano, José María and Enrique Puig were second-generation family members who took this company to the global stage. They made very important strategic moves to enter complex markets such as the United States and France. The four brothers assumed different executive positions over the years and instilled basic values in the corporate culture, which also translated to the board of directors and family shareholders.

Among those values, Puig highlighted the importance of meritocracy in attracting the best managers and professionals in the industry. In the late 1990s, they decided to improve corporate governance standards, separate ownership from governance functions and that the majority of board members would be external, independent directors. The family would limit its powers as shareholders and elect good board members to govern the company.

A related value was the importance of CEO succession and renewal. The second generation had been running the company for twenty-five years. In the late 1990s, they withdrew from senior management positions and allowed the members of the third generation to take on key responsibilities as board members. In 2004, Marc Puig became the new chair and Manuel Puig became the vice chair. They were the only two family members in governance and management positions in the company.

The values that the Puig family instilled in the company had a deep effect on the firm's governance, which remains very strong more than two decades after its approval. The Puig experience is shared by other companies, in particular, family businesses that combine the long-term commitment of shareholders with a high level of professionalism in management and governance. It reveals several positive values that can be underlined as drivers of effective boards of directors and good teams. I will develop this theme more deeply in Chapter 7.

In the Puig experience, some board directors' values and attitudes are particularly relevant. The first is professionalism. Professionalism in board members is slightly different from professionalism in senior executives or CEOs. The latter need to think, debate, decide and implement. Board members need to analyze situations with limited information and time. They should understand problems, judge and eventually make a decision, but – in most cases – not implement it. The wisdom to make a judgment, the capacity to ask the right questions and listen to different voices, the empathy to understand different human perspectives of the same problem and the commitment to accountability and transparency are very important components of their work. When recruiting new board members, senior executive experience is important, but the board nominating committee and the board chair should remember that board members need to embody these professional qualities.

Service is another central value at Puig. Board membership is about serving the company's common good and enabling its long-term development. Service requires the directors' attitude of collaboration and willingness to help the board work as a team. The chair of the board should emphasize the board's mission, guiding values and reasons why the board should serve the company and help the CEO and the top management team excel in their job of managing the organization. The Puig experience also highlights that the spirit of collaboration within the board, with the top management team and with shareholders and other stakeholders is critical for the success of the board.

6.5.3   The Board's Agenda

The board has some legal duties, such as approving the annual accounts and nonfinancial reports, appointing the CEO and making the final decision on strategic issues. The increasing level of regulation of boards of directors and the growing role of ESG factors make boards of directors legally responsible for the information's accuracy. The evidence in many boards of directors is that boards spend an ever-increasing part of their time reviewing management reports and compliance issues (Daems, 2020; Dessin, 2020). These are important, but there are ways to cover these legal requirements and prevent them from fully consuming the board's limited time. There is also evidence that the board may dedicate significant time to reviewing the firm's financial situation or past performance. As a result, the board is left with little time to discuss new challenges or strategic issues that the firm is facing. The balance between allowing time for compliance issues and finding time for strategic reflection is a delicate one.

The chairperson and the CEO can prepare the board's agenda for the next few years and a more detailed plan for the current year. From this plan, the content for every single board meeting will emerge. The chairperson should strike the right time allocation for relevant issues. Defining the board agenda is one of the critical tasks that the board chair and CEO should develop collaboratively. The board agenda is not only the agenda for a specific meeting; it also includes the range of topics that the board should work on based on the firm's strategic road map. The major goals, policies and initiatives included in the firm's strategy should be present in board discussions and meetings, not only to assess their progress and effectiveness but to truly understand their drivers and speed up their implementation.

The board needs to look into the future: It is the only way to govern the company for the long term. It should have a strong grasp of the company's main issues and challenges. These themes should regularly appear on the board's agenda and receive an adequate time allocation to facilitate a good debate.

Some boards of directors have adopted a policy of limiting the amount of time spent on formal presentations in their meetings, since board members can read and analyze them beforehand. The goal is that board members prepare board meetings in advance and use their time together to discuss these and other relevant issues. This is particularly important in compliance issues and financial reporting.

A reasonably good board in terms of its members and composition could do an outstanding job if the board agenda is comprehensive and thorough, and well managed by the board chair. A well-designed agenda can help the board focus on relevant issues. On the contrary, a good board in terms of makeup may do a mediocre job simply because the board chair wants the board to spend time on business reviews and compliance issues. These issues are important, but the company expects the board and top management team to be future-oriented.

6.5.4   The Board Chairperson

In board dynamics, the role of the chairperson is critical. Its relevance is so significant that corporate legal systems in some countries support the separation of the roles of chairperson and CEO, since the first should ensure that the board actually works and operates for the benefit of the organization.

The board chair leads the board (Cadbury, 2002; Banerjee, Nordqvist and Hellerstedt, 2020). This role is very distinctive since the board may comprise a group of talented individuals who have a part-time dedication to the company. Moreover, board members may have experience in managing a business but limited experience in serving on boards. The board chairperson needs to ensure the board can work as a functional team, with the qualities described earlier in this chapter.

The board chairperson should have the qualities required of other board members, as well as the ability to work with them and lead them with a wise and empathetic approach. The chairperson should encourage them to spend time on board affairs, work in specifically created groups to analyze challenges, pose questions to frame debates and if necessary, tame heated discussions, work cooperatively and stay a step ahead of the CEO on issues relating to the future of the organization. The board chair should also adopt an entrepreneurial approach for issues that are the sole responsibility of the board, such as CEO hiring, development and succession.

The role of the board in monitoring and advising the CEO and governing the firm for the long term depends very much on the quality of board meetings and the depth and richness of the board discussions. As mentioned earlier, most of the information used by the board in its deliberations comes from the CEO and senior management team. Nevertheless, during discussions, the board can pinpoint which elements of a problem might be missing and which might be overrepresented in the information provided by the CEO. Moreover, the board can also frame the type of analysis and diagnosis that the CEO prepares. At the same time, the chairperson should make sure the board does not overstep and tread on the CEO's functions.

The board chairperson also plays a vital role in leading board discussions. When proposals are met with a certain degree of unanimity, the board chair needs to ensure that dissident voices are heard, critical questions are asked and major arguments are taken into account. The board chair should also encourage participation, even when the level of agreement on a certain proposal is very high. It is also relevant that the board chair be the last person to offer an opinion on a critical issue. A board chair who comments on an issue before other directors may not be fulfilling the duty of effectively leading the board.

When the level of disagreement is high, the role of the board chair is also important, not only to try to reach a consensus but to ensure that the major questions or doubts around the proposal receive a reasonable explanation. In this process, the cooperation of the CEO is vital, since in many areas, his or her knowledge and experience with the business is essential. The role of the board chair in asking and framing good questions is paramount to ensure that the board of directors functions as a successful governing body.

The board chair also has another crucial responsibility: to make sure that shareholders, in particular, large shareholders – family offices, institutional investors or private equity firms – are fully aligned with the company, understand the major issues of the business, and help create an atmosphere of trust between the board and shareholders. At the same time, the chairperson should share the foremost concerns of shareholders and other stakeholders with the board. In particular, the board chair should pay close attention to shareholders' views of the CEO and top management team, offer shareholders more information to broaden their perspective on key issues and detect if the board's positions are promoting managerial inertia.

The relationship between the board chair and the CEO is critical. It should be based on professionalism, trust and accountability. The board chair should understand that the CEO, not the board, runs the company and is responsible for its performance. The board should support the CEO and top management team. At the same time, the CEO should understand that the board has the ultimate responsibility for the firm's long-term orientation and that top management should help the board by offering good analyses and proposals. Boards and the entire organization expect CEOs to work with professionalism, accountability and transparency, and lead by example. The development of a positive relationship between the CEO and the board chair – and the entire board of directors – is essential for the firm's success.

This complex task requires that board chairs have some special qualities. They include experience as a CEO or senior manager, a solid strategic understanding of different businesses and wisdom and empathy in interpersonal relations at the highest level. A board chair should show respect for every person and understand a variety of human situations – in particular, those arising from work pressure or cultural diversity. Finally, the board chair should be a great team player and be willing to assume responsibilities, while allowing other team members to contribute and receive recognition for their contribution.

6.5.5 The Board as a Social Group

In boards of directors, the desired diversity, aimed at encouraging a broader scope of perspectives and backgrounds, may also create challenges when decisions pertain to complex issues or need to be made at a certain speed. This is even more relevant when a corporate crisis erupts because of poor risk management or ethical blunders. This is the case when the board should make a decision within a limited timeframe, for instance, when faced with a hostile takeover or pressure from an activist investor who demands radical changes in the company's strategy and a seat on the board of directors (Khurana and Pick, 2005; Pick and Merchant, 2012).

An initial challenge emerges when, confronted with a crisis, board directors are unable to physically meet in the same place and are forced to hold meetings via videoconference. This is the case of highly diverse boards of directors whose members live around the world and have to fly to the firm's headquarters for in-person board meetings. COVID-19 has accelerated the use of videoconferencing for board meetings, and some CEO appointments and M&A deals have been executed completely through digital means. Nevertheless, it is also worth noting that business discussions may be less holistic and spontaneous when meetings are held online. Additionally, strategy discussions are encumbered, participants' inclination to speak up and share different views may be diminished, board members' moods may be harder to assess and the chair's role in moderating the debate, encouraging participation and synthetizing viewpoints becomes more difficult. Group behavior in a digital world is different than in-person interactions, and videoconferencing may make the board chairperson's job of managing the board more complex.

The second challenge of the board as a social group relates to a core characteristic of good boards of directors: Board members may have impressive professional profiles. In highly disputed issues, two or more sides of the discussion may arise, leading to different alliances on the board. Some people may not like "losing" their arguments and being left in a minority position within the board. Managing these tensions is indispensable for successful boards of directors. One way for the board chair to address them is to routinely pose questions to board members who have strong views on an issue. This approach helps them clarify their arguments and, if possible, respond to board members who do not see the value of certain options.

The third challenge is to build solutions that diverge from the original proposal and consider new perspectives that were opened up by the debate. Encouraging board members to address different issues and express their views is an essential task of the board chairperson. An explosive division on key issues could truly undermine the board, which is why encouraging distinctive views and enabling board members to discuss them with respect and rigor are indispensable qualities of good boards.

The board chair has an important role in ensuring board members have a well-defined and integrative perspective of the firm and in advancing proposals that the board can eventually consider and approve. A focus on the board's decision-making process is critical. It needs to make timely and wise decisions, at times with limited information. This is even more complex when there is an important lack of consensus among board members.

As the board of directors becomes increasingly diverse, the function of the board chairperson in managing underlying assumptions and beliefs about is indispensable. A high degree of board diversity also calls for renewed efforts to fully understand the firm's purpose and strategy, as well as the board's mission and how it works and operates. In particular, the culture of the board in examining proposals, exploring alternative decisions and reaching consensus are very relevant features of good and competent boards of directors.

The board as a social group is connected with the reality of its formal structure and, in particular, the board composition and the selection of its members. Cultural fit is also important in teams. There are excellent board directors whose fit on certain boards may be less than ideal because of an unavoidable gap between the individual and the group. Just as good companies hire for fit, good boards should follow suit by adding fit to their list of criteria when considering potential board members. Fit includes not only cultural fit with the board or the firm, but also fit with regard to the company's challenges. A case in point is the board of a family business that needs to plan the succession of the CEO or other senior executives who are also members of the family. In these firms, a deep understanding of the family business and expertise in framing and solving problems in a family business context are important qualities for potential board members.

The board of directors as a social group can become dysfunctional as a result of members' lack of fit (Charan, Carey and Useem 2014). This problem bears no relation to a lack of strategic vision. Very often, it stems from behavioral factors: lack of dedication to the board, lack of professionalism in dealing with board issues, disrespect for the firm's senior executives or peer board members and lack of flexibility in considering other options in board discussions. It is also the case that some board members may think their peers possess an inadequate strategic perspective. This dysfunctional behavior occurs in board meetings and might lead some boards of directors to fail in their mission. What some views of boards ignore is that boards of directors are groups of people that should work as effective teams. As a human and social group, the board is susceptible to this type of human weakness and personal behavior. Moreover, it is even inclined to display this conduct due to members' part-time dedication and limited contact with the company, which make interactions and opportunities to solve weaknesses less frequent.

The role of the board chair in addressing this problem is critical. One way to avoid or mitigate these situations when they arise is to conduct annual individual reviews of the board, its organization and performance. This assessment, which advanced jurisdictions currently require regularly, is an indispensable tool to make headway. The review process should be carefully designed to underscore its benefits as a highly valuable tool aimed at improving the quality of the board's work and governance effectiveness, as opposed to a formal procedure. This review should encourage board members to express their views in a professional and candid way. When done well, this evaluation gives rise to new perspectives on the board of directors as a group, including the perception of all members of the board as a social group and the fit of each board member. Reviews from individual board members should be considered by the board chair, who should offer personal feedback to each member on how the rest of the boards view her contribution. This is a very useful tool for the chairperson when considering board membership changes.

6.6 FINAL REFLECTIONS

The growing importance of boards of directors in corporate governance has advanced the notion of board structure and composition as determinants of success. This approach is necessary but not sufficient. The experience of some boards indicates that the best board structure and composition may fail if the board as a team is dysfunctional or not led by a competent board chair. This chapter explores the evidence on high-performance teams and its application to understanding boards. Their success underlines a number of critical factors: the team's mission, values and culture; the definition of clear goals;

optimal team structure, composition and leadership; the clarity of its membership, as well as its relationship with other teams and the rest of the organization; and specific conditions that enable team effectiveness.

Boards of directors are the top governing team in a company. The notion of successful teams suggests that boards of directors have some features that make it difficult for them to become effective teams. Board members have a limited dedication to the company; some of them may not know the business in depth; they do not have access to all the information available on some topics; they do not personally know some of the people involved in specific issues or decisions; and, except for critical decisions like hiring or firing the CEO, the board's decisions will be executed by the top management team.

In this chapter, I present a framework to promote the view of the board of directors as a team, and organize its qualities according to board architecture and identity. In terms of the board architecture, core attributes of good boards include, among others, the ownership structure of the company, with shareholders committed for the long term; the structure of the board and internal structure of different committees; board size; board composition and its diversity in terms of gender, race, culture, geography and experience; and the potential separation of the roles of board chairperson and CEO.

The architecture of the board needs to be functional. Nevertheless, what makes each board different is the board personality. The board is a team of individuals who share a common aim – to govern the firm for the long term. Successful boards require some personality features. The first is the need for a clear purpose of the board, one that encompasses and manifests the firm's purpose. The second is the culture and values of the board as a professional team. The third is the role of the board chairperson in leading the board and governing the interaction between the board and the CEO, and between the board and relevant shareholders. The fourth is the board agenda, and the themes the board needs to address in alignment with the firm's strategic plan. The fifth is how the board as a human group makes decisions and manages tensions. In particular, the role of the board chair in leading discussions, enabling dissenters to express their views, asking the right questions and eventually, leading the way when decisions need to be made, is critical.

7 From Compliance to an Engaging Corporate Culture

At the beginning of 2021, Amadeus was the leading global software company for the travel and hotel industry. The company was created in 1991 by four European airlines – Air France, British Airways, Iberia and SAS – to build their own digital reservation system. With business units distributed throughout the European Union, Amadeus had become the global leader in its industry and one of Europe's largest software companies (Masclans and Canals, 2020).

Amadeus' growth strategy was the result of internal innovation, corporate venturing, collaborations with start-ups and selective acquisitions. It was based on several principles. The first was its customer centricity and commitment to develop software solutions that truly added value to its clients' operations and allowed them to work easily with end customers. The second was the firm's global scope, with software teams and commercial teams in key countries. The third was a talent development and talent acquisition strategy centered on competencies, diversity, career opportunities and mission and values. People engagement at Amadeus was not grounded on transactional factors like compensation – although it was important – but on providing a unique professional context of learning, development and working with cutting-edge software solutions. The fourth pillar was the corporate culture that Amadeus had nurtured over the years, with specific customer-oriented values and principles.

Amadeus' commitment to exceptional customer support offered a reference for employees and a focus for strategic decisions. It also fostered internal cooperation. In software companies with a portfolio of solutions, the potential to create corporate silos is very high. Amadeus' culture actively encouraged internal cooperation across business units and software teams with the aim of creating value for customers. This was an influential driver for internal innovation since it brought together experts with distinct capabilities to address customers' challenges and design better solutions for them.

As this chapter will reveal through the experiences of various companies, the evolution of a corporate culture is the outcome of many decisions, behaviors and principles in the life of an organization, including the impact of its board of directors. Rather than a general discussion on corporate culture, this chapter will explore the board's role in corporate culture and the specific role they play in shaping it.

The experience of Amadeus' board of directors offers some interesting insights. The interaction between the board of directors and the CEO and his top management team was based on professionalism, respect, trust and accountability. The board of directors and the CEO fully understood their specific roles in the company's governance model. The board was conscious of its role: guide the company for the long term, sustain a profitable growth strategy and attract the right people to maintain industry leadership. Amadeus, as a software company, had to consider and leverage the clear benefits of scale, first-mover advantages in some markets and the advantages of forging long-term relationships with a limited number of customers.

In 2017, Amadeus was considering the acquisition of TravelClick, a US software company. Owned at the time by a private equity firm, TravelClick had developed a sophisticated portfolio of reservation software solutions for the low-cost segment of the US hotel industry. Its positioning focused on independent hotels and small hotel chains, as opposed to large hotel groups.

When Amadeus' top management began exploring this growth opportunity, TravelClick presented some interesting features. The first was its reputation for providing reliable software solutions to its main market segment, thanks to an excellent team of software developers. The second was its access to the US market, where Amadeus had an important but smaller presence than in Europe, and where there was significant growth potential. The third was its positioning as a software provider for independent US-based hotels, which represented 70 percent of total reservations in the US hotel sector.

The Amadeus board of directors considered this opportunity and had full confidence in its management team. Its chief concern was not only the financial dimensions of the deal: regular interactions between the board, CEO, CFO and the rest of the top management team had created a culture of trust and accountability, which facilitated communication between the board and top managers.

Rather, board members expressed to the CEO and his management team that the TravelClick acquisition might jeopardize Amadeus' corporate culture. To manage this risk, the board wanted to make sure Amadeus could thoroughly assess TravelClick's people and culture. The board also expressed concerns about whether the Amadeus management team could successfully integrate hundreds of TravelClick software designers. They had a different cultural mindset that was more focused on economic transactions and where economic compensation was the most important employee engagement factor.

Amadeus' board illustrated how boards of directors can shape corporate culture. They asked questions to learn more about TravelClick's corporate culture and values, its key people and their motivations, strategies to retain them and plans to proceed with the integration into Amadeus. In this process, the Amadeus board offered vital lessons on the role of corporate culture in boards' strategic decisions.

The first lesson is the importance of people and corporate culture in strategic decisions. They have the power to both reinforce a cycle of success or bring the company down. The GE acquisition of Alstom's energy business in 2015 was a deal that nearly pushed GE to the brink of collapse. People and cultural clash played a role in this. Corporate governance concerns how the company can develop and grow sustainably for the long term, creating value for all parties involved. Corporate culture is very relevant for effective governance.

The second lesson is the specific role of the board in shaping corporate culture. The board defines principles that shape the decisions to be made by the board or top management. These principles offer insights into the board's chief priorities, concerns and fundamental values. They are a powerful engine in defining corporate culture because they express what matters and what does not in the organization. Through its actions, the Amadeus board defined principles or reinforced the tenets of its corporate culture by emphasizing criteria that had underpinned the company's development over the years. The TravelClick acquisition was a very important strategic decision for the company, and by asking wise questions and pointing out potential challenges, the board exhibited its competence and commitment while not overstepping the role of the CEO. The way the board considers and decides on strategic decisions like acquisitions, the selection of a new CEO or a new executive compensation model, sends a very powerful signal to the rest of the organization, one that strongly shapes its corporate culture.

The third lesson is the board's time horizon for strategic decisions. Amadeus worked with customers who had a long-term perspective, and had frequent interactions with them. TravelClick was more focused on fewer client transactions. Since Amadeus was a customer-centered company, its board realized that the decision to acquire TravelClick could impact Amadeus' development and wanted to ensure that in this decision the top management was working with the same time horizon.

The fourth lesson is risk management. Corporate acquisitions have a very high failure rate (Fernandes, 2019). Even for a company such as Amadeus, which had generated very reliable cash flows over the years, the risk of a failed acquisition could be relevant. For the board of Amadeus, the major risk of the TravelClick acquisition was not financial but the financial fallout of a potential culture clash between the two firms. By sharing its concerns during the decision-making process, the board of Amadeus showed prudence and a clear understanding of where the primary risk factors lay for the company.

Mediocre risk management has an impact on a firm's financial strength and performance, but risk factors are often related to people's behavior, customer relationships and the global supply chain.

Corporate culture influences companies and corporate performance[1] and helps sustain long-term development, which is why it plays such a vital role in corporate governance. The board alone does not define the corporate culture. Corporate culture is shaped by numerous decisions made over the years, many under the oversight of the CEO and senior management team. But the role of the board is critical in shaping some of these decisions.

The board's role in corporate culture is the focus of this chapter. Culture is indispensable for a credible purpose, a successful strategy, leadership development and for the transformation of the board as an effective team. Corporate culture and the culture of the board underpin the major board's functions. Section 7.2 offers an overview of corporate culture and its fundamental elements. In Section 7.3, I outline what shareholders, top management and other stakeholders, including regulators, expect from the board in addressing corporate culture. Section 7.4 takes a deeper dive into the role of the board of directors in corporate culture. In Section 7.5, I address an important dimension of boards of directors associated with the collegial nature of boards in most countries: their work as a team and the quality of interaction among team members. The positive impact of boards of directors not only depends on the competence and diversity of its members, the company's potential or the economic cycle. It also depends on the board's ability to work as a team and serve as a role model, helping and serving top management and the organization as a whole.

---

[1] An exploration of the relationship between corporate culture and economic performance is offered by Guiso, Sapienza and Zingales (2015). For a managerial perspective, see Schein (1984), Kotter and Heskett (2006), Cameron and Quinn (2011) and Groysberg et al. (2018), among others.

7.2   CRITICAL FACTORS THAT SHAPE CORPORATE CULTURE

Headquartered in Gütersloh, Germany, Bertelsmann is the world's leading media and education company. It is a privately owned company founded by Carl Bertelsmann in 1832, with the majority of shares owned by the Bertelsmann Stitftung.[2] The company's global presence grew during the 1960s and through the 1990s under the leadership of its chairman, Reinhard Mohn. During this period, Bertelsmann became a global leader in media and book publishing.

Mohn highlighted the importance of Bertelsmann's culture and values in the firm's development. He inspired his senior managers and board members to make decisions based on the firm's values and supported unique policies such as a focus on customers, concern for employees and their education and well-being, respect for local cultures as the company expanded internationally, entrepreneurship, social commitment and trust. The company had a clear agenda of social responsibility. More recently, the board of Bertelsmann summarized these precepts in The Bertelsmann Essentials. These principles highlight Bertelsmann as a purpose-driven organization with two core values: creativity and entrepreneurship. These values encompass others that stand out in Bertelsmann's culture. They influence the board of directors and senior managers in their decision-making. They are not only visible in Bertelsmann meeting rooms and hallways, but often appear in senior management presentations and at the board level in some strategic decisions, including senior executive nominations. How do corporate values truly shape the firm's culture?

A corporate culture is defined by the implicit and explicit principles and values that shape how individuals behave and make decisions in an organization. Individuals bring their own values to the firm, but their behavior is influenced by what they consider to be

---

[2] Cardona and Wilkinson (2008) offer a good description of Bertelsmann's evolution and the role of its corporate values and culture.

acceptable and successful professional behavior in specific contexts. Groysberg et al. (2018) are more explicit on this point: Corporate culture is the tacit order of an organization that shapes people's attitudes and behaviors.

For senior executives, strategy can be expressed in a clear, rational way and be understood by different stakeholders. While most view corporate culture as a driving force in shaping the firm and its reputation, they consider it difficult to manage, express and change. Moreover, it seems to evolve with people's behavior – including top management decisions – which is not always consistent with the company's reason for being.

Over the past three decades, corporate culture has been studied and its driving factors better understood. The work of Schein (1984, 2017), Cameron and Quinn (2011) and Groysberg et al. (2018), among others, has helped shed light on corporate culture: its main elements, different forms and styles, how it is shaped by top managers and its impact on corporate performance.

Schein (2017) offered a unique perspective on the core dimensions that shape organizational culture. In his model of organizational culture, originated in the 1980s, he identified three different dimensions or levels in organizational factors that shape a corporate culture and help map it: artifacts, espoused values and assumptions.

The three levels refer to the degree to which a cultural profile is externally perceived and identified. Artifacts refer to tangible, overt or verbally identifiable components in organizations that can be easily observed by people who are not members of the organization. Artifacts include architecture, furniture, dress code or formal decisions.

Espoused values defined the organization's values and rules of behavior. Through espoused values, members represent the organization both to themselves and to others. This is often expressed in public statements of culture or corporate purpose.

The third level of culture is defined by shared assumptions. They are embedded, taken-for-granted behaviors that are usually unconscious, and constitute the essence of corporate culture. Tacitly integrated into the organizational dynamic, these assumptions are hard to identify and define.

Groysberg et al. (2018) offered a complementary perspective. They point out that strategy and culture are primary levers that CEOs can use to steer the company's direction. Strategy expresses goals and actions with formal, reasonable logic, and its assumptions and conclusions can offer clarity for all stakeholders. Corporate culture expresses goals through values and beliefs, and its articulation may be more ambiguous than strategy. These authors posit that organizations' cultural styles are defined by two dimensions and their related trade-offs. The first is the nature of people interactions and how people relate with one another (independence versus interdependence dimension). The second is members' response to change in an organization (flexibility versus stability dimension). Under this framework, Groysberg et al. distinguish eight distinct culture styles that reflect different combinations of people's interactions and their response to change. These customer styles suggest how people can interact inside an organization and the flexibility toward change within the organization.

Corporate culture includes some essential dimensions that define its influence on an organization. Cameron and Quinn (2011) analyzed thirty-nine indicators of organizational effectiveness and found statistical significance in two polarities. The first is internal focus and integration versus external focus and differentiation, a polarity that expresses whether the company is centered either on internal or external factors. The second polarity is related to the notion of stability and control versus flexibility and discretion, another very important trade-off in management. Using these two polarities as a base, they suggest the Competing Values Framework and present four potential types of corporate culture: hierarchy, market, clan and autocracy.

The Schein model helps identify different layers that define corporate culture. It provides a useful methodology for boards of directors and senior managers to better understand the main ingredients of a specific corporate culture. The framework of Cameron and Quinn (2011) and Groysberg et al. (2019) offers a complementary perspective to Schein's model. These models supplement each other and help analyze this complex theme. They are particularly relevant for boards of directors that care about the firm's culture.

7.3 CORPORATE CULTURE AND ITS ROLE IN CORPORATE GOVERNANCE

As corporate culture has refined its foundations, its influence on governance has also grown. According to the first contemporary code of corporate governance (Cadbury et al., 1992), corporate culture was supposed to act as a defensive barrier against unethical behavior in organizations. A good culture would protect companies from the unethical behavior of managers and employees. Research in this area eventually showed a positive relationship between a strong culture – exemplified by a competent and engaged workforce – and corporate performance (Kotter and Heskett, 2006). In this way, corporate culture began to be viewed as a cornerstone of strategy execution in organizations.

The 2008 financial crisis highlighted an additional dimension of corporate culture. Some financial institutions and other companies with a penchant for high-risk investments paid a high price during that crisis. In many of those organizations, exorbitant economic compensation tied to financial performance goals, combined with an aggressive growth culture, led to their near collapse. A corporate culture that puts the company at risk is not a healthy culture. Since then, corporate governance codes and institutional investors have developed frameworks and models of corporate culture and increased their pressure on boards of directors to monitor the company's culture. The COVID-19 pandemic and the ensuing crisis also inspired a new perspective on the relevance of corporate culture, particularly with regard to a company's reaction to a crisis, emphasis on "health and safety first," treatment of its people and customers and transparency with shareholders, creditors, capital markets and stakeholders.

This evolution has some very positive dimensions and places corporate culture at the heart of corporate governance, where it belongs, irrespective of the credibility given to it by senior managers. Nevertheless, this trend has a dangerous dynamic: turning corporate culture into one more factor to be considered by the board of directors due to additional compliance requirements or investors' checklists.

Some codes of corporate governance are trying to address this challenge. Among the most prominent initiatives is the new UK Unified Corporate Governance Code (2018), which states: "The board should assess and monitor culture. Where it is not satisfied that policy, practices or behavior throughout the business are aligned with the company's purpose, values and strategy, it should seek assurance that management has taken corrective action" (n.1.2.).

Large institutional investors are also emphasizing the importance of corporate culture and the need to adjust strategy and policies to the desired corporate culture. Unfortunately, corporate culture is more complex, ambiguous and difficult to define by the board than other governance issues. It is a fragile construction, difficult to develop and steer in the right direction, and very easy to destroy and debilitate with a few decisions that run counter to it.

The experience of Henkel, a leading global consumer goods company based in Dusseldorf (Germany), provides useful insights into the role of corporate culture in corporate governance. In particular, it shows the interaction between the founder's values, the family as shareholder and the firm's culture. Henkel is a family owned business founded by Fritz Henkel in Aachen in 1876 and was listed on the Frankfurt Stock Exchange in 1985. As of the end of 2020, Henkel family members held around 60 percent of its ordinary shares. It is a great company that survived two world wars and emerged strongly as an international company in the 1980s (Simons and Kindred, 2012).

Over the years, the role of the Henkel family diminished in terms of its shareholdings, especially after the company's IPO on the Frankfurt stock exchange in 1985, but the values of the Henkel family were present throughout the organization. The firm's headquarters were located in Düsseldorf, next to one of the Henkel factories.

In 2009, Albrecht Woeste, Henkel's chairman and a fourth-generation family member, retired from the firm. He and other board members had been thinking carefully about the succession process. Simone Bagel-Trah, a fifth-generation member of the Henkel family, was chosen as the new chairperson of the supervisory board. In 2008, the firm engineered another transition: Kasper Rorsted was named as the new CEO, replacing Ulrich Lehner. Rorsted had joined the firm in 2005, serving as the executive vice president of HR, purchasing and IT. In 2009, Henkel was a solid company, weathering the storm of the financial crisis. The change in the chairmanship was considered among the Henkel family members to be an opportunity to renew the company, strengthen its culture and make the company more competitive.

The Henkel family had instilled core values in the organization that played a role in shaping its culture: professionalism, commitment, long-term horizons, spirit of service and community outreach, among others. The challenge for the board, the top management team and the Henkel family was to preserve the firm's enduring values with a sense of urgency and accountability in performance across the organization. The Henkel family members serving as board members, the remaining nonfamily board directors and the top management team worked for months to renew the Henkel heritage and lay the groundwork for the company's future development.

This process had several repercussions. The first was a redefinition of the core values that would better reflect the company and what it hoped to achieve. In January 2010, Henkel's board approved a new company vision – "A global leader in brands and technologies" – and outlined five key corporate values: customers at the center, people, financial performance, sustainability and a future based on the Henkel family business foundation.

The second repercussion was a streamlining of the Henkel strategy, with a new focus on consumer satisfaction and global teams, in order to make the firm's international strategy more sustainable. The third was the revamping of talent development. The board of directors and top management team understood that the cornerstone of a healthy corporate culture was people development, including educational opportunities, career promotion and compensation. A new model of hiring, assessment and compensation was put into place to align people strategy with the company's overall aspiration. The alignment of the board and executive committee regarding a new direction was essential.

Henkel's family values played an important role in shaping corporate culture, which in turn influenced strategic decisions taken at the board level. At Henkel, with a large shareholder of reference with clearly defined values, the role of corporate culture in strategic decisions is extremely important.

The Amadeus and Henkel experiences highlight some relevant ideas and notions on culture governance. The first is that corporate culture is the dynamic outcome of the interaction among different factors. They include the values of the company founder, the personal leadership style of CEOs and senior managers, the priorities high-lighted by the board of directors and its decisions, the firm's formal statement of values, employee interactions, people's hiring and devel-opment process and the financial compensation model, among others. Corporate culture is defined by decisions, principles, formal rules and daily behavior. Each one of these driving factors interacts with the rest and shapes individuals' behaviors. It is also interesting to note that individuals bring their own values to the workplace, meaning that the interaction between corporate culture and individual values fuse into a dynamic process.

The second notion is that corporate culture is deeply shaped by the top management team, whose members take part in both daily decisions and long-term strategic decisions. The board of directors can help shape a corporate culture, but should work in cooperation with the CEO and top management team in helping forge a positive culture.

The third notion is the strong connection between corporate culture and purpose. As explored in Chapter 3, the recent spotlight on corporate purpose and its increasing relevance in corporate governance overlaps with emphasis on corporate culture and values. It is like a person with many types of intelligence: having more of one – for instance, cognitive intelligence – does not mean that others, such as cultural or emotional intelligence, are less important. Today, we have a better understanding of the multiple dimensions of human intelligence and how each contributes to human development.

In a similar way, purpose and corporate culture are interconnected and complementary. Purpose explains why a company is in business, and may reflect some of the values that are already at play throughout the company. At the same time, a company guided by a deep sense of purpose will nurture its culture by emphasizing why the company exists, through individual behaviors and corporate decision-making. Corporate culture is the pathway through which corporate purpose becomes a reality.

The fourth notion is that corporate culture is shaped by many factors and decisions. Nevertheless, people decisions – who gets hired, who gets promoted and who gets fired – and decisions on compensation and rewards are the most powerful transmission mechanisms of the values that define a firm's corporate culture. They send a clear message on how the board of directors and the top management team perceive the contributions of individual employees.

Consider the decision a board faces in preparing for a CEO transition. The board should consider all available options, including the possibility of finding a new CEO outside of the company. This might be the most sensitive option if the company requires a deep renewal and lacks a solid leadership pipeline of good internal candidates. Nonetheless, this situation is not foreign to the board's performance and duties. If the leadership pipeline is not robust, this could be the direct responsibility of the board of directors for disregarding this issue. If the board decides to seek external candidates, it should clearly explain its rationale to the top management team and its commitment to ensuring that potential candidates respect the company's positive dimensions and culture.

The fifth reflection is how the organization interprets the board's decisions on strategy and strategic investments. Some strategy decisions can exert a very powerful effect throughout the organization, both the decision itself and the process followed by the board to approve it. Strategic decisions that align with the organization's corporate purpose and culture will be better understood by its members. Strategic decisions deemed inconsistent with the firm's purpose will be more difficult to assimilate by the organization and may eventually decrease employees' engagement.

The decision-making process is also very important, with a relevant impact on corporate culture. Most strategic decisions entail the contribution of different managers and employees, who know the business situation better than most board directors. Boards will have a hard time gaining respect if their decision-making fails to consider the views of people with expertise and oversight of a concrete business issue. In some instances, these people could be wrong or express views that are not based on facts. If this is the case, the board should confront this situation in a straightforward manner.

In the next section, I describe the role of the board in corporate culture, with an emphasis on how the board can work in order to promote a healthy and sustainable corporate culture.

7.4   THE ROLE OF THE BOARD IN SHAPING CORPORATE CULTURE

The board of directors can play different roles in corporate culture. Each role depends largely on the nature of the firm, the composition of the top management team and who the key shareholders and stakeholders are.

The Cellnex experience in this respect is very rich (Canals, 2018). Starting in 2000, it had grown and evolved as a telecom business unit of Abertis, the world's largest highway management company, until its establishment as a new, independent company in 2015.

Cellnex was a business unit of a large holding company in which it was not the core business, a condition that shaped its organizational culture in three significant ways.

The first was that the customer was king. Technical competence to deliver outstanding customer service was deeply ingrained in the firm's culture. The second was that hiring and development was based on technical competence and customer orientation. The third dimension was an entrepreneurial mindset among the firm's top managers, who realized that corporate survival in a fast-moving business context required a customer focus, the ability to adapt and speed.

The Cellnex experience suggests that board of directors' structure alone does not determine performance. It was also the behavior of board directors, and in particular, the professional and personal styles of the chairman and CEO, which gave the new board the functionality of an excellent board capable of promoting the firm's growth. They were the ones who stressed to the board of Abertis the need for an advanced corporate governance model, characterized by a solid board made up of independent board members. They also supported a role for Abertis – as the main shareholder – that would generate trust among institutional investors. They also pressed for a diverse board of directors that could guide the international orientation of the company.

For a high-growth company in a highly risky business like telecoms infrastructure, both speed of change and prudence in strategic investment were essential. Excessive investment in too short a timeframe could derail the company. Too little investment at too slow a rate could render the company irrelevant. The combination of the top managers' entrepreneurial spirit and the board's long-term horizon led to outstanding governance and management. It also helps explain one of the most successful European IPOs in recent history.

Furthermore, the Cellnex experience shows how the board behaved in the face of strategic decisions: how it assessed these decisions, how it collaborated with top management to evaluate the risk profile of each strategic decision and how it gave top management the autonomy to execute. More importantly, the Cellnex board helped

Table 7.1. *The boards' role in shaping corporate culture*

• Assessing organizational culture
• People development and compensation
• Strategic decisions
• The collaboration between the board of directors and the CEO
• Engagement with customers
• Relations with shareholders

develop the management team and contributed to bolstering central principles, such as customer centricity, teamwork and a sense of entrepreneurship and accountability. These precepts were reinforced by the board in a high-growth context, where it would have been easy to lose some of these values because of the high-speed change the company underwent. The Cellnex board influenced the culture in very powerful ways by shaping core decisions, competently and judiciously interacting with top management and looking out for the firm's long-term evolution. In this process, the role of the chairman and CEO of Cellnex were critical to the firm's success.

Cellnex's experience reveals that corporate culture can play a major role in corporate performance and corporate governance. The specific shape of a corporate culture or its evolution after an organization's many years of existence is a complex issue, but the board of directors needs to understand and forge them.

The evidence of Amadeus, Cellnex, Henkel and Werfen highlights the board's critical role in forging corporate culture. Based on these experiences, several dimensions of the board's interplay with culture stand out (see Table 7.1). These dimensions are the focus of the next sections.

7.4.1 *The Role of the Board in Assessing Culture*

Werfen is a global leader in specialized diagnostics with headquarters in Barcelona, Spain, and a large footprint in the United States and

Asia.[3] Founded in 1966 as a family business, it boasts a successful R&D–driven strategy and strong corporate values that shape many decisions. The board and senior management team take these values seriously. In recent years, Werfen senior executives took part in hundreds of conversations with employees across the organization to gain a deeper understanding of what helped and what hindered them from bolstering their engagement and performance. Their answers provided additional insight into Werfen's values and it was a way for the board and the CEO to assess the state of the firm's culture and employees' engagement. Large surveys that include a rich diversity of questions and reach the majority of employees can offer a comprehensive diagnosis of the current state of the organization's culture and values. When well-designed surveys can be complemented with structured, one-on-one conversations with employees to learn more about their values, engagement and professional aspirations, the board can obtain deep knowledge on the role of culture and values in the firm, as well as its evolution over time.

The Amadeus, Cellnex and Werfen experiences underscore the strong link between corporate culture and sustainable corporate performance over the long term. The board should understand and assess this relationship. Corporate culture seems to have an impact on corporate performance through specific channels, of which I will highlight four. The first is in hiring and developing competent people, and the role of professional qualities and personal values in the decision. The second is the existence of explicit or implicit guidelines of acceptable company conduct in terms of individual behavior, risk-taking and customer relations. The third is how the board assesses and rewards the CEO and senior managers, and how senior managers reward employees. The fourth is the board and senior managers' focus on collaborative employee behavior, which helps reinforce purpose and trust, and serves as a reference for exemplary behavior. A company cannot prosper in the long term with a toxic or lackluster corporate

---

[3] Canals (2017) offers a description of its recent evolution and strategic challenges.

culture. In assessing the firm's culture, the board should explore these questions.

Amadeus' experience also offers a useful reflection. Amid the profound changes in the software industry, could Amadeus have seized its strategic opportunities and successfully exploited them without a healthy culture? A company can operate without an explicit corporate culture and even thrive for a few years. In this scenario, an implicit culture with tacit rules and principles would emerge. The chances of it developing as a healthy, sustainable culture are average. The main drivers of performance inspired by a positive corporate culture need to be nurtured and developed. Given the deep influence that corporate culture can have on a firm's long-term performance, it makes sense that boards take a more proactive role, as the Cellnex and Amadeus boards did. And the first step in this process is a solid diagnosis of what defines that culture, its main drivers and how the board and the top management team can positively impact them.

7.4.2 *People Development and Its Impact on Culture*

People development is at the heart of a healthy corporate culture. It is individuals' behaviors and decisions that set the example across the organization and encourage positive collaboration and engagement. For this reason, developing and hiring people are two profoundly influential drivers of culture.

When Cellnex launched its IPO in 2015, it decided that most of its top management team would be comprised of the same group of people who had worked together when the company was a small business unit inside Abertis. At the end of 2021, only two members of the top management team came from outside of the company. This conveyed a very powerful signal about the importance of teamwork, technical reliability and customer service, values that had been central to Cellnex's development. The CEO and his top management team could sow the seeds of the new company's corporate culture based on an atmosphere of collaboration among different divisions and units, entrepreneurship and meritocracy. These values were all highly important for the newly formed company.

The board should have conversations – with metrics, if possible – on the topic of corporate culture and its impact on people development. Both in Cellnex and Amadeus, the boards asked the CEO to work on employee development policies to reinforce the talent pipeline, better align individual and corporate performance, strengthen the corporate culture with a clear focus on customers and a healthy compensation system. The Cellnex, Henkel and Amadeus boards took the time to deliberate the new competencies their companies required, especially leadership capabilities. They did not outsource this reflection to external companies but instead dedicated time to exploring diverse approaches, generating good practices that had a clear impact on corporate culture.

7.4.3   Strategic Decisions and Corporate Culture

Those companies also offer some interesting reflections on the role of strategic decisions in shaping corporate culture. Since its IPO, the board of Cellnex worked toward its aim of becoming an international company with a strong presence in the EU and developing its management team and talent pipeline to make this aspiration a reality.

Cellnex's strategic orientation could have been different. As company based in Spain, it might have opted to grow in Latin American countries, where the language and other cultural factors were more familiar for Cellnex executives. By emphasizing growth in the EU, the board of directors of Cellnex signaled some important guidelines. The first was to operate in countries with stable regulatory systems and a certain degree of legal security, which is vital in regulated industries. The second was the determination to create cross-cultural teams in sales, technical positions, corporate roles and services in Europe that together could forge a truly international company.

The strategic decisions made by Henkel's board also shed light on how it can shape corporate culture. In the years following the 2008 financial crisis, when institutional investors in many large companies pushed for divestment from business units and geographies, the board of Henkel analyzed the firm's geographical scope with the CEO and top management team. It also headed the transformation and restructuring of some business units. In certain geographies, recent performance had not been as good as in other areas. It would have been easy for the board to reduce the firm's geographical scope. But it did not. The board decided to support the company's international character and commitment to develop a global leadership team and integrate and coordinate across geographies and business units.

Through these strategic decisions, the Cellnex and Henkel boards also showed their commitment to supporting the uniqueness of their companies. In strategy discussions, the shared understanding of the firm's sustainable competitive advantage is very relevant. When the goal is long-term value creation, companies need to focus more on the specific factors that enable them to assemble great people and help them work, innovate and serve customers well and sustain a competitive advantage. With this objective, the board should shift its focus from assets and resources to people, capabilities and corporate culture.

Corporate culture and values, when supported by a good board, is a key advantage for companies, one that truly helps create value for the long term. In the end, the board of directors communicates what makes the firm different in the eyes of customers, employees and shareholders.

7.4.4 Collaboration between the Board of Directors and the CEO

As discussed in Chapter 1, the notion of collaboration between the board of directors and the CEO seems at odds with the still-dominant view in corporate governance that boards of directors should mainly monitor the CEO. Independence from the CEO could help the board in this respect. At the same time, the board needs to offer advice to the CEO and make decisions – such as strategic investments – based on the reports prepared by the CEO and top management team. As Westphal (1999) and McDonald and Westphal (2003) discussed, boards' independence from the CEO makes their advisory role more difficult to fulfill. These studies suggested that social ties – and social networks – are particularly important when directors need to give advice to CEOs. And a collaborative view of the board and CEOs explains the complexity of board relationships better than pure agency theory, which emphasizes board independence from the CEO.

As evidenced by Amadeus, Henkel, Werfen and Cellnex, among others, positive collaboration between the board of directors and the CEO and top management team offers several benefits for the company and its corporate culture. The first is that collaboration reinforces a culture of commitment to the company, enriched by the knowledge and capabilities that both the board and the CEO bring to the organization. When teams have diverse members, cooperation improves the final outcome. The second benefit is that a culture of collaboration across the entire organization is conveyed. The interaction between the board of directors and the CEO is perceived by all parties involved – inside the organization and by external observers, such as institutional investors, customers and suppliers. Evidence suggests that, in companies with high levels of trust, performance will improve. People learn that collaboration pays off when they see it in the relationship between the board and top management.

When crises emerge, the need for the board of directors and the CEO to collaborate and positively interact on strategic decisions is extremely important, as witnessed by the global pandemic. New priorities need to be established, divestment decisions may need to be made, scheduled projects may have to be delayed and the firm's financial structure, liquidity and solvency may need to be strengthened. Moreover, the board and the CEO need to rely on fully committed senior managers and employees to develop the company for the long term. The collaboration between the board and the CEO is more important than ever.

Several factors influence the interaction between the board and the CEO. Based on the experience of the companies discussed in this book, I would highlight five main factors that shape this relationship. The first is the board's attitude of respect in its professional dealings with the CEO or senior managers. The second is the way directors frame their questions and challenge the CEO. The third is how directors assess CEO proposals, problems or decisions. The fourth is how directors provide feedback on senior managers' professional performance. The fifth is how they respect the autonomy and initiatives of senior management. These factors define and impact the culture of collaboration between the board and the CEO, as well as the human and professional quality of their interactions.

The Cellnex case reflects how a board of directors can be both very professional and demanding, a difficult balance to achieve, particularly in the technology sector, where the need for growth is so critical. The interaction I observed between the board and the top management team can be defined as one of respect and trust. The board outlined the boundaries of the decisions to be made, legitimized the autonomy of the CEO and top management team to implement them, encouraged top managers' initiative, reinforced accountability and fostered trust at the same time. The board knew that a culture of trust and collaboration was essential to ensure a top management team of outstanding professionals capable of leading the company to success. The board also understood that senior managers had to feel appreciated, respected and challenged, and would enjoy working with an experienced board of directors. It was an example of a demanding board in a very competitive industry helping the top management team do an outstanding job.

CEOs and senior management teams that earn recognition from their board of directors and the trust of board members need to be accountable and transparent. The CEO should be transparent and clearly explain the firm's challenges and opportunities, progress on its strategic decisions, evolution of its financial and nonfinancial performance and factors to consider in the near future. The CEO should help directors do their job, reciprocate the board's trust and generate ideas and pathways for action when unexpected events or decisions jeopardize corporate forecasts.

When top managers work with accountability and transparency, they bring humanity and candor to the corporate world. They also serve as role models for other managers and the rest of the organization. Trust can be nurtured by accountability and transparency. Trust and accountability should work in two directions: from the board to top management and from top management to the board of directors. These qualities should ripple out to the rest of the management team and the organization as a whole.

The quality of interaction between the board of directors and the CEO and senior management team – of which collaboration is a key attribute – strongly defines the professional and human interaction among employees. On the contrary, it is difficult to generate trust in a company when the board does not trust the top management team or vice versa.

7.4.5   Customer Knowledge and Engagement

The board should understand customers and their evolving needs, and remind top managers that serving customers is the primary reason the company exists. In this regard, it is important to observe the amount of time boards of directors spend on getting to know customers, understanding the value the company creates for customers and dedicating board meetings to understand and improve the commercial and emotional bonds between the firm and its customers. This is a very simple but sometimes overlooked reflection.

The 2015 Volkswagen carbon–emissions scandal was not only the outcome of cheating regulators, as well as deceiving customers: Volkswagen was selling a product whose attributes were different from what it promised to its customers. The recent Facebook crisis also reflects a lack of respect for customers, who were not a priority for the board nor for the firm's senior managers. The way the board of directors approaches, analyzes and considers customers shapes how the rest of the company regards customers.

In a customer-centric company, employees and people policies are essential. Employees design and sell products and services and nurture relationships with customers with the intent of serving them exceptionally well. A company exists to serve customers, which requires the professionalism and commitment of its people.

7.4.6 The Firm's Relations with Shareholders

The nature of the company's shareholders can be very diverse: family offices, founders, institutional investors, hedge funds, private equity, sovereign wealth funds or governments, among others. In all cases, the board and the CEO should engage shareholders by informing them of major events and decisions, getting their views on the firm and its performance and addressing any concerns they may have about the company's future. It is clear that shareholders have explicit rights. The board should ensure all shareholders have quality information about the firm and treat them all equally by providing them with the same type of data. The board needs to be particularly careful with the company information it shares with large shareholders. Conflicts of interest should be avoided and the breach of the duty of loyalty may provoke a serious reputational problem for the entire board, not just the investors and the board director who represents them.

In particular, the challenge for boards in dealing with shareholders is balancing the duty to avoid asymmetric information disclosures – and prevent investors from using them for insider trading – with the need to engage shareholders with ideas and suggestions for the company. Investors' advice could be beneficial in some strategic decisions and also help the board gain shareholder support for future strategic decisions.

7.5   BOARD CULTURE, TONE AT THE TOP AND CORPORATE CULTURE

This section explores the nature and impact of the culture of the board of directors – the tone at the top – on corporate culture. The board's internal work has a powerful influence on corporate culture and reveals how it expects the rest of the organization to behave in different professional settings. Board directors do not work full time for the company. The board's work, methods and style do not coincide with the nature of work performed by managers and other professionals. But they have a strong influence on how they work and perform as a team, and shape the firm's culture. The experience of the companies explored in this chapter suggests that directors' attitudes set an example for the rest of an organization and shape corporate culture.

7.5.1   Professionalism

The first board director's attitude is professionalism. A fresh wave of corporate governance rules and codes has charged boards with new duties to comply and inform. The increasing demands of investors have further pressured boards to fulfill their duties with higher levels of engagement and commitment. Shareholders and other stakeholders place a great deal of trust in boards of directors. They should be up to the challenge.

It might be simple to define the board of directors' overall mission – to help develop the company for the long term – yet its precise role is impossible to express in quantitative objectives. The board's supervision and collaboration with the top management team are functions or approaches that cannot be measured in the same way that a company measures sales growth, profits or gross margins. Senior managers rely on a team with a well-defined hierarchy and explicit goals and policies. In the board of directors' case, no such organization exists. In general, the board's goals are more ambiguous and senior management is operationally responsible for achieving them. The board helps the senior management team perform its job through deliberation, reflection and some decisions.

There is a strong case for professionalizing boards of directors. It is a very demanding role and one that carries significant responsibilities. Directors' work is ambiguous, requires deep knowledge of the business, broad management experience, prudence, wisdom and empathy to know when to act and when to wait in the face of important decisions such as replacing the CEO. When boards reflect on these qualities, they are able to work as an effective body of governance, helping the company for the long term and serving as a role model of professionalism for the entire company.

A significant dimension of the work of board directors is the holistic nature of their tasks and duties. It is holistic with regard to time horizons – including the ability to strike the right balance between long and short term in its decisions – and its rapid response when crises arise. Its role is also holistic in terms of scope (business units and geographies) and business challenges and functions (sales, people development, operations or finance). This is not an argument for board directors to have expertise in every single area of the company's operations. That said, the board collectively should have an overall level of competence and the capacity to work as a team to address the company's different challenges.

7.5.2   Integrity

One of the new features to emerge in corporate governance over the past two decades is the increasing demand for board-approved codes of ethics to establish standards of behavior. Unfortunately, the application of ethical codes did little to prevent the 2008 financial downturn and other large corporate crises of recent years, such as the diesel-emission scandal in the automotive industry, or the tax and data privacy issues of US technology giants. In these cases, the primacy of short-term financial results trumped decent behavior. Greed and financial success are regrettably, still linked to overall corporate success in the minds of some board directors. Experience shows that wrong actions never lead to long-term success, but rather to crisis and eventual failure.

The evidence suggests that codes of ethical behavior (Melé, 2009) can be useful tools when they reflect a company's positive experience and help clarify expected behaviors. But daily actions and exemplary conduct go first. Strategic and operational decisions made by the executive committee or the board should reflect the essence of these codes. Otherwise, they are useless.

The board of directors can help set the ethical tone of the company with a series of relevant decisions. The first is the decision to hire, develop or fire the CEO and other senior executives who should act as a reference in terms of their professional and decent behavior. The personal profile and style of CEOs and senior managers are very relevant in shaping corporate culture. The second decision relates to how the company recognizes and rewards good contributions by managers and other professionals, and the compensation structure. Compensation models with wide pay gaps within the company, or large divergences with same-industry firms, may reflect the substantial role of financial factors in engaging people, which is not the best driver of long-term performance. The same applies to the level and structure of compensation of board directors.

Boards of directors should carefully monitor any conflicts of interest they might have with the company or related companies. Board members are expected to serve the company to develop it for the long term. Board directors should not have conflicts of interest with the company on whose board they serve. Any potential collaboration that cannot be seen from this perspective or that may reflect the interests of other directors should be avoided.

7.5.3 Commitment to Service

Board directors serve companies as stewards of the firm's long-term survival. This requires a broad diversity of functions, as well as time dedication.

Serving on a board of directors does not simply entail attending board meetings. This is one of a board members' duties but not the only relevant part of their work. In fact, the quality and productivity of board meetings depends more on other factors: the executive committee's preparation of the issues for discussion with the board chairperson, the time spent by directors before board meetings and the many preceding conversations between board directors, the CEO and executive committee members.

The importance of the board's decisions and their impact requires board members to gain an in-depth awareness of the multifaceted dimensions of the company's challenges and the people who can help solve them. This demands the directors' availability and generous use of their time to delve into these issues outside of scheduled board meetings.

Board directors should also be available for extra meetings and conversations with the CEO. Through this attitude, they send a clear signal of their engagement and commitment, as well as what service and leadership mean in that specific company.

Gaining a solid grasp of a company is time-consuming for board directors. For this reason, it is highly recommended that companies retain high-performance directors who deeply understand the company for long periods of time. National codes of governance establish time limits. Short tenures also create mental boundaries and a transaction-based approach to directorships, by which directors shift from one company to another. Professional freedom notwithstanding, board stewardship requires board directors who, with shareholders' support, want to serve for the long term.

7.5.4 Collegial Teamwork

A defining attribute of the board's work is its collegial nature. Board directors achieve objectives through teamwork and collective action. How board directors work together shapes in many ways its overall success and influences corporate culture.

This spirit of collaboration is the glue that binds the board together. It also reinforces the idea that board members work for the long-term development of the firm. Effective teams have clarity on the mission and goals, strategies and policies to achieve them, available resources and well-defined notions of accountability and performance. As discussed earlier, this is not the case for boards of directors. They do not have specific goals, are not an organized team united by the pursuit of specific objectives and their unique contribution does not depend on resources but on their expertise and capacity for discernment and engagement. These features make the need for board members' collaboration even more urgent and compelling.

In such a singular type of team, some factors can make a difference. The first is a clear notion of the board's specific mission in the company. While not a legal requirement, it may be beneficial for boards to establish their own purpose or mission to help the company in distinctive areas, in coherence with the firm's purpose and corporate law. Communicating the board's purpose helps clarify the expectations that shareholders, stakeholders and board members have of this role.

The second dimension is the unique methodology that boards employ to address board issues. This includes the creation of meeting agendas, top managers' preparation of information, the board's approach to senior management assessments and how soft issues, such as corporate culture, are understood and discussed in board meetings.

The third factor is a clear sense of accountability and transparency. A board works as a trusted institution for shareholders and other stakeholders. It should seek the long-term development of the firm. It should serve the top management team and the rest of the company. And it should show that they are not above the standards of professional behavior expected from all employees. In sum, they foster a culture of accountability and transparency by acting as references in their work and decision-making.

The final factor relates to interpersonal relations. They are shaped by several qualities: respect for each board member; the conviction that the board as a team is more than the sum of its individual board directors; the availability to work with other board members; the sense of mission that brings board members together; and finally, a culture of candor and learning that emerges from working with other excellent professionals.

7.5.5 Accountability and Transparency

Boards and board members are accountable to shareholders, regulators and other stakeholders in order to comply with increasingly strict corporate laws. Yet another duty precedes the legal precept of accountability: It is derived from the board members' role as fiduciaries of shareholders, who expect them to govern effectively to promote the company's long-term survival and success. Boards of directors and individual board members should make accountability an ethical touchstone of their behavior, beyond legal duties. Accountability also encourages boards of directors to disclose more information than is actually required when the board considers it very relevant for shareholders or other stakeholders. Excellent boards of directors go ahead of the pack in reporting information. This is especially manifest in the way great boards report on environmental and people issues, far beyond the requirements of regulatory and accounting standards.

Transparency is related to accountability and the way reporting to third parties is developed and disclosed. The attitude of transparency is a deeper concept. It requires the board to work in such a way that, if its deliberations and discussions were ever to be made public – which is normally not the case – all major stakeholders would express satisfaction by its level of professionalism and integrity. Transparency is a key dimension of integrity. There is no greater requirement for a fiduciary than serving professionally and with transparency. This is a clear reminder that ethical attitudes are indispensable in any job, including that of a board director.

7.6 FINAL REFLECTIONS

The influence of culture on corporate governance and corporate performance has slowly but steadily been recognized by academic research, the investment community and regulators. The hypothesis is that corporate culture can influence behaviors that shape the firm's risk culture and management and impact corporate performance. This chapter offers a summary of applied research and good governance practices on the role of corporate culture: what defines it, what can influence it and what the board of directors can do to shape or change it.

The expectations are very high for what board of directors should accomplish in corporate culture. The board of directors may not be functional enough to shape culture. The effectiveness of its work in this and other areas will primarily depend on the level of collaboration with the CEO and the top management team. Corporate culture is forged by the daily actions of many people, and in particular, the actions of top and middle managers in how they make and follow up on decisions, engage employees, communicate and serve customers.

This chapter also explores the interaction between corporate culture and corporate governance. In particular, how the board of directors, as the top decision-making body in any organization, can influence corporate culture through the way it works, makes decisions and coordinates with the top management team. Board leadership differs from CEO leadership; it is also more ambiguous. But the board of directors can help shape the organization's culture through the way it understands problems, asks questions, challenges top managers, adds new dimensions to debates, makes decisions and becomes a reference in terms of commitment, professionalism, service and integrity.

Unfortunately, some of these dimensions cannot be captured in a structured reporting system. But board members should reflect on the corporate culture factors examined in this chapter and give thought to how they address them. The board should consider how it can improve the quality of their culture and, ultimately, the quality of the firm's culture. Corporate culture is a powerful force that contributes to the firm's long-term development.

8   Engaging Shareholders and Key Stakeholders

THEY ENGAGE SHAREHOLDERS?

On March 15, 2021, the board of directors of Danone announced its decision to replace Emmanuel Faber as the company's chairman and CEO in the wake of intense pressure from two global hedge funds: Bluebell Capital (United Kingdom) and Artisan Partners (United States). These activist investors began acquiring Danone's shares in the preceding months and launched an activist campaign against the firm and its CEO.

Danone, a French food–products company, was the world's largest maker of yoghurts. It had built a unique global brand name and a reputation for social responsibility and sustainability. Emmanuel Faber was named CEO of Danone in 2014 and chairman of the board in 2016. In 2020, Danone was recognized by French corporate law as a company with a purpose, underscoring its commitment to serve its stakeholders.

Although Danone's recent economic performance had been lagging competitors, the dismissal of Faber – a senior executive who was well respected in the company – came as a great shock. On March 1, 2021, compelled by both activist investors, Danone's board of directors unanimously approved Faber's proposal to separate the roles of chairperson and CEO (Danone press release, March 1, 2021). He would continue as Danone's chairman and the board would launch a search committee to select a new CEO. In hindsight, it seems clear that the board's position was not very strong in dealing with the activist investors. Two weeks later, this same board announced its dismissal of Faber.

Bluebell Capital and Artisan Partners, two small activist investors, were the driving forces behind Faber's departure. On January 18, 2021, the French media reported that Bluebell Capital had reached out to Danone's board, calling for Faber's dismissal as CEO. Bluebell was a two-year-old boutique hedge fund with only €70 million in assets, of which €20 million were recently acquired Danone shares (Fletcher and Abboud, 2021). The British firm was soon joined by Artisan Partners, another shareholder with a small stake in Danone that saw a business opportunity in Bluebell's campaign. These two funds expressed shareholders' increasing dissatisfaction with Danone's mediocre performance over the past few years. One of their arguments was the disputed governance arrangement by which Faber had been made chairman and CEO, a decision that contradicted many corporate governance recommendations to separate these roles. Bluebell argued that poor governance was the root of Danone's underperformance.

Some analysts believed the activists' attack on Danone was incited by Faber's excessive emphasis on sustainability issues. In this frame, the dispute between the activists and the board of directors was a remake of the classic debate on shareholder primacy versus stakeholder management. In this case, investors wanted to push the pendulum back toward greater investors' power and restore the firm's profitability. Faber's strong support of ESG factors and commitment to purpose and multi-stakeholder management made this a compelling argument. Nevertheless, the evidence also revealed that Danone's real challenge was not its focus on sustainability; it was its overall performance and ability to create long-term value, which had both been deteriorating in recent years.

Danone had been slower than Nestlé and Unilever in adapting to evolving consumer tastes and preferences. Danone had recently reorganized its functions and activities between headquarters and country subsidiaries, leading to a concentration of key corporate functions in its headquarters and a diminished influence of core local markets in strategic decisions. This reorganization was explicitly designed to improve efficiency and profitability, yet triggered negative effects on Danone's ability to effectively serve the changing consumer preferences in its main markets.

It is interesting to consider whether a different corporate governance model, with a division of the chairperson and CEO roles, would have offered the board of directors greater leverage in monitoring the CEO and senior management team. When the chairperson also serves as the CEO, management retrenchment may intensify and the board's ability to press for changes in management is more limited. Interpersonal dynamics play a very important role in boards' decision-making processes and it is difficult to know whether another governance system would have helped Danone's board better navigate this challenge. Nonetheless, there is evidence suggesting that, when companies confront serious performance problems, the concentration of the chairperson and CEO roles in the same person leaves the board with fewer options for the board to work with the CEO on reorienting the firm's strategy.

Another lesson from the Danone case is the capacity of two small activist investors – particularly small for a company with a €41 billion market capitalization in March 2021 – to organize a campaign against a board of directors and galvanize other shareholders who were displeased with the firm's performance. It also highlights how important it is for boards of directors to engage relevant shareholders. In the case of Danone, questions remain on whether the board had been active enough in engaging key shareholders – activist investors included – and communicating with them to better understand their views.

Positive interaction between boards of directors and shareholders is a cornerstone of good corporate governance. Successful companies have committed shareholders and boards of directors who regularly communicate with them.

The alignment between shareholders and boards of directors is a pillar of good corporate governance, as well as a source of potential friction between investors and companies. For decades in the twentieth century, when ownership structures remained largely in the hands of families or governments, this alignment was quite close. The dispersion of ownership and emergence of institutional investors with small shareholdings and other financial investors – for instance, venture capital firms – have made developing a positive relationship between shareholders and boards more critical. This is a critical point for good governance and the firm's long-term development. The Danone case also highlights the need for boards to engage shareholders and ensure they have a solid understanding of the company, and for directors to have a reasonable understanding of shareholders' concerns.

This chapter addresses these themes. The importance of striking the right balance between shareholders, the board of directors and the senior management team is the focus of Section 8.2. Special emphasis is given to the heterogeneous and diverse nature of shareholders. Most research on corporate governance still considers shareholders as a homogeneous group of people with similar, if not the same, preferences. Section 8.3 examines the duties of shareholders, in particular those associated with the quality of corporate governance and the board of directors. Boards' engagement with shareholders is the focus in Section 8.4. Finally, in Section 8.5, some criteria that boards might find beneficial to engage their stakeholders are highlighted.

8.2   SHAREHOLDERS, BOARDS AND CEOS:
AN UNSTABLE BALANCE

The critical role that shareholders play in corporate governance is indisputable. Efforts to protect them and the value of their investments have been focal points in corporate law and corporate governance in advanced countries over the past decades. Good legal protection of shareholders can be a driver of corporate growth and investment (La Porta, López de Silanes, Shleifer and Vishny, 1998, 2000). It is logical that this theme has gained prominence in corporate governance. Empirical evidence has also strengthened the notion that firms should be governed primarily to safeguard shareholders' interests, underlining the shareholder primacy model.

The challenge of finding the right shareholders for each company and business project is highly relevant. Shareholders are essentially as heterogeneous as individuals, with a diversity of personal and financial preferences. Even if most prefer to reap strong returns on their financial investments, their time horizons and the nature of their returns – including their tax treatment – vary widely. The same occurs with companies and their underlying business decisions. Each company has its own business project, strategic decisions, expected investment horizons and cash flows, with different levels of risk and returns.

In management theory, the dominant frameworks have focused on the qualities of the senior management team and their fit with the firm's specific features. For the most part, the alignment of the top management team with the board of directors and shareholders is a marginal issue. In corporate governance studies, the focus tends to be on how to align the board and CEO with shareholders' interests and goals. The need to align shareholders, boards and top managers on the firm's purpose and strategy has received less attention.

This alignment is indispensable for the firm's long-term success. In fact, one of the main reasons behind the success and longevity of family owned firms is the balance and close alignment between shareholders, the board of directors and CEO (see Figure 8.1).

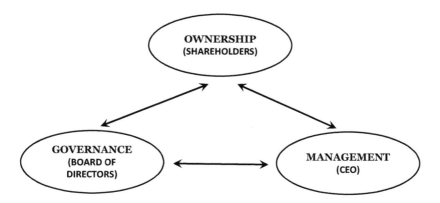

FIGURE 8.1 A delicate balance

A dominant presence of the family – as shareholder and overseer of the board and senior management – may lead to problems, such as the lack of external perspective. But the opposite is also true: Solid alignment among shareholders, the board and management can help guide companies for the long term. And misalignment among shareholders, the board of directors and management may lead to instability and underperformance.

8.2.1 Heterogeneous Shareholders

In the United States, families were the dominant type of shareholders until the 1920s. At that time, investment banks, investment funds and insurance companies invested more actively in the stock market, and shareholders in family owned companies gradually sold off their shares in search of liquidity and diversification. In Europe and Asia, the growth of institutional investors as shareholders started in the 1970s but at a lower speed than in the United States. In many continental European and Asian countries, family controlled and government-owned companies are still the dominant form of ownership (Franks and Mayer, 2017).

The rise of index-related funds and private equity – especially intense since the 1990s – are remarkable changes in corporate ownership (Dasgupta, Fos and Seitner, 2021; OECD, 2021). Among their repercussions is the increased prominence of these new investors in controlling companies, particularly, and their transition as main shareholders in lieu of families and governments (Table 8.1 and Figure 8.2). The role of new types of shareholders in listed companies in different countries is presented in Table 8.1 – Chapter 1, Table 1.1 includes some figures for the United States. In particular, by the end of 2017, institutional investors controlled 38% of equity in listed companies in Europe and 48% in Asia. Figure 8.2 presents the importance of different shareholders in listed companies in OECD countries at the end of 2020. Institutional investors controlled 43% of the equity in

Table 8.1. *A world with heterogenous shareholders (2017)*[*]

	Private Corporations (%)	Public Sector (%)	Families and Individuals (%)	Institutional Investors (%)	Others Free-Float (%)
Advanced Asia	17	23	7	23	30
Europe	13	9	8	38	32
China	11	38	13	9	28
Emerging Asia excl. China	34	19	10	16	21
Latin America	34	7	17	20	21
Other Emerging Countries	15	28	6	20	31
Global Average	**11**	**14**	**7**	**41**	**27**

[*]as a percentage of total capital in listed companies (10,000 largest listed companies)

Sources: OECD (2021), OECD Capital Market Series data set, FactSet, Thomson Reuters, Bloomberg

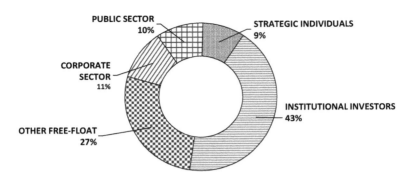

FIGURE 8.2 Investors' public equity holdings[*]
Source: OECD CORPORATE GOVERNANCE FACTBOOK 2021
* overall ownership share by the market value of the category of owners. OECD
countries. December 2020

the listed firms, followed by the corporate sector itself (11%) and
strategic individuals (family offices, etc.) who owned 9% of total
equity in listed companies. If privately held companies are included,
families controlled around 45% of equity in more than 28,000 companies in eighty-five countries (OECD, 2021).

One of the core features of this trend is new shareholders' shorter
time horizons and lower involvement compared to family owners and
governments. The hypothesis that all shareholders are equal and have
the same preferences is no longer true. Each shareholder has unique
goals, time horizons and expectations about the company, as well as
distinctive capabilities in influencing governance. These new types of
investors may not be as committed as families, which view companies
in terms of generations, but their financial power offers firms the
prospect of bolstering their long-term potential when they replace other
shareholders who prefer to sell their shares.

The relationship between shareholders and boards of directors is
shaped by the expectations shareholders have when they invest in the
company. Boards of directors should recognize the importance of
matching the company's profile and potential with the profiles and

expectations of investors. Otherwise, they will soon confront complex challenges.

A central function of the board of directors is to ensure a reasonable alignment between the firm's potential and investors' expectations. When this is not the case, the board should consider whether adapting the company to meet investor expectations is appropriate. While this option exists, it may not be possible for several reasons: Companies cannot change rapidly, investors' expectations might change and the firm may have minority shareholders, whose rights also need to be respected. The board should manage this complexity, facilitate the exit of shareholders with divergent expectations and seek other shareholders whose interests better match the firm's goals and prospects.

8.2.2 Family Business: The Case of Owners with Long-Time Horizons

The strategic decisions taking by family firms during the COVID-19 pandemic shed light on their perspectives of time horizons. As discussed in Chapter 4, in May 2020, the board of directors of Puig decided to acquire Charlotte Tilbury, an expanding and influential cosmetics company in the United Kingdom with phenomenal digital growth and a strong foothold in Asia. At a time of great uncertainty and ambiguity regarding the pandemic's long-term effects, Puig entered the cosmetics industry by investing in the British company. The Puig board faced a complex decision considering the size of the investment, its diversification into a new industry and the uncertainty unleashed by the global pandemic.

Puig was an extremely well-managed company owned by the Puig family, with second-, third- and fourth-generation family members as shareholders. Following the acquisition, Marc Puig, president of Puig, explained that the company's decisions aimed to have a positive impact with a very long-term time horizon. Its board was comprised primarily of external, independent board members. The decision to acquire Charlotte Tilbury would influence the firm's mid- and long-term development. Both shareholders and the board of directors understood this tension well.

Puig's acquisition of Charlotte Tilbury highlights another relevant dimension of shareholders and boards in strategic decisions. Some investments make sense for some shareholders, but not for others. Family offices and pension funds tend to be good investors for long-term projects. Hedge funds have shorter horizons. For companies, the attractiveness of a potential investor is not defined by its scale or reputation but by the investor's overall alignment with what the firm needs to drive its long-term development, and the stability that this support provides.

In deliberating about the shareholders the company may need in the future, boards of directors should consider several attributes. The first is to understand shareholders' reasons to invest in a specific company. Financial returns are an important motivating factor but not the only one. Other features, such as the nature and sustainability of the financial return, tax treatment and delivery over time, might also shape investors' motivations.

Time horizons of investors are also very relevant. Private equity firms have different time horizons from other shareholders. Investors with shorter time horizons also can play a positive role in companies by providing liquidity and better management, but boards of directors should consider the investors whose time frame best match the company's needs. Time horizons also impact how stable shareholders are. Activist hedge funds may offer good returns to investors, but their strategy is focused on the short term. It is not clear whether they are the best drivers to help the companies they invest in achieve better returns in the long term.

Investors' emotional connection with the firm is also relevant. In this criterion, family owned businesses are the best shareholders. Pension and retirement funds also tend to prefer companies where employee-related social dimensions are taken seriously. Corporate governance models and regulations should take into account that shareholders are essentially heterogeneous. In particular, boards of directors should be cognizant of these dimensions and seek the best shareholders possible for the company.

8.2.3   What Type of Shareholders Does a Company Need?

Boards of directors should understand the identity, motivations and expectations of shareholders who espouse different preferences (Table 8.2). Several distinguishing features of shareholders can help boards of directors assess their suitability for the company. The first is the nature of the shareholder and the type of investment. These include financial shareholders, who invest in the company and expect financial results, as well as industrial investors, who aspire to transform the company and eventually merge or combine it with another firm in the industry. The second feature is shareholders' ultimate purpose. Some investors only seek financial profitability. Other investors – for instance, institutional investors or pension funds – may pursue sustained, predictable profitability for their investment.

The third feature is investors' time horizon. In order to promote the firm's long-term development, it is very important for boards of directors to ensure alignment between the company's time horizons and those of the main shareholders. Otherwise, their views will clash on how to best deliver value for shareholders and lead to an untenable situation for the company.

The fourth feature is the nature of financial returns generated by the company. Some companies offer stable, predictable and recurrent

Table 8.2. *Which shareholders does a company need?*

- Understand the nature and reason why shareholders invest in the company
- Shareholders expected returns
- Time horizons
- Nature of returns
- Shareholders expertise in the industry
- Shareholders' stability
- Shareholders' presence in the board

returns, as occurs in well-managed utility firms. Some companies might not offer a large return on equity (ROE) and enjoy higher share prices instead of higher cash flows, as transpires in many growth companies. Cash flows can be less regular in companies prone to business cycles, such as automobile and industrial equipment firms. Boards should make sure that shareholders fully understand the nature of the business, as well as its sources of potential instability.

The fifth feature is shareholders' experience in the company's sector and its main geographic area. Private equity firms with vast experience in a specific industry can play a more transformational role when they invest in firms in the same sector or ecosystem. Companies and their boards of directors can greatly benefit from shareholders with core expertise in their industry.

The sixth feature is shareholders' turnover. Companies need capital to invest in the long term. Financial capital is generic. Shareholders are specific and heterogeneous. What matters is the specific identity of the shareholder who wants to invest in a company, and how well their preferences match the firm's profile and goals. Even in liquid and well-developed capital markets where, in normal times, share sellers can find investors who want to buy, the function of shareholders should transcend simply providing capital. Shareholders – in particular, relevant shareholders – should become stewards of the company. They should care about the firm's governance, strategy and performance, and exercise their legal right and influence to improve it along these key dimensions.

The final feature is shareholders' representatives as board directors. The influence that shareholders have in a company increases considerably if their representatives have some seats on the board. This opens up the discussion on the role of institutional investors who do not want to have a seat on the board. This also adds the question of whether the company will benefit from having those individuals or companies as board members.

8.2.4   Boards That Engage Shareholders in Strategic Decisions

Fluidra, a global firm in the pool industry, merged with Zodiac in 2017, as discussed in Chapter 4 (Msclans, Tapies, Canals, 2020). Before the merger, Zodiac was a leading company in the US market and Fluidra was the market leader in Europe. By joining forces, they turned into the worldwide industry leader. The role of shareholders in the newly created company added some complexity to the merger. Zodiac had been acquired by Rhône Capital, a US private equity firm, in 2016. Fluidra was a Spanish firm founded in 1969 by four families. It went public in 2007. By 2017, the founding families controlled around 50% of its shares and the remainder were on free float on the Madrid stock market, with large institutional investors as shareholders.

When deciding on the merger with Zodiac, one of the Fluidra board's main objectives was that the company remain listed on the stock market and follow best practices in corporate governance, including having a board with a large number of independent board members. After long discussions between the Fluidra and Zodiac boards, the terms of the merger deal were approved in October 2017, with a new ownership structure: 40% of shares of the new company would be owned by Rhône, 30% by Fluidra's family shareholders and 30% would be traded on the stock market. This solution reflected the financial valuations of both companies reasonably well and paved the way to the merger and its corporate governance structure.

The new board of directors knew Zodiac was a good shareholder but reflected a different time horizon and investment cycles than the Fluidra founding families. For the board of directors and, in particular, for Eloi Planes, board chairman and one of the family shareholders, a crucial challenge was reflecting on the type of shareholders the company would need in the future in consideration of Rhône's eventual exit. In 2021, roughly four years after the merger, Fluidra was a listed company with a free float of around 50%, with excellent growth prospects and stable cash flows. At the same time, its board of directors and senior management team observed new opportunities for future growth. The company would continue investing in the future and need capital in order to pursue its expansion plans.

Eloi Planes and the board of directors were convinced that the nature of Fluidra's business would greatly benefit from long-term investors – the founding families and other family offices as shareholders – to provide continuing stability to the company. It would also benefit if a higher percentage of its shares were in free float. The board and senior management team would need to take into account the diversity of shareholders. They also believed the firm's governance and management would benefit from the discipline required of a listed company with a substantial part of the shares in free float.

The Fluidra board of directors' reflection on the type of shareholders the company would need in the future is a reference for all boards. In time, this consideration becomes more urgent and decisions must be made. For this reason, it is a core issue for the company's long-term development, as well as the reputation and credibility of its governance. Boards of directors and the companies they serve would benefit from regularly discussing this theme in board meetings.

8.2.5   Shareholder Preferences and the Firm's Purpose

Shareholders' perspectives of the firm's purpose and long-term orientation are also very relevant in how boards of directors should engage them. For this reason, boards of directors should refrain from adopting a concrete purpose without first involving relevant shareholders – if not all shareholders – in the discussion. The firm's purpose aims to reflect the firm's integrative and holistic nature and guide its long-term development. To be effective, purpose should influence strategy, business model and other core corporate policies. It defines the firm's essence, which is why the board of directors should ensure shareholders take part in the conversation.

Boards of directors should not involve shareholders in approving the firm's purpose simply because it is a "nice to have" or as a shield to protect the firm from reputational challenges or mounting regulatory pressure. In this case, it would be a useless exercise. Shareholders may have an interest in the firm's purpose if it influences its strategy and business model, and helps it forge a unique identity and potentially attract talent.

As in long-term investments, family offices and institutional investors may have a predilection for intangible assets and values that do not directly translate into short-term economic results but that nourish the firm's culture and values. This is also the case of foundations as shareholders. Foundations are trusts created within the framework of national laws whose founders seek to leave part of their wealth to promote a social-impact project whose funding will come from shareholdings' returns (Tomsen et al., 2018). In continental Europe, there are many large, relevant companies whose founders or descendants left part or all of the firm's shares to a foundation. An example is Bertelsmann, wholly owned by several foundations set up by Reinhard Mohn, its longtime chairman and CEO. This is also the case of Siemens and Bosch in Germany, Ikea and Ingka in the Netherlands and CaixaBank in Spain, which are all partially or wholly owned by foundations.

These foundations have the explicit mission of pursuing the firms' long-term development. By their very nature, these foundations serve as long-term stewards of their companies. Because foundations tend to be separated from the founding families, they can take a more neutral approach to company issues. At the same time, their boards of trustees are passionate about the firm's long-term development. Foundations may also adopt a more pro-social perspective on specific areas. This is the case for Ikea and Ingka, which have been at the forefront of climate change initiatives by promoting a holistic sustainability strategy.

In companies that are doing well financially, foundations offer some functionality to pursue specific social goals. This is the case of CaixaBank, Spain's largest retail bank. Fundación Bancaria La Caixa is its largest shareholder, with roughly a 30 percent stake. The bank is professionally managed by a board of directors, with a majority of independent board members. The foundation's values, culture and goals are part of what CaixaBank aspires to achieve, with a focus on financial inclusion and sustainable finance. They make the bank's strategy profile different from competitors that do not have foundations as shareholders.

In these cases, a clear picture emerges. Not all shareholders are equal, neither in terms of their size, nor in terms of their nature, goals and expectations. Boards of directors should engage shareholders and gain a firm grasp of their expectations. Boards should also strive to secure the right type of shareholder to promote the firm's long-term development.

8.3   SHAREHOLDERS AS STEWARDS AND THE FIRM'S COMMON GOOD

In advanced countries, corporate law guarantees shareholders some rights to protect the value of their investment. These vary slightly across major jurisdictions and usually include the right to vote on concrete issues: the appointment, confirmation or removal of board directors and the approval of some strategic decisions, senior-executive compensation policy or dividend policies. As crucial decisions, it is natural for corporate law to require shareholders to vote on them. To ensure this voting process is meaningful, shareholders expect the board of directors to regularly send them updated, high-quality and in-depth communications to ensure they can make informed decisions.

As explored in Chapter 1, a company is not a collection of financial or physical assets that can be bought or sold with no impact on its internal effectiveness. A company is an organization of people with unique capabilities and motivations who, with a management team, use capital and physical or intangible assets to pursue the firm's purpose and goals. Shareholders provide financial capital and should look after the company for several reasons. The first is that, by tending to the company, shareholders also protect their investment. Second, shareholders are accountable to the original owners of capital – for instance, families in family offices or final investors in private equity funds. By taking care of the company, shareholders also help protect their final investors' financial investment. This situation is generally referred to as investors' stewardship and is widely used by institutional investors to explain their investment duties.

Third, a shareholder is a part of a wider social network. Shareholders should monitor the companies in which they have invested not only out of self-interest, but to ensure these companies are better off because of their financial and governance support.

Shareholder rights come also with some responsibilities and duties. Unfortunately, legal systems do not provide a clear description of the duties shareholders should assume, beyond avoiding illegal activities like insider trading or abuse their power over minority shareholders. The shareholder's chief duty is to promote the company's governance and long-term value creation. Shareholders guided by this motivation become good stewards of those companies. Family businesses and foundations are naturally aligned with this perspective. It is the natural reaction of owners with significant assets invested in a company. It is also common for private equity firms to become highly involved in governance issues after investing in a company. In this case, the challenge for companies is to assure that both parties' time horizons coincide. As vulnerable institutions, companies also need protection from third parties that may want to use them for their own purposes.

For institutional investors, the notion of stewardship is more complex (Fisch et al, 2020; Gordon, 2021). In principle, they are long-term asset managers who should take care of their own investors, the actual owners of the invested capital. Institutional-investor stewardship usually refers to their responsibilities regarding their investors. This is the view that institutional investors take. BlackRock's philosophy on investment offers some insight:[1] "BlackRock has the responsibility to monitor and provide feedback

---

to companies, in our role as stewards of our clients' investments ... through engagement with management teams and/or board members on material business issues."

A broader view of shareholder stewardship would also include investors' duties toward the company they have invested in. In other words, the company's board of directors will have trouble developing an open, positive attitude toward institutional investors if the latter do not serve as good stewards of the company they have invested in. As Mayer (2020) expresses, there is not good stewardship if investors only act on self-interest.

What does good stewardship toward a company mean? Shareholders can engage companies through voice or exit. They can engage through "voice" by voting in general shareholders' meetings and working with the board of directors and senior managers to better understand the firm's strategy and make more informed decisions. They can also do it through "exit" by selling the company's shares.

In their interactions with companies, institutional investors rely on governance experts to engage with firms, spend time with their boards and senior management teams, learn about their business and how they create value, understand their governance provisions and get to know the companies' CEO and senior managers. These activities require a considerable amount of time and the involvement of people with high levels of expertise and experience (Bebchuk and Hirst, 2019; Fisch, Hamdani and Solomon, 2020). Unfortunately, even the largest institutional investors have small teams of people dedicated to stewardship. Some investors own shares in thousands of companies and hire staffs to engage with them, yet these teams typically lack the scale required to hold regular meetings with companies' senior management. Moreover, institutional investors prefer not to sit on boards of directors to avoid conflicts of interest with their own final investors.

Private equity firms are more active in promoting positive stewardship even though they are more motivated by self-interest to protect and grow their own investments. These firms or their representatives serve on the firm's board of directors, try to gain a stronger grasp of their challenges and get involved in strategic decisions. Unfortunately, their time horizons do not always coincide with the firm's horizon and they may put their own interests ahead of those of the firm and other shareholders. This is also the problem with activist investors. On the positive side, they often uncover some of the firm's essential weaknesses and strive to define and address them. Unfortunately, their incentives to deal with these issues do not always lead to the best outcomes for the firm.

In this context, deeper reflection is needed on what share ownership means and what companies and society should expect from shareholders that benefit from this legal instrument. Mayer (2020) introduced the notion of trusteeship, based on the concept of trust, which is essential to foundations. Trusts that invest in companies have a duty to develop them for the long term. The interests of trusts dovetail nicely with the interests of the company, which is also the case with many family owned firms. Mayer explains that the evolution of trusteeship as a mechanism of social cooperation among different parties to achieve common goals, is what makes a trusteeship different.

There is a complementary perspective to Mayer's observation that can shed light on the role of investors in companies and society. Companies are institutions whose effectiveness requires cooperation. In markets, competition prevails; in organizations, coordination, cooperation and team building are more effective. Without cooperation, very few organizations can thrive and survive. Rather than external agents, shareholders are part of the company. They do not work in the company yet provide the firm with indispensable assets. They entail the voluntary cooperation of managers and employees, who work together to offer customers a unique proposition and drive economic value in this process. The company's ability to attract talent in the future depends greatly on its corporate culture and overall reputation (Canals, 2010a).

By working well professionally, companies as organizations also contribute to the common good. Common good, as defined by

Aristotle, is the set of qualities in a society that allows its citizens to develop their own personal and professional projects successfully. In the business world, companies benefit from being part of societies that are safe, respectful of human rights, dynamic, innovative, environmentally conscious and that boast robust legal and educational systems, among other qualities. Companies cannot be free riders; they also need to do their part to promote the common good. The common good is not something companies should take for granted at no cost to them. Regulation plays a very important role in this respect but it is not enough.

To this end, shareholders should nourish this cooperative attitude, as well as consider their concerns about their investment value and the financial returns they can generate. There are trade-offs and conflicts with this perspective. But emphasizing shareholders' duty to promote the organization's common good is relevant: Shareholders should protect the value of their investment, which is associated with the firm's long-term success. The lack of alignment between shareholders and the company in terms of financial performance or time horizons may lead to relevant disagreements. Good corporate governance requires engaged shareholders.

8.4   BOARDS OF DIRECTORS THAT ACTIVELY ENGAGE SHAREHOLDERS

Boards of directors have specific legal, fiduciary duties. They can be summarized as the duty of care to the company and its long-term development, and the duty of loyalty to the company, which requires members to avoid acting against the best interest of the firm. Both are conditions for the firm's good governance.

The duty of care is sometimes interpreted through the lenses of shareholder value maximization and shareholder primacy, themes explored in Chapters 2 and 3. Maximizing shareholder value has become the overriding aim of firms since the 1970s. Shareholder primacy was a direct outcome of this hypothesis, establishing an order of access of different parties' rights to the firm's value creation process. In this respect, one offshoot is the view that boards of direct-ors should prioritize shareholders and commit to maximize share-holder value. As discussed in Chapter 2, the board should bolster the firm's efforts to create as much long-term economic value as possible for all shareholders and stakeholders and to establish a clear dividend policy.

Shareholder heterogeneity is a principle that corporate govern-ance should assume. Each shareholder has unique expectations about the firm, returns, time horizons and social preferences. Shareholders have rights in the firm but so do other parties. Companies need capital, shareholders provide it and boards should protect sharehold-ers' interests. Boards need to convince shareholders that their com-pany offers them a unique investment opportunity.

The notion of engagement in corporate governance is generally associated with activities developed by institutional investors, as a manifestation of their duty of stewardship toward their final client investors. As part of their efforts to protect their clients' investments, institutional investors should engage with companies to ensure they have proper governance, strategy and policies in place.

There is a complementary view of engagement in corporate governance, one that is less developed. It refers to the tasks carried out by boards of directors to assure the firm has the right type of shareholders, who are there for the long term because of their affinity for the company. As the former US Securities and Exchange Commission chair Mary Jo White stated, "[t]he board of directors is – or ought to be – a central player in shareholder engagement."[2] The reason why boards need to engage shareholders is the assumption that, in listed firms, shareholder relations were and still are essen-tially a function delegated and executed by the CEO, CFO or director of investor relations. Boards are the main channel of communication with investors regarding the firm's performance and major decisions.

[2] Mary Jo White, Remarks at the 10th Annual Transatlantic Corporate Governance Dialogue, Washington, DC, December 3, 2013.

Over the past few years, additional factors have emerged that help explain why boards should pay attention to shareholder engagement. The first is the CEO and boards of director leadership in the dialogue with shareholders on issues unrelated to the firm's financial performance or execution of strategic plans. These themes are linked with the firm's governance issues, senior leadership pipeline and successions plans, and board composition, among others (McNabb, Charan and Carey, 2021). The second factor is the sharpened focus on ESG factors advocated by some investors, including the board's governance of the firm's environmental and social impact and its approach to governance mechanisms. The third factor is the need for companies to cultivate a positive relationship with shareholders on nonfinancial issues and also benefit from their insights.

In the companies examined in this book, their boards of directors engaged shareholders on concrete issues. Cellnex's board of directors – through its CEO, its CFO and its director of investor relations – engaged shareholders to discuss its growth strategy and ensure it could rely on them for its ambitious growth plans. It also defined corporate governance guidelines to convince them that the company would adopt the best practices to guarantee an outstanding governance structure, including a highly competent and diverse board of directors. Unilever also counted on shareholders to support its Sustainable Living Plan and management of its environmental impact. Fluidra dedicated significant efforts to align shareholders' different time horizons and reflect on the best shareholder structure for the future. These are just a few examples of leading companies that successfully anticipated the need to engage shareholders and ensure they had a deep understanding of the company. Table 8.3 summarizes some core features that define the board of directors' shareholder engagement.

8.4.1   Board Accountability and Transparency

The first feature is shareholders' expectation of professionalism and integrity from a company and its board is directors. Accountability

Table 8.3. *Boards of directors: Key areas for engagement with shareholders*

- Board directors' professionalism, accountability and transparency
- Relevant information about the firm's performance and potential
- Board of directors and senior management team
- Corporate culture and the culture of the board
- A culture of collaboration
- The firm's overall impact

and transparency are complementary attributes of board directors' professionalism. The board's accountability not only encompasses its legal obligations but the basic duty of protecting the financial resources invested by third parties, who expect to be reasonably informed of the board's actions in order to manage their investments. Board directors are accountable to shareholders in terms of how they conduct operations and carry out their duties.

National corporate law offers details on the board's duties with regard to accountability. Nevertheless, there is a basic principle of fairness: The board should foster shareholders' trust toward the board and the company. Firms need the cooperation of shareholders. The accountability of boards should not be limited to the confines of corporate law but broadened to include actions to foster shareholders' trust. Achieving this goal may require the board to enhance how it engages and communicates with shareholders.

8.4.2   Boards' Disclosure of Relevant Information

The second feature in developing positive engagement with shareholders is to offer holistic information about the company, its performance and its potential. The development of capital markets over the past few decades, coupled with the dominance of financial indicators in assessing the firm's performance, has led to a framework of corporate reporting in which financial variables have practically excluded other dimensions of performance. The balanced scorecard and its variations tried to offset the dominance of financial variables. Only recently, amid growing evidence of the material impacts of companies' decisions on the environment and society, have regulators and institutional investors called for other indicators of performance, such as ESG factors.

This effort is plainly insufficient. The so-called S factors (social) include dimensions that may be hugely important in some countries, such as race discrimination or slave labor. These factors are undoubtedly important and companies that aspire to gain social esteem should respect everyone, especially their employees and customers. Unfortunately, in most of the cases, the S-factor dimension does not address another essential component of corporate performance: the P factor (people), as discussed in Chapter 5, manifest in the firm's attractiveness to hire and retain people. Most institutional investors and proxy advisors request very limited information in this realm. This contradicts the notion of people development – including senior managers' succession – as one of the most important and complex policies that boards should monitor and govern.

Another area where the quality of information disclosed by boards can improve is corporate strategy. Most companies spend time with investors to inform and update them on their strategic plans and decisions, but the board's attention to strategy is limited. The CEO and senior management team are the ones who work with strategy and propose it to the board once it is nearly developed and finished. This also contradicts the board's duty to look after the firm's long-term orientation and corporate strategy. Boards should take additional steps to understand the firm's strategy and discuss it with the CEO, as outlined in Chapter 3. Many boards should strengthen their grasp of the firm's strategy and ability to share it with shareholders by thoroughly understanding how the firm creates long-term value.

Strategy is an area that highlights another challenge inherent in the board's engagement with shareholders. Boards of directors can engage individual and relevant shareholders who want to dedicate time to better understand the company. Boards of directors need to strike a delicate balance to avoid asymmetric information disclosures that benefit some shareholders over others, and the right of shareholders to deepen their knowledge of the firm's performance and potential. Each national law system offers its own solutions. Insider information is an enormously delicate issue and one that can have criminal implications. Boards and shareholders should conduct themselves with extreme caution, fully understand the company's legal context and act under its precepts. Investors have the right to gain a deeper awareness of the firm's long-term projects, which is why adequate and well-structured information is so relevant.

Listed companies or companies that operate in organized debt markets also share information regularly with financial analysts. Good investors do not expect to receive copious amounts of information. Boards of directors should recognize the type of quality information that their good, long-term investors need in order to remain committed to the company. Conceptual clarity about strategy and execution, and the professional qualities of the board and the senior management team, are more important than a myriad of financial indicators.

8.4.3   The Composition of Boards of Directors and Top Management Teams

The composition of the top management team and the board of directors is an important aspect of nonfinancial information. Board members are not mere agents of shareholders but directors that shareholders have appointed to govern and manage the company for the long term. In its interactions with shareholders, the board should present consistent and holistic information about the board, as well as its competence and diversity. It should focus on the senior management team and the future leadership pipeline that the company needs: the current situation, its evolution, future development and the central policies adopted by the board and the CEO to bolster the management team.

Over the past two decades, consulting firms have developed new indicators to measure the effectiveness of human capital. At the same time, more and more companies are making talent their top priority and showing how much they care for their people, but the chasm between words and action is still large. According to various surveys (see Edelman, 2021), younger generations show record levels of disconnection from their employers. If this situation reflects the company's reality, it is a serious problem. Boards of directors should ask the CEO to provide evidence of the company's progress in this respect. Board directors should understand the firm's people-development function, monitor its progress and properly disclose relevant information to shareholders.

8.4.4   Corporate Culture and the Culture of the Board

In light of institutional investors' growing interest in corporate culture and values, boards should consider them core hubs of the firm's governance. Chapter 7 explores the relevance of corporate culture and the culture of the board itself to improving the quality of board decision-making in highly uncertain contexts. For boards of directors, reporting on this core area of interest for shareholders is highly complex. With respect to the board's culture, some approaches have been discussed but still fall short of offering effective policies or guidelines.

Boards should learn how to evaluate and improve the culture of the firm, as well as its own. Devising an inventory of initiatives is not enough. As suggested in Chapter 2, a framework that connects corporate purpose with corporate culture and values, vision, strategy, the business model and other corporate policies is highly relevant. Corporate culture should be understood and nourished from the firm's purpose. The board's reporting on corporate culture should not be used solely as a protective shield from corruption and ethical misbehavior; it should also promote a positive culture that enhances the firm's level of professionalism and inspires collaboration and innovation to serve customer needs.

8.4.5   Collaboration

A vital ingredient of the firm's culture and governance model is the internal cooperation among its different parties to achieve corporate objectives and fulfill its overarching purpose. Unfortunately, models based on agency theory and the practices of some boards have led to confrontation and mistrust between boards and shareholders. This is the exact opposite of what shareholders' positive engagement requires. The board should promote a positive relationship with shareholders, guided by professionalism, integrity, accountability and transparency, and earn their support for the firm's long-term development.

Developing this culture of cooperation between boards and shareholders is a complex endeavor. It requires a combination of board qualities and prudent policies. A culture of cooperation should also be reflected in interactions between boards of directors and top management teams. Boards of directors' collaboration with shareholders and top management teams has the potential to permeate the entire organization and reinforce this very important organizational dimension. It is essential for companies that strive to create value for the long term.

8.4.6 The Firm's Overall Impact

Boards should also understand and assess the firm's overall impact and, in particular, to what extent it has reached its purpose. Chapter 9 delves more deeply into how boards can develop a holistic understanding of companies' impact. In this section, I would like to highlight that investors need a comprehensive view of the firm's total impact beyond financial performance. If shareholders aspire to be good stewards of the company they invest in, they should have a clear picture of the firm's overall performance.

Companies are complex organizations. Some business functions, such as manufacturing or logistics, are relatively straightforward while others, such as innovation or people development, are more complex. But companies are sophisticated institutions, capable of organizing collaborative efforts to profitably serve customers. The board of directors should embrace this holistic view of the firm and should consistently share it with shareholders. Obviously, environmental and social effects of companies should form part of this picture. Shareholders, and particularly institutional investors, should recognize that the E (environmental) and S (social) factors are important but not the full story. As highlighted earlier, the understanding of people policies (P) is essential since culture, values and strategy are driven by people and their behavior, not the other way around.

Boards should also understand – and be able to explain – how purpose, strategy and major policies shape the firm as an organization of individuals – a human group – over the long term; how decisions foster trust among employees and customers; how policies reinforce corporate culture, and most importantly, how decisions change the soul of the organization for the better. Considering the overall impact of different decisions and policies on the organization as such, is very relevant.

In gaining a deeper awareness of the company's overall impact, it is worthwhile to reflect on its major stakeholders – employees, customers, shareholders, suppliers and the environment, among others – and its interactions with them. This is a long list of stakeholders, which poses a challenge for boards. Nonetheless, this list comprises the different parties the company interacts with in one way or another. Companies are communities and networks of different people and parties that collaborate with each another, grounded on mutual trust. This is a quintessentially human challenge: people working and cooperating with other people to achieve explicit goals in an atmosphere of trust. In this process, sharing a common purpose not only helps the company as an organization to achieve its goals. In some cases, legal systems and regulations will force companies to adhere to certain policies. In other areas, it is managerial discretion and prudent business judgment that drive boards of directors and senior managers to establish priorities, goals and policies. A good board of directors has the capability to weigh different perspectives and ensure that the decisions adopted support the firm's development.

8.5   THE BOARD OF DIRECTORS AND STAKEHOLDER ENGAGEMENT

Boards of directors should promote positive engagement with shareholders, as described in the previous section. It is not a clear governance principle that boards should also engage other stakeholders, as discussed in Chapter 1 (Mayer, 2018; Edmans, 2020; Henderson, 2020; Polman and Winston, 2021). The nature and content of engagement with stakeholders is different in terms of specific goals and policies. Nevertheless, if boards consider certain stakeholders to be vital to the company's development, they should consider how to best engage them, whether directly or through the top management team.

For board directors or senior executives, embracing a positive view of stakeholder engagement is not a matter of personal preference; it arises from the notion of the company as an organization whose performance depends on the contribution of different parties: employees, managers, shareholders, suppliers and others to work together to serve customers and solve explicit customer needs. It stems from the understanding that a company's activities affects the world around them, from local communities to the environment, which might not be wholly internalized in its pricing system. The company also needs to consider these external effects.

Once the company has complied with all legal requirements relating to people, communities, taxes and the environment, and internalized these factors, some shareholders or boards of directors may want to expand their efforts to support specific social causes. This is reasonable as long as they reflect shareholder preferences and approval, are fully disclosed and promote the firm's long-term development. The notion of key stakeholders as an important consideration for the board is relevant to the company's future success. In this respect, it is useful to distinguish different types of shareholders in terms of their commitment to the company.

8.5.1   Core Stakeholders: Customers and Employees

In assessing how to interact with and eventually engage stakeholders, boards of directors need to distinguish between different types. The company's core stakeholders are customers and employees. Board members should understand customers well: They are the foremost reason the company exists. Board members should spend time discussing customer-related issues and interact with customers whenever feasible. This is very relevant since very few of the reporting models of institutional investors or rating firms consider how relevant customers are to the firm's long-term development. This has implications. Few boards of directors prioritize customers. Projects centered on customers and their satisfaction are rarely included in board agendas unless they are related to growth projects.

The company's employees are the other core stakeholder group. They organize and execute the operations necessary for the company to adequately serve its customers, as well as provide new ideas and projects. They are familiar with customers, serve them, respond to their needs and requests and consider their future needs and the best way to address them. Among institutional investors, there is rising interest in employees as stakeholders. Part of this interest stems from a longer list of S factors that companies need to disclose. As generally occurs with ESG factors, institutional investors' sphere of interests in recent years is more of a reflection of their concerns about the risks the company is taking. In particular, the risk of not adopting better policies in specific realms, such as gender or racial discrimination, pay gaps, child labor or employment practices that restrict personal freedoms. As important themes, companies should adopt policies that ensure legal compliance.

As discussed in the previous section, these factors are important and entail legal obligations, but alone, they are not enough. If engaging core stakeholders is so essential, is it enough for companies to assure they are not infringing on any laws? The answer is probably not. People-development experts highlight several factors that help strengthen bonds of trust and engagement between individuals and organizations. These factors are not an option for a company, they are a duty. Enhanced engagement boosts corporate performance and fosters commitment, cooperation and creativity, among other benefits.

People's engagement also positively affects another central board duty: succession planning, in particular, the CEO and senior managers. A productive succession-planning process requires a pipeline of candidates whose qualities – academic profile, knowledge, professional capabilities, soft skills and personal attitudes – are sufficiently robust to offer the company an internal source of talent to meet its current and future needs. Good succession planning does not occur in a vacuum; it is more consistent and reliable when the company has a good pipeline at all functional levels. This should include organization-wide people development and engagement.

8.5.2 *Other Key Partners*

More and more, the firm's long-term success depends on the successful evolution of its partners. The digital economy has given rise to new, complex networks of companies, both in the real and virtual world. These companies interact and depend on one another. In their search for efficiency, companies have also sought a narrower and disintegrated scope of operations. As a result, companies rely increasingly on the goods and services of other companies. In particular, the acceleration of globalization and a more integrated global economy have led firms to rely more on globally dispersed suppliers. Global value chains have been established based on speed and efficiency. Sadly, new trade wars, geopolitical conflicts and the COVID-19 pandemic have compelled companies to rebalance the role of efficiency in their decision-making and consider the resiliency of their business model. In this context, supplier relations have become more relevant than ever. For many companies, the pandemic has prompted the need for deeper cooperation with their core suppliers.

In services and most notably, in the e-commerce realm, inter-company collaborations are growing. The outsourcing of IT and cyber-security services to essential partners is soaring. The co-creation of solutions, such as electronic payments, is also on the rise. This upsurge in joint ventures in core operations that directly impact the firms' long-term development requires the board to establish govern-ance criteria for these activities. The board cannot simply ignore them and assume the management team will take care of them. These activities are critical. The board should know and monitor them and define clear guidelines on how to engage partners. There is much at stake, not simply access to raw materials, products or services; these collaborations also define the company's access to core strategic resources or its ability to develop strategic capabilities with the right partners. For boards of directors, the risk of not overseeing this dimen-sion is too high. This is a clear case where good board governance involves much more than simply monitoring contracts with stakeholders.

8.5.3   Local Communities and the Environment

Companies develop their activities in local communities. Even if firms have global operations, their impact on customers, people and suppliers is typically localized in specific regions. Companies contrib-ute to communities by investing, paying salaries, funding public spending through taxes and other specific initiatives. At the same time, companies benefit from the prosperity of communities – or suffer from the lack of it. Cities with safe environments for individ-uals and families, solid educational systems, educated residents, stable and fair laws and effective public institutions offer companies a better context for their operations.

Companies should contribute to the long-term success of the communities where they operate. They reap numerous benefits from the community's success and often pay only a fraction through taxes and other concepts. Companies develop better in friendly commu-nities. On the contrary, it is difficult for companies to thrive in decaying communities or regions: Good talent and customers may be scarce. This is a common phenomenon in emerging countries, which cannot easily escape this conundrum. It is natural for companies to spearhead different initiatives to improve the conditions of their communities of operations. This is not philanthropy; it is a recognition of the company's debt to the community and the positive future repercussions from investing in it. Firms that positively engage with local communities will not only improve their reputation. They will fulfill a civic duty and become an institution of reference for others.

This reflection is also relevant when boards of directors consider the company's impact on the natural environment. For many years, the environmental effects of companies were not considered relevant by most of society. The growing carbonization of the atmosphere from rising emissions and its impact on climate change have turned environmental effects into a major concern for society, governments, investors and boards of directors. The risks of negative environmental impacts – pollution, climate change and extreme weather, among others – on both the firm and society are too high to be ignored by companies.

This universal risk affects all companies. No one can hide and escape from this risk. Although regulation has a major role in tackling this challenge, companies also need to do their homework. In this area, boards of directors should also take a leadership position as advocates of the firm's long-term development. Chapters 3, 4 and 9 discuss how boards can introduce governance criteria to address the firm's environmental effects. Within the framework of this section on firms' third-party relations, it is appropriate to consider that their environmental effects generate costs that need to be taken into account. Firms should try to minimize or cover these costs and offset them through specific policies. Measuring these costs is very complex. In the end, regulators will step in and define the applicable carbon tax for each industry. But paying the actual costs of negative environmental effects is only one dimension.

Companies should also work and develop creative solutions to mitigate and offset the firm's environmental impact. These solutions are neither easy nor cheap. Companies should work with governments to devise solutions that can bring these effects to zero. Innovation is a big part of the solution and the creativity of entrepreneurs should play a defining role.

In this respect, it is important for companies to take a holistic view of their environmental effects by considering the entire supply chain. Boards of directors and senior managers should evaluate which elements of the value chain the company should feel responsible for, beyond regulatory expectations. Chapter 3 included an overview of Unilever Sustainable Living Plan. The company felt responsible for the entire value chain, from the farmers who cultivated its raw materials to the end consumer. This was a difficult and expensive decision but one that drove innovation and pushed Unilever to develop new, more sustainable products.

Local communities and the natural environment provide a context where companies can grow and develop, or stagnate. It is true that solving these problems requires more than the actions of individual – or countless – companies. But firms can and should contribute to this effort. As in other core dimensions of the firm's activities, the board of directors should take an active role in overseeing the company's effects on third parties and ensuring that it monitors and controls its negative externalities on stakeholders, and develops positive policies to help alleviate these wider problems. At stake are not only social challenges that need solutions, but the firm's long-term development.

8.6   FINAL REFLECTIONS

The role of shareholders as contributors to the firm's long-term development goes beyond their shareholdings. Responsible shareholders need to have a sound understanding of the companies they invest in and awareness of their competitive advantages and potential for growth, as well as weaknesses. They should know who serves on the board and senior management team, and how leadership development and succession plans are organized. In short, shareholders should not consider their shareholdings as a mere financial investment. Firms are far more than financial assets.

The growing dispersion of shareholders has tilted the balance of power in organizations. If shareholders do not exercise their duty of stewardship in the companies in which they have invested, corporate governance will lose an important pillar of development. Boards should consider that companies need shareholders who are well aligned with their goals. For this reason, it is vital for boards to cultivate shareholder engagement. Boards of directors can help shareholders exercise this duty by engaging them and assuring they have useful and comprehensive information about the company, recent performance, core challenges and future development.

Although the relationship with each stakeholder is unique, boards of directors, as stewards of the firm's long-term orientation, should also govern this relationship, even if nurturing the day-to-day relationship with them is the responsibility of management. In a global business arena where networks are growing in all industries, the need to cultivate relationships with key partners is essential. Suppliers, joint-venture partners and product or software codevelopers have become indispensable pillars for firms. When these relationships are strategic, the board should have clear criteria on how to govern them and coinvest with them.

The board should also have governance criteria on how the firm's operations impact the natural environment and the local communities where it operates. Regulations may force companies to behave a certain way. Companies are also social institutions that operate on the foundation of trust in their relationships with others. For this reason, companies cannot be free riders. They should continuously reflect on the evolution of their relationships with key stakeholders, including local communities and the environment, in addition to strategies to offset and minimize their negative environmental and social impacts. In a word, companies should not only adhere to the law but reflect on how they can improve their overall impact and develop into a positive reference in society.

9 Assessing the Firm's Overall Impact

9.1 THE CHALLENGE OF ASSESSING THE FIRM'S PERFORMANCE

In January 2021, Ingka CEO Jesper Brodin and deputy CEO Juvencio Maeztu were discussing the firm's strategic challenges. Although the pandemic had taken a heavy toll on the retail company, its financial performance was very resilient. The CEOs reflected on Ingka's commitment during the pandemic and its central priorities over the last two years. The firm's purpose, aimed at making comfortable homes more affordable and accessible through concrete initiatives, was very relevant in assessing the firm's impact. Ingka's progress on major initiatives such as its digital transformation, the opening of new Ikea city centers and investments in more sustainable products and the circular economy were core elements of this assessment.

Ingka's experience suggests that companies across a range of industries are not only facing complex challenges such as the pressure to mitigate their environmental impact or growing bottlenecks in global supply chains. Companies are also trying to design new business models that allow them to operate successfully from a financial standpoint while tackling these wider challenges. In some industries, companies may need longer timelines to attain some sustainability goals. In the oil and gas industries, for instance, the transition to more sustainable energy sources and net zero emissions will take years. Against this backdrop, the relevant point for companies and their boards of directors is not only to report and disclose data on these initiatives in a transparent and comprehensive way. It is also how to assess the firm's overall impact and progress, integrate financial and nonfinancial dimensions of performance and take into account all of the company's impacts on customers, people, shareholders, the planet and other stakeholders.

Ingka's recent challenges highlight the conundrum of firms with successful performance records and a commitment to protect the environment or local communities. The economic slowdown following the COVID-19 crisis, mounting trade barriers, geopolitical tensions, changing consumer preferences and decarbonization initiatives are having a negative impact on the performance of many companies. Moreover, not only investors but consumers, employees and other stakeholders are putting growing pressure on companies to disclose their effects on the environment and society at large, beyond financial indicators.

Nevertheless, the biggest challenge for companies is not the diversity of themes and indicators that boards of directors need to monitor and disclose but rather the lack of consistency among them and their weak connection with the firm's purpose and strategy. Comparisons of nonfinancial indicators of companies in the same industry are difficult to carry out. Some performance indicators are required by national regulators. These include, among others, disclosure of financial performance, executive pay and carbon emissions. Other indicators, such as ESG factors, are strongly supported by institutional investors and proxy advisors. ESG rating firms also provide some special scores and rankings on these issues, but the diversity of criteria and methodologies are not functional, not even for investors. The European Commission, the SEC and other relevant regulators are working on this issue, but it looks like a common framework to report on ESG is still a work in progress.

Some firms also use certain indicators related to the unique nature of each company. Specific corporate performance dimensions such as innovation rates, productivity and customer satisfaction fall into this category. Boards may consider them useful, but investors do not seem to pay too much attention to them, and, in most cases, they do not ask about them. Unfortunately, the lack of connection between these factors and the firm's overall strategy is one reason why they are not considered relevant by some investors. The gap between what investors want to hear and what regulators expect, on one hand, and what the board considers relevant, on the other, is still very large.

In this chapter, I address some challenges that boards of directors face when assessing the firm's overall impact and highlight three themes to help firms more coherently integrate financial and nonfinancial performance with strategy. The first theme relates to the firm's performance, which should focus not only on its financial results but on its connection with purpose, vision, strategy and its business model, as well as the capabilities and resources it has developed over the years. This connection and search for consistency highlight dimensions that make companies unique.

The second theme is that companies should have a clearly defined strategy that can create sustainable value in the long-term. Sustainability in value creation requires firms to adopt a unique approach of serving customers by investing in assets and resources and developing some special capabilities (Ioannou and Serafeim, 2019; Porter and Serafeim, 2019). The board should ensure the firm's strategy is clear and sustainable and report on it. Financial performance looks at the past; strategy considers how the firm will create value in the future.

The third theme is how to consistently integrate financial and nonfinancial indicators. In this pursuit, the challenge is not only the creation of standards, although these are necessary and helpful; compliance is very important but not enough. The genuine challenge is how uniquely a firm – under the leadership of its board – establishes its long-term strategy and assesses its overall performance and impact over time, in the context of its purpose and strategy.

Before presenting a holistic framework to understand the firm's performance, it is also relevant to consider some central questions: What is the firm's overall impact and for whom?

9.2 CORPORATE PERFORMANCE AND OVERALL IMPACT: WHAT SHOULD THE FIRM'S GOALS BE?

Boards of directors should monitor the senior management team and oversee the firm's performance. This is an established principle in good corporate governance practices. Over the past decades, this board duty focused on monitoring the CEO and making sure that the company tried to maximize shareholder value. Investors, investment bankers and consultants developed different tools that highlighted how companies could create shareholder value and how they should report on value creation (Fama and Jensen, 1983; Rappaport, 1986). The increasing importance of nonfinancial factors, such as those behind ESG dimensions, and the emergence of the notion of multi-stakeholder governance, has caught boards and investors unprepared to deal with the complexities of working with indicators other than financial ones.

The reflection on the firm's disclosure of performance brings the discussion of shareholder primacy versus broader stakeholder interests back to the table. As elaborated in Chapters 1 and 2, companies are institutions that have a clear raison d'être in society: serving customer needs while simultaneously creating economic value. National law grants companies the license to operate under this tenet and protect its shareholders with limited responsibility. Companies should generate profits to allocate them toward R&D, learning opportunities and capital investments, and pay shareholders a good return on their investment. Competitive capital markets put pressure on companies to pay shareholders well.

Effective customer service, people development and environmental-protection initiatives should not be viewed by boards of directors as constraints on a company's value creation process. Rather, the initiatives are the true drivers of customer loyalty and brand power, employee engagement and innovation, as illustrated in Chapters 2–4 with the experiences of Amadeus, Cellnex, Fluidra, Ingka, Unilever and Schneider Electric. In the same way that companies consider their legal duties to perform, they should consider what it takes to continuously meet and serve customer needs, and develop and engage their employees. Customer loyalty and employee engagement lead to more creative environments, enable the development of new capabilities and products and help firms remain competitive in the long term.

As Edmans (2011, 2020), Eccles and Serafeim (2014), Flammers (2015) and Gartenberg, Pratt and Serafeim (2019), among others, showed, there might be some trade-offs between companies' profitability and their caring about customers, people and the environment in the short term, but firms should adapt their strategy and business model to take those relevant realities into account. Companies need to hire good people, pay them well, invest in their development and prepare them to serve customers in alignment with the firm's mission. Only companies that truly care about their customers, employees and the environment can successfully compete for the long term.

The experiences of Ingka, Schneider Electric and Unilever also show that good financial performance does not intrinsically contradict ambitious goals around employee engagement or positive environmental policies. These experiences are also consistent with the hypotheses offered by Porter and Kramer (2011) and Henderson (2020), among others. Companies that take employees' expectations seriously and aspire to offer customers sustainable products are also better poised to create a positive culture of innovation, product design and development that contributes to generating new competitive advantages. The challenges that companies voluntarily choose to address are transformed into drivers of innovation and change, helping them develop new capabilities and, eventually, new competitive advantages.

The trade-off between shareholder objectives and the interests of other stakeholders arise when companies do not have a clear purpose or strategy, or when they execute strategy with mediocre business models. The 2021 Danone governance crisis reveals that companies with purpose are not a problem in terms of financial performance. The real problem emerges when purpose is not fully integrated into strategy and the business model, leading the firm to underperform. The role of the board of directors in this context is critical. The board should discuss the purpose-versus-profit debate with the CEO, deeply analyze its arguments and adopt and own a position that it can communicate to investors.

The debate between shareholders and other stakeholders is relevant in this context. The criticisms against stakeholder management are incomplete and incoherent with actual business experience. As Hart and Zingales (2017) rightly argue, it is shareholders who should decide on the philanthropy initiatives of the companies they invest in. Nevertheless, relevant stakeholder management is not about philanthropy. By developing people, channeling resources to innovation to better serve customers, working with suppliers to improve their effectiveness or offsetting the firm's negative environmental impact, firms take these social issues seriously and invest and innovate to create sustainable value.

Boards of directors are fiduciaries who should look after the firm's overall impact and assess the sustainability of its performance. In this role, boards and senior management teams need to consider several dimensions. Sometimes, these factors are clearly regulated by law, such as minimum wages or carbon emissions. In other cases, board members should use their business judgment to consider these factors, discuss them with the CEO and weigh their potential impact on the firm's performance and reputation. If shareholders disagree with the directors' business decisions, they can express their views and opt not to reelect them in the next shareholders meeting.

Friedman (1970) and Fama and Jensen (1983) simplified the argument by underscoring the primacy of shareholder value, but they also introduced uncertainty in some areas. In particular, by highlighting the focus on profits, they did not explicitly consider the negative externalities generated by the firm's activities. Moreover, some policies relevant for stakeholders may help the firm create value for the long term but require investment and expenses in the short term. The timeframe of value creation is also very relevant. Time horizons are different for different types of shareholders; they are heterogeneous, so centering the focus only on shareholder value may not be a good guide for the debate. Unfortunately, the contemporary versions of shareholder primacy do not contemplate these critical features.

Bebchuk and Tallerita (2020) are also right in some of their criticisms of companies whose CEOs explicitly supported the 2019 Business Roundtable statement on corporate purpose and multi-stakeholder management. They are right in highlighting the contradiction of these CEOs in supporting purpose while not changing any major corporate policy or submitting it to a shareholder vote. However, their argument is incomplete. As the experiences of many innovative companies presented in this book reveal, it is possible to integrate purpose into strategy and business model, develop multi-stakeholder management and create long-term value.

A word of caution in this debate is needed. As mentioned in Chapter 8, shareholders in the abstract are a simplification. In the real world, shareholders are diverse, heterogeneous and driven by different motivations and expectations that evolve over time. Listed companies in capital markets are not the majority of firms. Family-business and private-equity backed firms are dominant in the corporate world outside of the United States and United Kingdom. In these companies, the alignment between shareholders, boards of directors and CEOs is quite high.

Agency problems are real in most listed companies but are not the biggest governance concern in other firms with shareholders of reference. Privately owned companies have some governance problems as well, but shareholders are more involved with the company and able to remove CEOs and change the board more flexibly than in public companies. Some problems that arise in the debate between shareholder primacy and stakeholder perspective are more relevant in the context of highly dispersed ownership in listed companies. When shareholders, boards and senior managers share the same long-term vision and are fully aligned, the debate between shareholders and other stakeholders is less relevant. Shareholders and stakeholders alike have an important share in the firm's destiny.

The growth of distributed ownership in listed companies in the United States led to the lack of proper monitoring of boards of directors by shareholders and the dominance of powerful CEOs. The rise of managerial capitalism did not have the checks and balances necessary for good corporate governance. This explains the call for independent, external board members that regulators in Western countries began demanding in the 1990s.

Unfortunately, these problems have yet to be resolved. Institutional investors are dedicating more time and effort to considering companies' long-term prospects, as reflected in their stewardship reports. Despite this rising interest, it is important to note that these reports disclose a mere handful of engagements – direct contacts with boards of directors or senior managers – out of the myriad companies they have invested in. Most institutional investors are not spending the time needed to serve as good shareholders of their investees. A significant problem in assessing the firm's performance is shareholders' genuine interest in acting as responsible investors who care how companies are governed and managed. This requires time and commitment. The relevant role that shareholders should play in corporate governance is threatened when they fail to spend sufficient time monitoring the board and engaging in positive conversations with directors.

In this context, boards and CEOs with disconnected shareholders are open to attacks from activist shareholders, who will emerge when the firm's performance falters. Supporters of shareholders' primacy should remember that companies are not machines. They are human groups, most of whom aspire to serve their customers' needs and create economic value in this process. Shareholders should dedicate efforts to better understand the companies they invest in and positively engage with management teams and boards to discuss the firms' long-term horizons.

Although the notion of shareholder primacy seems to have the advantage of simplicity, it does not give the complete picture on the firm's performance. As Mayer (2018), Edmans (2020) and Henderson (2020) point out, academia should also acknowledge that, in many companies, the nature of this debate is different. In the real world, the debate is between companies that are well governed, effectively managed, driven by a clear purpose or mission, guided by a coherent strategy and that have a good financial performance; and companies whose shareholders and boards are more focused on short-term value creation and their short-term horizon tend to underinvest in people, R&D or new products and services. Carefully framing the terms of the debate is very relevant for corporate governance.

9.3   A HOLISTIC PERSPECTIVE OF THE FIRM'S PERFORMANCE AND IMPACT

The board of directors' duty to monitor top management and corporate performance calls for more holistic models to assess the company's overall performance and impact. This is not only a question of whether shareholders should have primacy over other stakeholders; it is about establishing a credible framework that explains how a company promotes and sustains value creation for the long term. Firms create long-term value with a clear strategy and unique business model to help them better serve their customers.

Andrews (1971), Porter (1980, 1996) and Rumelt (2011) described the notion and relevance of business strategy for the firm's long-term performance. They identified the need to serve customers in a unique way, the role of strategy to help develop competitive advantages, the importance of the core idea of the business and the decisive contribution of people to strategy and, in particular, people with managerial responsibilities. Unfortunately, these contributions were disregarded by most financial analysts and capital markets.

Since the 1980s, investment banks, scholars and consulting firms have created new indicators of financial performance, all aimed at assessing a company's financial returns. Part of this effort was useful; for instance, it helped identify firms with good accounting profitability that were not generating enough cash flow to invest in new projects, sustainably managing debt levels and paying decent shareholder returns. This became the dominant culture in corporate reporting over the past four decades.

In the 1990s, the new strength of stakeholder management (Freeman, 1984) and the consideration of the three Ps of the triple bottom line – people, planet and profit – began to emerge in discussions on performance assessment and corporate reporting. In parallel, the increased focus on corporate social responsibility emerged and created additional challenges for the shareholder primacy perspective. Unfortunately, the early stages of this new perspective were timid and non-holistic, and the dominance of financial indicators continued.

Porter and Kramer (2011) went one step further with the notion of shared value, by which companies pursue social goals in a way that also drives additional shareholder value creation. Porter and Kramer were right in underlining that companies' pursuits of environmental and social initiatives that are detached from corporate strategy are doomed to fail. Unfortunately, this notion probably fell short in assessing the firm's overall impact.[1]

Only with the very recent sea change in the way large institutional investors consider ESG dimensions and the upsurge of impact investment has a new perspective emerged in the corporate performance and reporting debate. The early innovators in integrating financial and nonfinancial reporting such as the GRI (Global Reporting Initiative) and SASB (Sustainable Accounting Standards Board) have been joined by new initiatives, including the Carbon Disclosure Project(CDP) or the World Economic Forum's Stakeholder Management framework, promoted in cooperation with the Big Four auditing firms (World Economic Forum, 2020).

Despite recent progress, the quality of ESG performance indicators is still a work in progress. There is the challenge of comparing

---

[1] The Boston Consulting Group launched the "Total Societal Impact: A New Lens for Strategy" initiative in 2017. This framework helps companies think about ESG–related strategic growth opportunities.

corporate performance across industries, as well as between same-industry firms that apply different indicators. Also, there is a lack of clear standards of materiality,[2] measurement and reporting. In financial accounting, materiality designates all material issues that should be properly reported in financial statements. As a result, financial performance is tangible, clear, well defined and highly monitored by audit firms. On the contrary, nonfinancial performance is still non-standardized, with different institutions setting references and standards and offering scores and rankings, without an overall view of the information that they bring or how they can promote a more holistic perspective of the company's performance.

Fortunately, there are some initiatives underway to create international sustainability standard frameworks to report on ESG factors, including recent efforts by leading voluntary standard-setting institutions, including CDP, the Climate Disclosure Standards Board (CDSB), GRI, the International Integrated Reporting Council (IIRC) and SASB. The Enacting Purpose Initiative, promoted by the British Academy, also offers a powerful framework for measuring purpose in an integrated way. In November 2021, the IFRS Foundation announced the creation of the International Sustainability Standards Board (ISSB), which would develop a new set of sustainability standards based upon the existing frameworks.

This development of standards is good news. Nevertheless, the lack of standards in nonfinancial factors is not the chief obstacle in measuring firms' performance. The presence of different standards and the evolution of sustainability reporting have led to both greater awareness and confusion regarding this issue. According to Pucker (2021), increased integrated reporting has not significantly contributed to offsetting negative environmental impacts.

Far before the emergence of nonfinancial performance indicators, companies such as Ingka, Schneider Electric, Nestlé, Pepsico and

---

[2] Materiality is a quality related to the impact of noneconomic factors – including ESG factors – on financial performance.

Unilever, among others, reported on their activities from a holistic vantage point, combining financial and nonfinancial information, and clearly integrating them. In this way, investors, customers, employees and other stakeholders have been able to better evaluate the performance and overall impact of these firms, beyond the specific benefits they derive from them.

These companies and their governance frameworks have a common thread: They all have connected purpose, values and ESG with strategy, business model and stakeholder managament. These dimensions are relevant factors in the firm's performance. But they also share another similarity: Their boards and top management teams have been able to successfully articulate these building blocks and create a governance and management model that integrates these critical dimensions. As explored in Chapters 2 and 3 with the Unilever and Schneider Electric experiences, this process requires time and a firm determination to extend its scope to include investors and key stakeholders. Once the model is holistic and reasonably consistent, it becomes a powerful lever in helping firms bolster the quality of their governance frameworks and management teams.

In the following sections, I present an overview of how some of these companies are governing their long-term evolution and measuring their performance by expanding the board and senior management's focus to consider both business performance and the firm's impact on people, customers and environmental and stakeholder dimensions.

9.3.1 Unilever

When Paul Polman and his team began working on the Unilever Sustainable Living Plan in 2009, they reflected on the best way to address changing consumer needs, enhance employee engagement and consider Unilever's environmental impact across the value chain. The board gave Polman and his team the explicit goal of improving Unilever's financial performance. What might have looked like a huge conundrum for the CEO was actually an opportunity to rethink the company's strategy.

Unilever's management team embraced the challenge, sparked a well-structured and creative organizational change process and consistently defined the firm's purpose, which became integrated into Unilever's strategy, business model and strategic decisions. A few years later, the governance and management model they developed was clear and distinguishable. More importantly, it was recognized by investors as unique.

Although it was ultimately successful, the transformation that Polman unleashed at Unilever was not simple. On the contrary, it was a complex process for a large company with eight business units, wholly owned subsidiaries in more than 100 countries and a dual shareholding structure and headquarters in the Netherlands and the United Kingdom. Moreover, Unilever needed to regain the respect of investors following years of mediocre financial performance.

In 2010, Unilever unveiled a new corporate purpose, "[m]aking sustainable living common place." It was complemented by a well-structured vision, coherent goals, strategy and business model, and disciplined execution. As Polman and other board directors shared (Canals, 2019), the hardest part of this transformation process was not defining a clear purpose; what was truly complex was achieving a viable integration of Unilever's purpose into its strategy and business model to ensure it could create sustainable economic value. Once this framework was well defined and operational, accountability and performance assessment also became more functional.

Unilever's governance model put purpose at the center of its activities. At the heart of purpose, the commitment to customers, employees and key stakeholders, including shareholders, was made explicit. The company's disclosures on its impact on each of these realms was not an artificial experiment or a ratings game. Unilever started to report on the main themes and dimensions that the management team and board of directors felt best reflected the company's performance.

IMPROVING HEALTH AND WELL-BEING		ENHANCING LIVELIHOODS		
HEALTH AND HYGIENE	**NUTRITION**	**FAIRNESS IN THE WORKPLACE**	**OPPORTUNITIES FOR WOMEN**	**INCLUSIVE BUSINESS**
TARGET By 2020 we will help more than a billion people to improve their health and hygiene.	**TARGET** By 2020 we will double the proportion of our portfolio that meets the highest nutritional standards, based on globally recognized dietary guidelines.	**TARGET** By 2020 we will advance human rights across our operations and extended supply chain.	**TARGET** By 2020 we will empower 5 million women.	**TARGET** By 2020 we will have a positive impact on the lives of 5.5 million people.

REDUCING ENVIRONMENTAL IMPACT			
GREENHOUSE GASES	**WATER**	**WASTE**	**SUSTAINABLE SOURCING**
TARGET Halve the greenhouse gas impact of our products across the life cycle by 2030.	**TARGET** Halve the water associated with the consumer use of our products by 2020.	**TARGET** Halve the waste associated with the disposal of our products by 2020.	**TARGET** By 2020 we will source 100 percent of our agricultural raw materials sustainably.

FIGURE 9.1 Unilever Sustainable Living Plan (2020 goals)

Polman and his team strived to improve Unilever's effectiveness and financial performance, while simultaneously focusing their attention on three ESG-related areas that the company felt responsible for and that could help Unilever boost sales growth and make a positive difference (Figure 9.1). Each area had a few well-defined KPIs, which were directly linked with product development, operations and sales. The first area was – and still is – health and well-being. Its aim was to help more than a billion people take action, with two main themes: (1) health and hygiene and (2) nutrition.

The second area was "Enhancing Livelihoods" and comprised three major initiatives: (1) fairness in the workplace; (2) opportunities for women and (3) inclusive business. The third area was environmental impact, with four major themes: (1) greenhouse gas emissions;

(2) water usage; (3) waste and (4) sustainable sourcing. It took some effort, but employees and shareholders gradually appreciated and understood what Unilever was trying to accomplish and how it was planning to assess its performance along these new dimensions.

These areas firmly connected Unilever's impact with its purpose and offered a comprehensive view of progress on its financial and commercial goals while advancing its efforts to enhance people's health and nutrition, promote fairness and inclusiveness and reduce its environmental impact, all articulated in well-designed policies, careful investments and a disciplined innovation process. While some of these initiatives have worked better than others, their overall impact has been very positive for Unilever. It has undoubtedly blazed new trails both in its adoption of purpose and stakeholder management, and the coherent integration of financial and nonfinancial themes in its reporting.

9.3.2   Ingka

As examined in Chapter 2, in 2018 Ingka's board and senior management team decided to accelerate the company's transformation process in the face of evolving digitalization and a stronger commitment to sustainability. At the heart of this transformation was Ingka and Ikea's sense of purpose: to make customers' lives more comfortable and the products they need more affordable.

In 2018, Ingka's board approved the 2019–2021 strategic plan, which included ambitious revenue growth, margins and cash-flow objectives. Achieving these goals would require new strategic initiatives, most of which related to ESG dimensions: the affordability of Ikea products for consumers, accessibility via an omni channel approach and sustainability throughout the value chain. Ingka's board fostered the firm's growth along these three dimensions, which were closely connected with Ikea's purpose.

Ingka's approach shows how purpose and ESG dimensions can dovetail with strategy and business model. Moreover, it illustrates how some themes of purpose, such as the affordability of products and services, sustainability and promotion of the circular economy, can turn into the driving forces of innovation and change in companies. It is true that a firm might face trade-offs in the short term: Costs might go up for a while, required investments will require financial resources and traditional products – less affordable or less sustainable – might still see strong demand and be more profitable than newer offerings. Transformation toward more sustainable products or services and more environmentally friendly processes may entail higher costs and lower profitability in the short term. The same can be said of policies aimed at improving employee education and training.

Any corporate transformation process sparks disruption, as evidenced in the 1990s with the advent of e-commerce or in current times with the emergence of artificial intelligence applications in different business functions. Companies need to adapt and discover new opportunities for growth if they want to survive. Those that adapt and enhance their agility will be better poised to develop new products and services, serve customers in a unique way and attract top talent. In addressing purpose and sustainability, boards and senior managers need to embrace the same approach: understand the implications of different options and the risk of inaction; discover opportunities and explore alternatives; establish criteria to assess the various options; define areas where the company can experiment; and finally, adopt a broad map for change and transformation.

The takeaway from Ingka's experience shows that these goals add some complexity, but they can be successfully interwoven into the business model. When the board of directors approves the transformation process with a broader set of goals, the scope of the company's business and its performance become far more holistic. In turn, investors gain a better understanding of the company and different stakeholders can observe how the company balances diverse goals and trade-offs.

Ingka's reporting extended beyond financial performance and ESG dimensions. Its approach was integrated and holistic, with the board of directors focused on sustainable growth around affordability,

01	02	03	04	05
Create strong position leading from our Purpose.	Create a home furnishing movement.	Create a simple and unique digital Customer.	Create affordable services to make IKEA convenient.	Create a new world of IKEA in every city.
06	07	08	09	10
Create the IKEA stores of tomorrow.	Create a people people- and planet-positive IKEA	Create a relevant and affordable offer.	Create a simpler and better IKEA, designed for the future.	Create a people movement and make our culture and values a living reality.

FIGURE 9.2 Ingka: Ten jobs to be done
Source: www.ingka.com/newsroom/media-resources (April 29, 2021)

accessibility and sustainability. Ingka's challenges and opportunities emerging from these three themes were translated into ten initiatives (ten jobs) (see Figure 9.2), each one with some specific goals in a three-year timeline (2019–2021).

Each of these jobs had specific targets, policies and action plans. An interesting point is how Ingka's top management defined job number 7: "Create a people- and planet-positive Ingka." This job was defined by three areas. The first was "healthy and sustainable living," with three specific commitments and five targets. The second was "circular and climate-positive," with three specific commitments and five targets. The third was "fair and inclusive," with three commitments and three targets. It is important to note that some of these initiatives and targets were not simply discretionary choices made by the board to promote sustainability. Rather, they were fully integrated into product development and sought to positively influence consumer behavior, not to simply sell more units of specific products. Ingka's efforts to promote recyclable products, phase out plastics in its products and promote the use of renewable energies, both internally and by customers, reflect the interplay between its environmental focus and product innovation.

9.3.3   Schneider Electric

Two overriding forces were behind Schneider Electric's profound transformation over the past fifteen years: the need to fight climate change through the use of clean energy, and the application of digital solutions to improve its energy-usage effectiveness. Under the leadership of Jean-Pascal Tricoire, Schneider's board of directors and senior management team transformed these challenges into important opportunities to reinvent the company and better serve customers. In this way, two major sources of potential disruption – digitalization and electrification – became the catalysts of change for Schneider. The firm's purpose to create a world where innovation, effectiveness and sustainability in energy use could intersect became the driver of the firm's transformation.

This was a long journey, with many obstacles along the way. But the board and the senior management team were convinced of the need to transform the company through a coherent model of change that encompassed the aforementioned dimensions and effectively transmitted its related goals and commitments to employees, shareholders and other stakeholders. The new sustainability goals might have been viewed as additional obstacles to the firm's performance. On the contrary, Schneider Electric viewed them as opportunities to develop new products and services and strengthen their business.

In 2021, the company released the Schneider Sustainability Impact, which disclosed information on financial performance and six other areas of impact: climate, circular economy, trust, equity, generations and local. Each area had specific performance goals and indicators and clear targets to be achieved by 2025 (see Figure 9.3). This model was the outcome of Schneider Electric's long-standing efforts to disclose nonfinancial information. The company also strived to connect their company-specific targets with the seventeen United Nations Sustainable Development Goals.

What is truly relevant is that Schneider's objectives were all adopted voluntarily: All significantly exceeded the minimum legal

CLIMATE	BASELINE	Q1 2021	2025 TARGET
1. Grow our green revenues	70%	72%	80%
2. Help customers save CO_2 emissions	265M	276M	800M
3. Reduce CO_2 emissions from top 1,000 suppliers	0%	in progress	50%
RESOURCES			
4. Increase green material content in our products	--	in progress	50%
5. Plastic-free and recycling	--	in progress	100%
TRUST			
6. Suppliers who provide decent work to their employees	--	in progress	100%
7. Confidence of our employees to report unethical conduct	81%	in progress	+10 PTS
EQUAL			
8. Increase gender diversity (Hiring/Management/Leadership)	41/25/24	44/25/25	50/40/30
9. Provide access to green electricity to 50M people	30M	30.7M	50M
GENERATIONS			
10. Double hiring opportunities for interns, apprentices and fresh graduates	4,939	x1.11	x2.00
11. Train underprivileged people in energy	281,737	287,601	1M
LOCAL			
12. Country presidents with local commitments	0%	100%	100%

FIGURE 9.3 Schneider Sustainability Impact: Long-term commitments
Source: Schneider Sustainability Impact 2021–2025 (Q1 2021)

requirements in their countries of operation. Moreover, the firm integrated these targets into its business model and main activities. Some of them, such as climate and circular economy, were fully incorporated into Schneider Electric products, solutions and customer services. They were tightly interwoven into the offer that Schneider Electric was making to its customers. Others were connected with people policies to enhance employee well-being, especially in emerging countries with limited access to education, training, health services and social assistance benefits.

Even more remarkable, Schneider's integrated pursuit of these goals and transparent disclosure became the focal point of its regularly published reports and presentations for analysts and investors. By jointly presenting financial, social and environmental performance, Schneider Electric not only highlighted its commitment to sustainability and social dimensions; it showcased its efforts to wholly integrate these factors into its business operations.

9.3.4 Assessing Overall Impact: Beyond Integrated Reporting

The Unilever, Ingka and Schneider Electric's experiences reflect pioneering examples of how companies can integrate ESG factors into their purpose, strategy and business model, and also deliver very strong economic performances. While pathbreaking, they are extremely useful for all boards of directors in deciding which ESG and other nonfinancial factors to closely monitor, which performance indicators to follow and how these factors can connect with financial performance. As these companies show, the firm's impact goes beyond financial reporting and its integration with nonfinancial reporting. This is an important step but, in the end, companies should be able to communicate internally and externally who they are, why they are in business, how they create value and their overall impact. It is not merely a question of people preferring to engage with socially conscious companies, whether as customers or employees: A growing number of investors want to know the overall impact of the firms they invest in.

9.4 A FRAMEWORK TO ASSESS CORPORATE PERFORMANCE AND IMPACT: THE ROLE OF THE BOARD OF DIRECTORS

The tidal wave of nonfinancial factors that companies must now consider, coupled with institutional investors and regulators' mounting pressure for additional ESG-related disclosures, have created an enormous challenge for boards of directors. For many firms, reporting on financial performance and nonfinancial issues is significant, but integrating them in a meaningful way is difficult. The expectation from the board is to produce longer reports on nonfinancial dimensions, which unfortunately often result in an information overload, regardless of whether these factors are material to the company's expected performance and results. I will begin this section by first exploring some principles to better understand the firm's global performance based on the experiences outlined in this book. I also present a framework for thinking about the firm's impact.

9.4.1   Insights on the Firm's Impact from the Business World

Although the experiences of companies presented in this book are unique, they offer useful insights for boards of directors and senior managers in a broad range of companies, both listed and privately held. The first is that companies keen on improving their environmental and social impact should clearly delineate their areas of impact based on the material importance of nonfinancial factors for the firm's performance, P&L and balance sheet. At Unilever, Polman and his team did not casually choose environmentally focused areas as a public relations exercise. Unilever chose areas in which the company had a negative effect and made concerted efforts to track its performance and reduce its adverse impact within a reasonable timeframe. In this sense, firms should choose their ESG themes wisely and closely monitor their impacts, including those which are material for the company's operations. By indirectly reminding people of its purpose, a company can reinforce its commitment to sustainability, social goals and consideration of all costs – including those not explicitly reflected in financial reports.

The second insight is that the impact of environmental and social factors on the firm's performance transcends explicit costs or additional investments. Companies with good governance and effective management are able to coherently integrate these challenges into the firm's strategy and business model. Moreover, tackling these issues may spark additional innovation to help design novel products or services at premium prices, boost demand with new offerings or reduce costs. Empirical evidence also shows that purpose and ESG factors help intensify employee engagement, which also yields a positive impact on the firm (Gartenberg, Pratt and Serafeim, 2019).

The third insight is to consider the overall material impact of environmental and social factors on the firm. This material impact goes beyond costs and can be divided into six specific areas (see Figure 9.4). The first area is the potential for new revenues that come from product innovation, a different customer value proposition and better margins. The second area is the impact on expenses – both positive and negative. Responsible companies should consider negative impacts – for example, pollution – as costs to take into account, even if regulations in a country do not force companies to do so. The third area is the impact on the firm's balance sheet and, particularly, its capacity to raise new equity or issue debt with a lower cost of capital in light of its environmental and social profile, and the management of stranded assets that are losing value due to energy transition. The fourth area is the impact on the firm's reputation, in particular, among customers and employees – including future hiring – and other stakeholders as well. The fifth is the company's risk profile, including financial, reputational, regulatory, environmental and social risk. The sixth area of impact is the ability to engage long-term shareholders, who may be better aligned with the firm's purpose and strategy.

The fourth insight is that improvements in this complex area do not happen overnight. It is important for the management team to define aspirational but reasonable goals that are well integrated with the firm's strategy and provide it with a sense of direction, while the firm continues to perform well. The experience of these firms also shows that mistakes can be made in this process. Establishing overly ambitious goals can negatively impact the firm's reputation and demotivate employees if the firm fails to attain them.

ENVIRONMENTAL AND SOCIAL FACTORS' IMPACT	**REVENUES**	• REPUTATION • BRAND AWARENESS • NEW CUSTOMERS • GROWTH • PREMIUM PRICE PRODUCTS
	EXPENSES	• EXPLICIT ENVIRONMENTAL AND SOCIAL COSTS • COSTS OF INACTION
	BALANCE SHEET	• NEW INVESTMENT • EQUITY • DEBT • STRANDED ASSETS
	REPUTATION	• CUSTOMERS • PEOPLE HIRING AND DEVELOPMENT • STAKEHOLDERS
	RISK PROFILE	• FINANCIAL • REPUTATIONAL • REGULATORY • ENVIRONMENTAL • SOCIAL
	SHAREHOLDERS	• SHAREHOLDERS' ENGAGEMENT • NEW EQUITY • DIVIDEND POLICY

FIGURE 9.4 Environmental and social factors: A holistic view of materiality

The fifth insight is that goals should have a clear link to the firm's purpose, strategy and business model.[3] Unilever's chosen areas

---

[3] Porter and Serafeim (2019) argue that sustainability standards in and of themselves are not a source of competitive advantage. Companies need to discover a way to

were fully consistent with its purpose. As a matter of fact, they were established almost in parallel with the development of the firm's purpose. Goals should also be coherently integrated into the firm's strategy and business model since this enables the company to create value. The company's performance between 2009 and 2020 was clearly above average among its peers in the food, beverages and home products sectors. It is a prime example of how a company can grow while considering environmental and social dimensions in product development, and create long-term economic value for all, including shareholders, by considering different stakeholders in its decisions.

The sixth insight is that the board's level of aspiration is important in order to mobilize employees and suppliers to achieve the defined goals and boost their commitment to serving customers. The companies discussed in this chapter were both aspirational in the selection and simplicity of their chosen goals and the KPIs selected to monitor them.

The seventh insight is that, in a world dominated by technology and software, companies can become true innovators, architects of successful business models and magnets for talent and development. And as these firms prove, this is possible even in mature industries like food and beverages, or retail. At the time of writing, Unilever was rated among the world's best employers, along with large technology firms. The incredible impact of integrating financial and nonfinancial performance cannot be overstated. In this process, the firm's purpose can play a very relevant and positive role.

The final insight is on ESG regulation (Coffee, 2020). Companies should comply. But Ingka, Schneider Electric and Unilever began their process of defining purpose and ESG areas and goals years ago, when regulation in this area was practically nonexistent. What is truly remarkable about these firms is not only their pioneering role in integrating ESG with their strategy and business

integrate environmental factors into strategy and offer a unique customer value proposition.

model; it is the fact that they chose areas that were material to their business and others where they could make a unique impact. Moreover, they included ESG factors most relevant to the company and its different stakeholders. The lesson here is that companies should define their own purpose and appropriate ESG factors. Firms should take regulatory duties into account, but regulators will not tell them which areas they should emphasize and monitor. This responsibility falls to the board and the top management team (Canals, 2019; Polman and Winston, 2021).

This lesson leads to an important reflection for companies, regulators and scholars. In corporate governance, there is a school of thought that believes companies should simply follow the law and comply with formal regulation, with no need to move beyond this scope of duties. The experiences of Unilever, Schneider Electric and Ingka show that this is a limited view. They chose which ESG areas and goals to pursue (well ahead of regulation), explained their materiality to shareholders and the investment community and effectively integrated them into their strategy and business model.

No company, no matter how large, can single-handedly resolve the challenge of climate change or other complex social issues (Yan, Almandoz and Ferraro, 2021). But it is also true that regulation alone will fall short. Regulation is imperfect, subject to political bargaining and lobbying, slow and dependent on enforcement. The voluntary adoption of ESG dimensions is rational, embeddable into the firm's business and capable of making the company more competitive in the long term. Moreover, good governance practices will trigger a positive ripple effect. Regulation is indispensable in ESG areas. But the experiences of these firms offer a powerful lesson, showcasing the effectiveness of good boards of directors and CEOs and serving as a reference to many companies around the world.

As the companies discussed in this book suggest, the lively academic debate on the firm's goals as defined by shareholder primacy versus stakeholder management perspectives is incomplete. More and more companies – along with some investors – view this debate as obsolete. Well-governed companies should develop their strategy and business model to efficiently serve customers, engage their people and make a positive impact on other stakeholders while creating economic value. While considering this wider perspective may seem more complex, it is dynamic: It opens up new business models and fosters innovation. The board and the CEO need to make prudent decisions to ensure this process is sustainable.

9.4.2   A Holistic Framework for Impact Assessment

Within the boundaries of legal and regulatory duties, boards of directors and senior managers have the discretion of defining and prioritizing the ESG factors they deem most closely related to the firm's purpose, culture or business. In the end, the business judgment of the board is essential. In the cases of Unilever, Ingka and Schneider Electric, their boards of directors defined and approved a way to report on ESG factors when standards on this type of reporting were nonexistent. They chose specific areas of interest and key indicators because they were closely connected with basic customer needs, as emphasized in their firms' purpose. This was essential in determining where the company would place its ESG-factor focus, beyond the requirements of national laws and regulations.

The board of directors and senior management team should assess the firm's impact, not only for reporting purposes. As stewards of the firm's long-term development, they should develop a framework to assess performance. Adopting a generic framework of performance is not enough. The board should take into account the firm's characteristics, its industry, its whole value chain and how it sustainably creates value. This approach should allow investors and other interested parties to monitor the firm's performance reasonably well and draw comparisons with other industry peers. This way of assessing performance and impact has a direct outcome: It helps the board of directors and the senior management team track the company's progress in core areas. Disclosure and reporting come later.

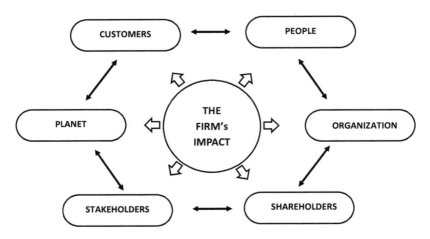

FIGURE 9.5 The firm's impact on stakeholders

The first party interested in assessing impact should be the board of directors itself.

The firm's performance and impact should consider the holistic perspective explored in the previous section with the experiences of Unilever, Ingka and Schneider Electric. The board and the CEO should work together to understand the firm's primary areas of impact and the consideration of relevant stakeholders (see Figure 9.5) and should design and select performance indicators that are truly relevant for the company.[4] The firm's impact on shareholders is very relevant in terms of continuing to attract capital, but it should also focus its efforts on sustainably creating value for customers and attracting and developing people with the best professional and personal competencies. To this end, the board and senior management team should firmly understand the firm's purpose, vision, strategy, business model

---

[4] The balanced scorecard is a widely used framework among senior managers that integrates key indicators of performance, beyond financial factors (Kaplan and Norton, 1992). It tried to expand traditional financial views on the firm's performance by including four major themes: financial performance, customer perspective and satisfaction, internal business processes, learning and growth. It did not include any of the current nonfinancial factors considered relevant in corporate governance today.

and corporate policies, and how they are interconnected. A good framework to understand the firm's performance should take these dimensions into account.

The design of the holistic framework should integrate the main drivers of the firm's value creation. Figure 9.6 presents a summary of the firm's performance assessment framework presented in this chapter. It has three major building blocks: governance and management, people, strategy and corporate policies, and impact on specific stakeholders. The first block is related to the firm's governance and includes some main governance pillars: the firm's shareholders, board of directors, management team and its purpose (why the company exists and what it tries to achieve).

The second block is related to people, strategy and main corporate policies. This block suggests that management hires and develops people, defines a strategy and a business model to serve customers, establishes an organizational structure and approves corporate policies. The third block expresses the company's impact on key stakeholders stemming from the firm's governance and management. The governance and management decisions have some effects on customers, employees, economic value creation and shareholders, stakeholders, the environment and the organization's overall strength. The firm's impact is not static but dynamic. Impact assessment may lead companies to rethink their governance and management models, as well as some specific policies.

This framework can be beneficial for different companies. But each company is unique. In designing a model for impact assessment, the board and senior managers should consider the firm's unique features, its specific industry and set of activities and other factors, as well as their internal logic that makes sense in each case.

First and foremost, this framework considers that organizations come into being because there are some entrepreneurs, founders or investors who set it up. In many cases, founders appoint a board of directors and select a CEO and senior management team. At times, the board, senior management team or investors want to highlight

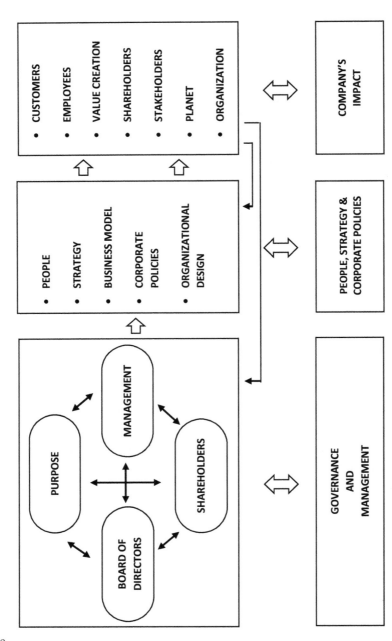

FIGURE 9.6 Corporate performance assessment: A holistic framework

a special purpose for the company. These four ingredients are the initial pillars of the company: shareholders, boards of directors, managers and a purpose.

The second block of this model highlights that managers hire and develop people, and define a strategy, business model and an organization to create value for customers. These decisions involve some specific choices on corporate policies that will determine the firm's evolution.

The third block of this model assesses the firm's impact. Performance assessment should aim to gather information on the firm's activity in a holistic way. Its operations will affect customers (satisfaction, retention or reputation), employees, as well as economic value creation, shareholders, other stakeholders (suppliers, partners and local communities), the planet (environmental effects) and the organization itself, starting with its own people and their ability to learn and create value in the future.

This description of the firm's effects and outcomes is more complex than purely financial information and involves some logical linkages and trade-offs. It is certainly difficult to reduce it to an index or a rating. It is understandable that some investors would prefer to simplify the complexity of a firm's operations and performance by using indexes, like the ESG State Street R factor or Morningstar Sustainability ratings, among many others.

Indexes and rankings are useful but sometimes overlook relevant factors. Moreover, they do not consider the consistency of ESG policies with the firm's strategy and business model. They do not discuss whether the index is rich enough to capture all factors relevant in the firm's performance, as well as their underlying causality relations. Some investors may narrow their focus to financial performance or simple indexes that offer a synthesis of other factors. But there are other investors who aspire to serve as good stewards of a firm. To this end, they should first gain a deep understanding of the firm, its strategy, its business model and how different dimensions of performance are connected with them.

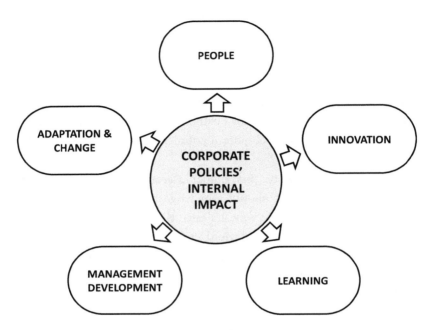

FIGURE 9.7 The firm's impact on the organization

Beyond investors' preferences, boards of directors and senior managers need to develop a model based on logic and causality that helps them integrate the firm's purpose and expected goals into strategy, strategic choices, business model and other central decisions. Moreover, they should carefully consider how past decisions regarding the board of directors, governance, senior managers and people recruitment and development have influenced strategy and strategic choices.

With these relationships in mind and the understanding that performance entails a range of factors, the evidence from the companies discussed in this book suggests several areas where firms should focus their performance assessments, all of them related to the key stakeholders (see Figure 9.5). The first is impact on customers: customer satisfaction, engagement, brand power and loyalty to the firm's products and services. The second is the firm's impact on people and employee development. The third area is the impact of the firm's policies on the organization itself: its learning, innovation and adaptability to change, among other dimensions. The fourth is the impact on shareholders, including both total financial returns as well as the quality of governance, stewardship and engagement. The fifth area is the impact on key stakeholders, including suppliers and the local communities where the company operates. The sixth area includes the company's environmental impact.

When the firm deploys its strategy and operations, its performance is not limited to its impact on external parties: customers, shareholders or the environment. The firm also has an internal impact on the organization through its decisions, policies and operations (Figure 9.7). The board of directors should assess this impact as well. It is possible to distinguish several areas of internal impact on the firm itself. The first area of the firm's internal impact is on its own employees and their motivation, engagement, compensation and development, and the basic policies the firm has in place: compensation, development and learning, diversity, inclusiveness and dimensions of the firm's culture such as collaboration, cross-functional learning or new opportunities. This set of indicators assesses how the learning occurs inside an organization, including both tacit and explicit knowledge.

The second is the impact on the organization and its capability to innovate and develop new initiatives to expand the firm's scope and better serve customers. Innovation, new investments and new business ventures fall under this umbrella. The third is the organization's ability to learn from external and internal changes, and its own decisions, in particular, wrong decisions and organizational mistakes.

The fourth is an assessment of leadership and management development. This is a complex dimension, but organizations that aspire to have a positive external impact also need to help their people grow. An indicator of success is the evolution of a richer and more diverse leadership pipeline. The fifth is the capacity to adapt and change in facing new challenges. This is particularly important in times of disruption. These challenges pose a risk for many companies but also offer opportunities. When senior managers consider them as such, they can be a source of innovation and help their employees grow and develop.

Boards of directors should understand these interlocking relationships within the unique context of their companies and work with the CEO and senior managers on a specific performance assessment model. As illustrated by the experiences of Unilever, Schneider Electric and Ingka, the board does not need to come up with a long list of indicators. Rather, they should focus on those that are truly relevant for both the nature of the company itself – including regulatory requirements – and the firm's explicit purpose.

In some cases, firms may want to highlight particular attributes or features in their notion of purpose, such as customers, people or environmental issues. Boards are free to expand the scope of these dimensions but need to connect them to the company's wider purpose and ensure they are tightly integrated into its strategy and business model.

9.5 FINAL REFLECTIONS

Assessing the firm's overall performance is a complex challenge. It should consider the diverse stakeholders to whom the firms and its board of directors are accountable. It should also include relevant financial and nonfinancial dimensions, which are properly integrated to avoid long lists of disconnected factors.

The experience of companies like Unilever, Ingka, Nestlé and Schneider Electric in reporting their overall performance offers interesting insights and reflections for all companies. The first is that companies that care about their environmental and social impact should clearly define which fundamental areas they want to emphasize beyond meeting regulatory standards. These areas should reflect their material importance for the firm's performance, P&L and balance sheet.

The second reflection is that boards of directors may want to be more ambitious in their objectives, by setting their sights over and above legal compliance. This was Unilever's tack when it defined targets aimed at enhancing the health and hygiene of millions of global consumers. In a similar vein, Schneider Electric minimized its negative environmental impact on an accelerated timeline, and promoted solutions for customers who want to reduce their carbon footprint.

These experiences highlight the need for firms to wisely choose and closely monitor specific impacts that are material to their activity and highlight an essential element of their purpose. Boards should explain the criteria behind these themes and their connection with the firm's overall strategy and business model. They should also make an effort to make sure that shareholders understand the framework and get them on board.

The third reflection is that companies need to consider the broader implications of their environmental and social impacts. These impacts can include a growth in revenues through innovation and premium prices, as well as positive and negative impacts on expenses and the firm's balance sheet, especially its capacity to raise equity or issue debt at lower costs due to a better environmental risk profile.

The fourth reflection is the need for the ESG goals and areas chosen by the board to be firmly integrated into the firm's purpose, strategy and business model. As the companies profiled in this chapter attest, there is clear evidence supporting the connection between ESG factors and value creation, which is an overarching responsibility for the board. This approach also shows that when companies consider different stakeholders in their decision-making, this process helps in building stronger and sustainable economic value for all, shareholders included.

The board's assessment of the firm's performance should be approached as more than a mere fulfilment of their duties. It is indispensable to shed light on how economic and noneconomic value are created through the company's policies and decisions, and assess the firm's potential to continue creating value sustainably in the future. This is an essential function of boards of directors and a key competence that they should develop.

10 Effective Boards of Directors for Better Corporate Governance
Creating a Masterpiece

The speed and depth of current disruptive changes that most companies should tackle make the role of boards of directors in the firm's governance more relevant than ever. Boards of directors are facing huge challenges in governing companies. Unfortunately, the assessment of the generation of boards of directors that was born in the 1990s is not particular positive and the pressure to rethink their role and functions in this time of widespread disruption is enormous. Understanding the factors that make boards of directors effective governance institutions is very relevant for companies, investors and society at large.

Theoretical and empirical studies on corporate governance provide some useful ideas for the design of boards of directors. But turning the board of directors into a more effective institution requires additional ingredients. In this book, I worked on detailed clinical studies of international companies, with dozens of structured interviews with their chairpersons, CEOs, board members and senior managers. Companies' clinical studies can offer a better understanding of the internal dynamics, competencies and evolution of an organization over a longer time frame. They also offer a more holistic and cross-functional perspective of a company. From this effort, some additional insights emerged on what good boards of directors do. In using clinical studies, prudence is indispensable to avoid undue generalizations.

In this book I present a holistic model of boards of directors, based upon these clinical studies: the board as the firm's steward. This model highlights six core functions that boards should assume to help firms deal with disruptive challenges effectively. To perform these functions successfully boards require some competencies, beyond the individual competencies that each board director has or should have. This framework has limits related to the companies considered in this book but provides some insights to reflect on the areas where boards of directors can actually improve their effectiveness. I would like to highlight in this section some ideas and reflections stemming from those companies and their boards of directors.

The first is that boards should pay attention to compliance. But the board's duty of care drives board members to do much more than just make sure that firms comply. Their duty as the firm's steward is to help develop the firm as an institution that serves a purpose and creates economic value sustainably. They should serve as stewards of the firm and the firm's purpose. They should help create value for shareholders and other stakeholders, and make sure that they can continue making the commitments that the firm needs for its long-term development. For boards, the option is not either profits or purpose to serve customers better. It is both profits and purpose, as discussed in Chapter 1. This requires some unique competencies and special work by boards of directors. But boards that govern with this criterion in mind can help companies develop for the long term.

The second is that the board is a governing institution – not only a mediating institution – appointed by shareholders, but whose responsibilities go beyond protecting shareholders. Companies should develop a strategy and a business model that serves their specific purpose and generates economic profits sustainably. Boards should govern companies and understand and help make the firm's strategy and business model work. Sustainable economic value creation points out that companies as organizations should be focused on serving customers' needs, and require the collaboration of people – their own employees, suppliers and other partners.

Companies operate in the specific context of local communities, and should respect them and contribute to them. They should also take care of the environment and reduce carbon emissions. When companies face challenges and constraints – raw material shortages, dominant suppliers, demanding customers, etc. – the entrepreneurial mindset of the CEO and her team, with the support of the board of directors, should help create business models that take into account these dimensions and create economic value. Boards of directors should govern companies by taking shareholders' needs and concerns into account, engaging core stakeholders (customers, employees and suppliers, among others) and making sure that these stakeholders can also benefit from the firm's activities in a fair way.

It falls upon the judgment of the board – taking into account legal and company provisions – how to consider stakeholders' expectations in the firm's business model, value creation and value distribution. The debate between shareholders' primacy and multistakeholder management does not provide an accurate picture of the real business world. Good boards should govern by engaging key stakeholders in order to create sustainable economic value for all. This requires that the board should make some decisions on specific trade-offs, since not all stakeholders are equal or have the same rights. Making these hard choices in a professional and fair way is what defines the quality of stakeholder management.

The third idea is that companies and their boards can greatly benefit from defining an explicit corporate purpose that explains why the company is in business and which specific social needs it tries to serve in a profitable way. A corporate purpose is not only an inspirational notion for employees or customers. It is a commitment that a company makes to explain why it exists and why a society gives it a license to operate. Moreover, it is also a reference for the type of products and services that the company wants to offer customers – avoiding, for instance, the pitfalls of reckless diversification. It also serves as a glue that can keep different stakeholders together with a purpose that goes beyond the individual and legitimate interests of each party. The firm's governance requires a long-term orientation, and purpose can be extremely useful in this process, as discussed in Chapter 2. Companies discussed in this book also show that purpose can have a deeper impact on companies when it is fully integrated into the firm's strategy, business model and major corporate policies. Purpose is at the heart of strategy and major strategic decisions.

The fourth idea is that boards should govern companies for the long term: This is a perspective that benefits almost all shareholders and stakeholders. Corporate strategy offers companies and its shareholders and other stakeholders a long-term orientation. Boards should have the competencies to discuss strategy and strategic issues with the CEO and the senior management team, and challenge managers' views, while contributing to improve their perspectives. The strategy function of boards – as discussed in Chapter 3 – goes beyond understanding the firm's strategic plan and the company's financial projections. It encompasses the set of key decisions that serve customers in a unique way and organize resources and capabilities to do so and create economic value sustainably.

The fifth is that strategy-making involves sometimes major corporate transformations. In this process, the firm's survival can be at stake. Orchestrating organizational change in a complex and disruptive context is a huge challenge for boards of directors, as presented in Chapter 4. They should steer the company toward a new destination, while still offering current customers what they need and creating economic value. In a nutshell, they should generate trust in what they do; and at the same time they should earn trust for what the company is not doing yet and plans to do in the future. The evidence from the companies discussed in this book and other empirical evidence is that corporate transformation is a complex process but one that truly needs the expertise, competence, guidance and support of the board of directors.

The sixth idea is that CEO nomination, development and eventual replacement is one of the most consequential decisions of boards of directors. The CEO nomination and succession processes are complex challenges for boards. The board should establish policies for leadership and employee development that go beyond the CEO appointment. In fact, the quality of the CEO appointment process goes hand in hand with the quality of the policies that the board has for people's hiring, engagement and development, as discussed in Chapter 5. Organizing the work of the board to allocate time to this important function is a critical function of the board. The board governs the company, but the firm's management is the responsibility of the CEO and her senior management team. The board should also pay careful attention to the process of hiring, developing, assessing and eventually replacing the members of the senior management team.

The seventh idea is that the board's decision-making process is not simple and linear. The board is a collegial group of persons who should work together to take care of the firm's governance. To become an effective governance institution, the board should work as an effective team, even if it has some structural features that do not make it easy, as discussed in Chapter 6. The way a board of directors is structured – its composition, members, mission, goals, method of work, culture of the board and personal values – has a direct influence on the decisions the board makes and the quality of the firm's governance. In particular, the way to define the relationships between the board and the CEO matters a lot, especially when companies face significant disruptions. The culture of the board also influences the firm's culture, as discussed in Chapter 7. Shareholders who care about the culture of a company should also place some attention on the culture of the board and the dynamics of the board as a human group.

The eight idea is that the board should also govern the engagement of shareholders and key stakeholders. In most cases, the board itself won't do so but will delegate this function to the CEO. Understanding that shareholders are heterogeneous is very relevant for corporate governance and the role of boards of directors, as presented in Chapter 8. Different shareholders have diverse expectations and time horizons. This is one of the reasons why the generic assumption of shareholder primacy is not a useful principle, since each shareholder is different from the rest. Effective boards should understand the different type of shareholders that they have, and take care of both shareholders and stakeholders. Failure to do so may have a negative impact on the firm's ability to create sustainable value in the long term. In the same way that good boards should understand the business well, they should also understand the contributions of different stakeholders well, and design the governance guidelines to engage with shareholders and stakeholders..

The final idea is that effective boards make sure that the firm delivers good economic value and also cares about the firm's overall impact, as presented in Chapter 9. This impact is not only reflected through ESG factors and indicators. Some ESG ratings may be partial and of limited value in predicting the firm's performance. The board should make sure that each company has a way to report on its activities and performance, connecting purpose with strategy and performance in some key areas (customers, people, economic value creation or the environment). In doing so, firms should follow the criteria and guidelines suggested by the international standards-setting bodies. But the specific areas of impact depend on the business model of each company and the type of stakeholders and shareholders that the company has. The board along with the CEO should make a careful assessment of which areas of impact to choose and why, and explain it clearly. Corporate purpose should influence this election.

It is not the job of boards to save capitalism. It is to make sure that the company they serve in is well governed so that it can achieve its purpose and goals, while the different shareholders and stakeholders keep making the necessary commitments that the company needs for its development. Good governance by boards is an unending process and board members should undertake it with the competence, passion and determination of great artists. Board directors can help create a unique masterpiece: sustainable companies that innovate and promote wealth and jobs for many people. In this time of great disruption, society needs well-governed companies that last and can generate prosperity. Boards can and should play an indispensable role in this extremely relevant challenge that contemporary societies have.

References

Adams, R. B. (2017). "Boards, and the Directors Who Sit on Them." In B. E. Hermalin and M. S. Weisbach, eds., *The Handbook of the Economics of Corporate Governance*, Volume 1. Amsterdam: North Holland, 291–382.

Adams, R. B. (2016). "Women on Boards: The Superheroes of Tomorrow?" *The Leadership Quarterly*, 27 (3), 371–386.

Adams, R. B. and D. Ferreira (2009). "Women in the Boardroom and Their Impact on Governance and Performance." *Journal of Financial Economics*, 94 (2), 291–309.

Adams, R. B., B. E. Hermalin and M. S. Weisbach (2010). "The Role of Boards of Directors in Corporate Governance: A Conceptual Framework and Survey." *Journal of Economic Literature*, 48 (1), 58–107.

Adams, R. B., M. Keloharju and S. Knupfer (2018). "Are CEOs Born Leaders? Lessons from Traits of a Million Individuals." *Journal of Financial Economics*, 130 (2), 392–408.

Adams, R. B. and T. Kirchmaier (2016). "Women on Boards in Finance and STEM Industries." *American Economic Review*, 106 (5), 277–281.

Aguilera, R., K. Desender, M. Lopez Puertas and J. H. Lee (2017). "The Governance Impact of a Changing Investor Landscape: Foreign Investors and Managerial Earnings Forecasts." *Journal of International Business Studies*, 48 (2), 195–221.

Aguilera, R., V. Filatotchev, H. Gospel and G. Jackson (2008). "An Organizational Approach to Comparative Corporate Governance: Costs, Contingencies and Complementarities." *Organization Science*, 19 (3), 475–492.

Alchian, A. and H. Demsetz (1972). "Production, Information Costs and Economic Organization." *American Economic Review*, 62 (5), 777–795.

Almandoz, J., Y. T. Lee and A. Ribera (2018). "Unleashing the Power of Purpose: Five Steps to Transform Your Business." *IESE Insight*, June.

Amit, R. and C. Zott (2021). *Business Model Innovation Strategy*. New York: John Wiley.

Andrews, K. R. (1971). *The Concept of Corporate Strategy*. Homewood, IL: Dow Jones Irwin.

Argandoña, A. (2008). "Integrating Ethics into Action Theory and Organizational Theory." *Journal of Business Ethics*, 78 (3), 435–446.

Argandoña, A. (1998). "The Stakeholder Theory and the Common Good." *Journal of Business Ethics*, 17, 1093–110.

Aristotle (2002). *Nichomachean Ethics*, edited by S. Broadie and C. Rowe. Oxford: Oxford University Press.

Azar, J. (2020). "The Common Ownership Trilemma." *The University of Chicago Law Review*, 87 (2), 263–296.

Azar, J., M. Duro, I. Kadach and G. Ormazabal (2021). "The Big Three and Corporate Carbon Emissions around the World." *Journal of Financial Economics*, 142 (2), 674–609.

Azar, J., M. C. Schmalz and I. Tecu (2018). "Anticompetitive Effects of Common Ownership." *Journal of Finance*, 73 (4), 1513–1565.

Azar, J. and X. Vives (2021). "General Equilibrium Oligopoly and Ownership Structure." *Econometrica*, 89 (3), 999–1048.

Bainbridge, S. M. (2018). "The Board of Directors." In J. N. Gordon and W. G. Ringe, eds., *The Oxford Handbook of Corporate Law and Governance*. Oxford: Oxford University Press, 275–333.

Bainbridge, S. M. (2018). *Outsourcing the Board*. Cambridge: Cambridge University Press.

Banerjee, A., M. Nordqvist and K. Hellerstedt (2020). "The Role of the Board Chair: A Literature Review and Suggestions for Future Research." *Corporate Governance International Review*, 28 (6), 372–405.

Barca, F. and M. Becht (2001). *The Control of Corporate Europe*. Oxford: Oxford University Press

Barnard, C. I. (1938). *The Functions of the Executive*. Cambridge, MA: Harvard University Press.

Barney, J. B. (2018). "Why Resource-Based Theory's Model of Profit Appropriation Must Incorporate a Stakeholder Perspective." *Strategic Management Journal*, 39 (13), 3305–3325.

Barney, J. B (1991). "Firm Resources and Sustained Competitive Advantage." *Journal of Management*, 17 (1), 99–120.

Bartlett, C. A. and S. Ghoshal, (1994). "Changing the Role of Top Management: From Strategy to Purpose." *Harvard Business Review*, November–December, 79–88.

Barton, D. and M. Wiseman (2014). "Focusing Capital on the Long Term," *Harvard Business Review*, 92 (1–2), 44–51.

Bebchuk, L. (2007). "The Myth of the Shareholder Franchise." *Vanderbilt Law Review*, 93, 675–700.

Bebchuk, L. (2005). "The Case for Increasing Shareholder Power." *Harvard Law Review*, 118 (3), 833–865.

Bebchuk, L., A. Brav and W. Jiang (2015). "The Long-Term Effects of Hedge Fund Activism." *Columbia Law Review*, 115 (5), 1085–1155.

Bebchuk, L. and J. Fried (2004). *Pay without Performance: The Unfulfilled Promised of Executive Compensation.* Cambridge, MA: Harvard University Press.

Bebchuk, L. and S. Hirst (2019). "The Specter of the Giant Three." *Boston University Law Review*, 99, 721–741.

Bebchuk, L. and R. Tallarita (2022). "Will Corporations Deliver Value to All Stakeholders." *Vanderbilt Law Review*, 75 (4), 1031–1091.

Bebchuk, L. and R. Tallarita (2020). "The Illusory Promise of Multistakeholder Governance." *Cornell Law Review*, 106, 91–178.

Becht, M., P. Bolton and A. Röekll (2003). "Corporate Governance and Control." In Constantinides, G. M., M. Harris and R. Stulz, eds., *Handbook of the Economics of Finance*, Volume 1. Amsterdam: Elsevier, 1–109.

Becht, M., J. Franks, J. Grant and H. F. Wagner (2017). "Returns to Hedge-Fund Activism: An International Study." *Review of Financial Studies*, 30 (9), 2933–2971.

Becht, M., J. Franks, C. Mayer and S. Rossi (2009). "Returns to Shareholder Activism: Evidence from a Clinical Study of the Hermes UK Focus Fund." *Review of Financial Studies*, 22 (8), 3093–3129.

Becht, M., A. Polo and S. Rossi (2016). "Does Mandatory Shareholder Voting Prevent Bad Acquisitions?" *Review of Financial Studies*, 29 (11), 3035–3067.

Becht, M. and A. Röell (1999). "Blockholdings in Europe: An International Comparison." *European Economic Review*, 43 (4), 1049–1056.

Berle, A. A. (1931). "Corporate Powers as Powers in Trust." *Harvard Law Review*, 44, 1049.

Berle, A. A. and G. C. Means (1932). *The Modern Corporation and Private Property.* New York: Transaction Publishers.

Berrone, P., L. Gómez-Mejía (2009). "Environmental Preferences and Executive Compensation: An Integrated Agency-Institutional Perception." *Academy of Management Journal*, 52 (1), 103–126.

Birkinshaw, J., N. J. Foss and S. Lindenberg (2014). "Combining Profit with Purpose." *MIT Sloan Management Review*, 55 (3), 49–56.

Blair, M. M. (1995). *Ownership and Control: Rethinking Corporate Governance for the 21st Century.* Washington, DC: Brookings Institution.

Blair, M. M. and L. A. Stout (1999). "A Team Production Theory of Corporate Law." *Virginia Law Review*, 85 (2), 247–328.

Bloom, N., R. Sadun and J. Van Reenen (2012). "Americans do I.T. Better: US Multinationals and the Productivity Miracle." *American Economic Review*, 102 (1), 167–201.

Bloom, N. and J. Van Reenen (2007). "Measuring and Explaining Management Practices Across Firms and Countries." *Quarterly Journal of Economics*, 122 (4), 1351–1408.

Blount, S. and P. Leinwand (2019). "Why Are We Here?" *Harvard Business Review*, 97 (6), 132–139.

Boivie, S., M. C. Whiters, S. D. Graffin and K. G. Corley (2021). "Corporate Directors' Implicit Theories of the Roles and Duties of Boards." *Strategic Management Journal*, 42, 1662–1695.

Bolton, P. (2021). "Company Valuation and the Effects of ESG Factors." Presented at the 2020 IESE ECGI Corporate Governance Conference. *Journal of Applied Corporate Finance*, 33 (2), 50–59.

Bolton, P. (2014). "Corporate Finance, Incomplete Contracts and Corporate Control." *Journal of Law, Economics and Organization*, 30, S1, 64–81.

Bolton, P., M. Brunnermeier and L. Veldkamp (2013). "Leadership, Coordination and Corporate Culture." *Review of Economic Studies*, 80 (2), 512–537.

Bolton, P., T. Li, E. Ravina and H. Rosenthal (2020). "Investor Ideology." *Journal of Financial Economics*, 137 (2), 320–352.

Bower, J. L. (2007). *The CEO Within: Why Inside Outsiders Are the Key to Succession.* Boston: Harvard Business School Press.

Bower, J. L. (1970). *Managing the Resource Allocation Process.* Boston: Harvard Business School Press.

Bower, J. L. and L. S. Paine (2017). "The Error at the Heart of Corporate Leadership." *Harvard Business Review*, May–June, 50–60.

Bratton, W. W. (2021). "Team Production Revisited." *Vanderbilt Law Review*, 75, 102–142.

Brav, A., W. Jiang, F. Partnoy and R. Thomas (2008). "Hedge Fund Activism, Corporate Governance, and Firm Performance." *Journal of Finance*, 63 (4), 1729–1775.

Brown, S. L. and Eisenhardt, K. M. (1998). *Competing on the Edge: Strategy as Structured Chaos.* Cambridge, MA: Harvard Business Review Press.

Cadbury, A. (2002). *Corporate Governance and Chairmanship.* Oxford: Oxford University Press.

Cadbury, A. et al. (1992). *Financial Aspects of Corporate Governance.* London.

Caldart, A. and J. Canals (2018). "Almirall." IESE Publishing, Case.

Cameron, K. S. and R. E. Quinn (2011). *Diagnosing and Changing Organizational Culture Based on the Competing Values Framework.* San Francisco: Jossey Bass.

Canals, J. (2019). "Unilever." Case, IESE Publishing.

Canals, J. (2018). "Cellnex." Case, IESE Publishing.

Canals, J. (2017). "Werfen." Case, IESE Publishing.

Canals, J. (2012). "Rethinking Global Leadership Development: Designing New Paradimgs." In J. Canals, ed., *Leadership Development in a Global World*. Houndmills: Palgrave Macmillan, 29–61.

Canals, J. (2010a). *Building Respected Companies*. Cambridge: Cambridge University Press.

Canals, J. (2010b). "Rethinking the Firm's Mission and Purpose." *European Management Review*, Special Issue, 7 (4), 195–204.

Canals, J. (2000). *Managing Corporate Growth*. Oxford: Oxford University Press.

Cappelli, P. (2013). *Strategic Talent Management: Contemporary Issues in an International Context*. Cambridge: Cambridge University Press.

Cappelli, P. and J. R. Keller (2014). "Talent Management: Conceptual Approaches and Practical Challenges." *Annual Review of Organizational Psychology and Organizational Behavior*, 1, 305–331.

Cardona, P. and H. Wilkinson (2008). "Bertelsmann." Case, IESE Publishing.

Carpenter, M. A. and J. D. Westphal (2001). "The Strategic Context of External Network Ties: Examining the Impact of Director Appointments on Board Involvement in Strategic Decision Making." *Academy of Management Journal*, 44 (4), 639–660.

Carson, J. B., P. E. Tesluk and J. A. Marrone (2007). "Shared Leadership in Teams: An Investigation of Antecedent Conditions and Performance." *Academy of Management Journal*, 50 (5), 1217–1234.

Carter, C. B. and Lorsch, J. W. (2003). *Back to the Drawing Board*. Boston: Harvard Business School Press.

Casadesus-Masanell, R. and J. E. Ricart (2011). "How to Design a Winning Business Model." *Harvard Business Review*, January–February, 100–107.

Cassiman, B. and G. Valentini (2018). "Open Innovation: Are Inbound and Outbound Knowledge Flows Really Complementary?" *Strategic Management Journal*, 37 (6), 1034–1046.

Chandler, Jr., A. D. (1990). *Scale and Scope: The Dynamics of Industrial Capitalism*. Cambridge, MA: Harvard University Press.

Chandler, Jr., A. D. (1977). *The Visible Hand: The Managerial Revolution in American Business*. Cambridge, MA: Harvard University Press.

Charan, R., D. Carey and M. Useem (2014). *Boards That Lead*. Boston: Harvard Business School Publishing.

Cheffins, B. R. (2020). "Stop Blaming Milton Friedman." ECGI Law Working Paper, 523/2020.

Cheffins, B. R. (2019). *The Public Company Transformed*. Oxford: Oxford University Press.

Cheng, J. Y.-J., B. Groysberg, P. Healy and R. Vijayaraghavan (2021). "Directors' Perception of Board Effectiveness and Internal Operations." *Management Science*, 67 (10), 5969–6627.

Cleary Gotlieb Steen and Hamilton (2019). "Hertz Pursues Novel Theory to Hold Former Management Team Personally Liable for Restatement and Ensuing Legal Proceedings." May 7, 2019, Clearly M&A and Corporate Governance Blog.

Coffee, Jr., J. C. (2020). "The Future of Disclosure: ESG, Common Ownership and Systematic Risk." ECGI Law Working Paper.

Coffee, Jr., J. C (2006). *Gatekeepers: The Professions and Corporate Governance.* Oxford: Oxford University Press.

Collins, J. C. and J. I. Porras (1996). "Building Your Company's Vision." *Harvard Business Review*, September–October, 65–77.

Collis, D. J. (2021). "Why Do So Many Strategies Fail?" *Harvard Business Review*, 99 (4), 82–93.

Collis, D. and M. Rukstad (2008). "Can You Say What Your Strategy Is?" *Harvard Business Review*, April, 82–90.

Colvin, G. (2019). "What the Hell Happened at GE?" *Fortune*, May 24.

Cornelli, F., Z. Kominek and A. Ljungqvist (2013). "Monitoring Managers: Does It Matter?" *Journal of Finance*, 68 (2), 431–481.

Cossin, D. (2020). *High Performance Boards.* Chichester: John Wiley.

Cossin, D. and O. Boon Hwee (2016). *Inspiring Stewardship.* Chichester: John Wiley.

Crooks, E. (2018) "Industrial Stalwart GE Contemplates an Overhaul." *Financial Times*, October 5.

Cuñat, V., M. Giné and M. Guadalupe (2012). "The Vote Is Cast: The Effect of Corporate Governance on Shareholder Value." *Journal of Finance*, 67 (5), 1943–1977.

Cusumano, M. A., A. Gawer and D. B. Yoffie (2019). *The Economics of Business Platforms.* Boston: Harvard Business School Press.

Davies, R., A. G. Haldane, M. Nielsen and S. Pezzini (2014). "Measuring the Costs of Short-Termism." *Journal of Financial Stability*, 12, 16–20.

Daems, H. (2020). *Insights from the Boardroom.* Brussels: Lanoo Campus.

Daily, C. M. and C. Schwenk (1996). "Chief Executive Officers, Top Management Teams and Boards of Directors: Congruent or Counterveiling Forces?" *Journal of Management*, 22 (2), 185–208.

Dasgupta, A., V. Fos and Z. Sautner (2021). "Institutional Investors and Corporate Governance." ECGI Finance Working Paper 700/2020.

Davis, G. (2016). *The Vanishing American Corporation*. Oakland, CA: Berrett-Koehler Publishers.

Davis, J. H., D. Schoorman and L. Donaldson (1997). "Toward a Stewardship Theory of Management." *The Academy of Management Review*, 22 (1), 20–47.

Davoudi, L., C. McKenna and R. Olegario (2018). "The Historical Role of Corporation in Society." *Journal of the British Academy*, 6 (1), 17–47.

DeHaan, E., D. F. Larcker and C. McClure (2019). "Long-Term Economic Consequences of Hedge-Fund Activist Interventions." *Review of Accounting Studies*, 24 (2), 536–569.

Donaldson, G. and J. W. Lorsch (1983). *Decision-Making at the Top*. New York: Basic Books.

Dodd, E. M. (1932). "For Whom Are Corporate Managers Trustees?" *Harvard Law Review*, 45, 1145–1163.

Doz, Y. and A. Cuomo (2019). "Corporate Governance 4.0: Facing Interdependency and Speed in a Complex World." Insead Working Paper.

Drucker, P. (1973). *Management: Tasks, Responsibilities, Practices*. New York: Harper and Row.

Drucker, P. (1955). *The Practice of Management*. New York: Harper and Row.

Du, S., C. B. Bhattasharya and S. Sen (2007). "Reaping Relational Rewards from Social Responsibility: The Role of Competitive Positioning." *International Journal of Research in Marketing*, 24 (3), 224–241.

Duane Ireland, R. and M. A. Hitt (1992). "Mission Statements: Importance, Challenge and Recommendations for Development." *Business Horizons*, 35 (3), 34–42.

Eccles, R. G. and S. Klimenko (2019). "The Investor Revolution." *Harvard Business Review*, 97 (3), 106–116.

Eccles, R. G., I. Ioannou and G. Serafeim (2014). "The Impact of Corporate Sustainability on Organizational Processes and Performance." *Management Science*, 60 (11), 2835–2857.

Edmans, A. (2020). *Growing the Pie*. Cambridge: Cambridge University Press.

Edmans, A. (2011). "Does the Stock Market Fully Value Intangibles? Employee Satisfaction and Equity Prices." *Journal of Financial Economics*, 101, 621–640.

Edmans, A. and X. Gabaix (2016). "Executive Compensation: A Modern Primer." *Journal of Economic Literature*, 54 (4), 1232–1287.

Edmans, A. and C. G. Holderness (2017). "Blockholders: A Survey of Theory and Evidence." In Hermalin, B. E. and M. S. Weisbach, eds., *The Handbook of the Economics of Corporate Governance*, Volume 1, Amsterdam: North Holland, 541–636.

Edmonson, A. C. (2018). *The Fearless Organization: Creating Psychological Safety in the Workplace for Learning, Innovation and Growth.* New York: John Wiley.

Edmonson, A. C. (2012). *Teaming: How Organizations Learn and Compete in the Knowledge Economy.* New York: John Wiley

Eeckhout, J. (2021). *The Profit Paradox.* Princeton, NJ: Princeton University Press.

Eisenhardt, K. M. (1989). "Building Theories from Case Study Research." *Academy of Management Review,* 14 (4), 532–550.

Eisenhardt, K. M. and M. E. Graebner (2007). "Theory Building from Cases: Opportunities and Challenges." *Academy of Management Journal,* 50 (1), 25–32.

Ess, H., J. Gabrielsson and M. Huse (2009). "Toward a Behavioral Theory of Boards and Corporate Governance." *Corporate Governance: An International Review,* 17 (3), 307–319.

Faeste, L. and J. Hemerling (2016). *Transformation.* Boston: Boston Consulting Group.

Fama, E. F. and M. J. Jensen (1983). "Separation of Ownership and Control." *Journal of Law and Economics,* 26 (2), 301–325.

Fernandes, N. (2019). *The Value Killers.* Houndmills: Palgrave Macmillan.

Ferrell, A., H. Liang and L. Renneboog (2016). "Socially Responsible Firms." *Journal of Financial Economics,* 122 (3), 585–606.

Finck, L. (2019). "A Fundamental Reshaping of Finance." Letter to CEOs. www.blackrock.com (January 30, 2019).

Financial Reporting Council (2018). *UK Corporate Governance Code.*

Finkelstein, S. (1992). "Power in Top Management Teams: Dimensions, Measurement and Validation." *Academy of Management Journal,* 35, 505–538.

Finkelstein, S. and D. C. Hambrick (1990). "Top-Management-Team Tenure and Organizational Outcomes: The Moderating Role of Managerial Discretion." *Administrative Science Quarterly,* 35 (3), 484–503.

Finkelstein, S., D. C. Hambrick and A. A. Canella, Jr. ed. (2009). *Strategic Leadership: Theory and Research on Executives, Top Management Teams and Boards.* New York: Oxford University Press.

Fisch, J. E., A. Hamdani and S. D. Solomon (2020). "The New Titans of Wall Street: A Theoretical Framework for Passive Investors." *University of Pennsylvania Law Review,* 168, 17–72.

Fisch, J. E. and S. M. Seep. (2020). "Shareholder Collaboration." *Texas Law Review,* 98, 863–920.

Fisch, J. E. and S. D. Solomon (2021). "Should Corporations Have a Purpose?" *Texas Law Review,* 99, 1309–1346.

Flammer, C. (2015). "Does Corporate Social Responsibility Lead to Superior Financial Performance? A Regression Discontinuity Approach." *Management Science*, 61 (11), 2549–2568.

Flammer, C. (2010). "Corporate Social Responsibility and Shareholder Reaction: The Environmental Awareness of Investors." *Academy of Management Journal*, 56 (3), 758–781.

Flammer, C. and P. Bansal (2017). "Does a Long-Term Orientation Create Value? Evidence from a Regression Discontinuity." *Strategic Management Journal*, 38 (9), 1827–1847.

Fletcher, L. and L. Abboud (2021). "The Little Known Activist Fund Who Helped Topple Danone's CEO." *Financial Times*, March 24.

Franks, J. and C. Mayer (2017). "Evolution of Ownership and Control around the World: The Changing Face of Capitalism." In Hermalin, B. E. and M. S. Weisbach, eds., *The Handbook of the Economics of Corporate Governance*, Volume 1, Amsterdam: North Holland, 685–735.

Franks, J. and C. Mayer (2001). "Ownership and Control of German Corporations." *Review of Financial Studies*, 14 (4), 943–977.

Franks, J., C. Mayer, P. Volpin and H. J. Wagner (2012). "The Life Cycle of Family Ownership: International Evidence." *Review of Financial Studies*, 25 (6), 1675–1712.

Freeman, R. E. (1984). *Strategic Management: A Stakeholder Approach*. New York: Cambridge University Press.

Friedman, M. (1970). "The Social Responsibility of Business Is to Increase Its Profits." *New York Times*, September 13.

Friedman, M. (1962). *Capitalism and Freedom*. Chicago: University of Chicago Press.

Garg, S. and K. M. Eisenhardt (2017). "Unpacking the CEO–Board Relationship: How Strategy-Making Happens in Entrepreneurial Firms." *Academy of Management Journal*, 60 (5), 1828–1858.

Garg, S. and N. Furr (2017). "Venture Boards: Past Insights, Future Directions and Transition to Public Firm Boards." *Strategic Entrepreneurship Journal*, 11, 326–343.

Gartenberg, C. M., A. Prat and G. Serafeim (2019). "Corporate Purpose and Financial Performance." *Organization Science*, 30 (1), 1–18.

Gartenberg, C. M. and G. Serafeim (2019). "Corporate Purpose and Firm Ownership." SSRN (August 20).

Gast, A., P. Illanes, N. Probst, B. Schaninger and B. Simpson (2020). "Purpose: Shifting from Why to How." *McKinsey Quarterly*, April.

Ghemawat, P. (1991). *Commitment: The Dynamic of Strategy*. New York: Free Press.

Ghemawat, P. and B. Cassiman (2007). "Introduction to the Special Issue on Strategy Dynamics." *Management Science*, 53 (4), 529–536.

Ghoshal, S. and C. A. Bartlett (1997). *The Individualized Corporation*. New York: Harper Business.

Ghoshal, S. and P. Moran (1996). "Bad for Practice. A Critique of the Transaction Cost Theory." *Academy of Management Review*, 21 (1), 13–47.

Gilson, R. J. (2018). "From Corporate Law to Corporate Governance." In J. N. Gordon, and W. G. Ringe, eds., *The Oxford Handbook of Corporate Law and Governance*. Oxford: Oxford University Press, 3–28.

Gilson, R. L. and J. N. Gordon (2019). "Boards 3.0: An Introduction." *The Business Lawyer*, 74, 351–366.

Gompers, P. A., S. N. Kaplan and V. Mukharlyamov (2016). "What Do Private Equity Firms Say They Do?" *Journal of Financial Economics*, 121 (3), 449–476.

Gordon, J. N. (2021). "Systematic Stewardship." ECGI Law Working Paper, 566.

Gordon, J. N. and W. G. Ringe, eds. (2018). *The Oxford Handbook of Corporate Law and Governance*. Oxford: Oxford University Press.

Gorton, G. B., J. Grennan and A. K. Zentefis (2021). "Corporate Culture." SSRN Working Paper.

Grant, A. M. (2008). "Does Intrinsic Motivation Fuel the Prosocial Fire? Motivational Synergy in Predicting Persistence, Performance and Productivity." *Journal of Applied Psychology*, 93 (1), 48–58.

Grossman, S. and O. Hart, O. (1986). "The Costs and Benefits of Ownership: A Theory of Vertical and Lateral Integration." *Journal of Political Economy*, 94 (4), 691–719.

Groysberg, B., J. Lee and J. Price (2018). "The Leader's Guide to Corporate Culture." *Harvard Business Review*, 96 (1), 44–52.

Guiso, L., P. Sapienza and L. Zingales (2015). "The Value of Corporate Culture." *Journal of Financial Economics*, 117, 60–76.

Haas, M. and M. Mortensen (2016). "The Secrets of Great Teamwork." Harvard Business Review online, June 17.

Hackman, J. R. (2002). *Leading Teams: Setting the Stage for Great Performances*. Boston: Harvard Business Review Press.

Hambrick, D. C. (2007). "Upper Echelons Theory: An Update." *Academy of Management Review*, 32 (2), 334–343.

Hambrick, D. C. (1987). "The Top Management Team: Key to Strategic Success." *California Management Review*, 30, 88–108.

Hambrick, D. C. and P. A. Mason (1984). "Upper Echelons: The Organization as a Reflection of Its Top Managers." *Academy of Management Review*, 9, 193–206

Hambrick, D. C. and T. J. Quigley (2014). "Towards More Accurate Contextualization of the CEO Effect on Firm Performance." *Strategic Management Journal*, 35 (4), 473–491.

Hambrick, D. C. and A. J. Wowak (2021). "CEO Sociopolitical Activism: A Shareholder Alignment Model." *Academy of Management Review*, 46 (1), 33–59.

Hamel, G. and C. K. Prahalad (1994). *Competing for the Future*. Boston: Harvard Business School Press.

Hansmann, H. (1996). *The Ownership of Enterprise*. Cambridge, MA: Harvard University Press.

Hart, O. (2017). "Incomplete Contracts and Control." *American Economic Review*, 107 (7), 1731–1752.

Hart, O. (1995). *Firms, Contracts and Financial Structure*. Oxford: Oxford University Press.

Hart, O. and L. Zingales (2017). "Companies Should Maximize Shareholder Welfare Not Market Value." *Journal of Law, Finance and Accounting*, 2, 247–274.

Haskel, J. and S. Westlake (2018). *Capitalism without Capital: The Rise of the Intangible Economy*. Princeton, NJ: Princeton University Press.

Helfat, C. E. and M. Peteraf (2003). "The Dynamic Resource-Based View: Capability Lifecycles." *Strategic Management Journal*, 24 (10), 997–1010.

Henderson, R. (2020). *Reimagining Capitalism in a World of Fire*. New York: Bloomsbury.

Henderson, R. and G. Serafeim (2020). "Tackling Climate Change Requires Organizational Purpose." *American Economic Review, Papers and Proceedings*, 110, 177–180.

Henderson, R. and E. Van den Steen (2015). "Why Do Firms Have Purpose? The Firm's Role as a Carrier of Identity and Reputation." *American Economic Review*, 105 (5), 326–330.

Hermalin, B. E. and M. S. Weisbach (2017). *The Handbook of the Economics of Corporate Governance*, Volume 1. Amsterdam: North Holland.

Hermalin, B. E. and M. S. Weisbach (1988). "The Determinants of Board Composition." *RAND Journal of Economics*, 19, 589–606.

Hill, J. (2020a). "The Conundrum of Common Ownership." *Vanderbilt Journal of Trasnational Law*, 53 (3), 881–906.

Hill, J. (2020b). "Shifting Contours of Directors' Fiduciary Duties and Norms in Comparative Corporate Governance." *UC Irvine Journal of International, Transnational and Comparative Law*, 5 (1), 163–183.

Hinchliffe, E. (2021). "The Number of Women Running Global 500 Businesses Soars to an All-Time High." *Fortune*, August 2.

Hitt, M. A., R. Duane Ireland and R. E. Hoskinsson (2015). *Strategic Management: Competitiveness and Globalization*. Boston: Cengage Learning.

Holmstrom, B. (1982). "Moral Hazard in Teams." *Bell Journal of Economics*, 13, (82), 324–340.

Holmstrom, B. and P. Milgrom (1991). "Multi-task Principal Agent Problem: Incentive Contracts, Asset Ownership and Job Design." *Journal of Law, Economics and Organization*, 7, Special Issue, 24–52.

Holmstrom, B. and P. Polman (2021). "Corporate Purpose and the Theory of the Firm." Special Session in the 2020 IESE ECGI Corporate Governance Conference. *Journal of Applied Corporate Finance*, 33 (2), 60–69.

Holmstrom, B. and J. E. Ricart i Costa (1986). "Managerial Incentives and Capital Management." *Quarterly Journal of Economics*, 101 (4), 835–860.

Holmstrom, B. and J. Tirole (1989). "The Theory of the Firm." In R. Schmalensee and R. Willig, eds., *Handbook of Industrial Economics*, Part 1. Amsterdam: Elsevier, 61–133.

Hoskisson, R. E. and M. A. Hitt (1994). *Downsizing*. Oxford: Oxford University Press.

Hoskisson, R. E. and R. A. Johnson (1992). "Corporate Restructuring and Strategic Change: The Effect on Diversification Strategy and R&D Intensity." *Strategic Management Journal*, 13, 625–634.

Huse, M. (2018). *Value Creating Boards*. Cambridge: Cambridge University Press.

Huse, M. (2007). *Boards, Governance and Value Creation: The Human Side of Corporate Governance*. Cambridge: Cambridge University Press.

Ioannou, I. and G. Serafeim (2019). "Corporate Sustainability: A Strategy?" Harvard Business School, Working Paper 19-065.

Ioannou, I. and G. Serafeim (2015). "The Impact of Corporate Social Responsibility on Investment Recommendations: Analysts' Perceptions and Shifting Institutional Logics." *Strategic Management Journal*, 36 (7), 1053–1081.

Ioannou, I. and G. Serafeim (2012). "What Drives Corporate Social Performance? The Role of Nation-Level Institutions." *Journal of International Business Studies*, 43 (9), 834–864.

Jensen, M. C. (1989). "The Eclipse of the Public Corporation." *Harvard Business Review*, September–October, 61–75.

Jensen, M. C. and Meckling, W. H. (1976). "The Theory of the Firm: Managerial Behavior, Agency Costs and Ownership Structure." *Journal of Financial Economics*, 3 (4), 305–360.

Johnson, R. A., R. E. Hoskisson and M. A. Hitt (1993). "Board of Director Involvement in Restructuring: The Effects of Board versus Managerial Controls and Characteristics." *Strategic Management Journal*, 14 (Special Issue): 33–50.

Joly, H. (2021). "How to Lead in the Stakeholder Era." *Harvard Business Review* online, May 13.

Kahneman, D. (2011). *Think Fast and Slow*. London: Allen Lane.

Kantor, J. and D. Streitfeld (2015). "Wrestling Big Ideas in a Bruising Workplace." *The New York Times*, August 15.

Kaplan, R. S. and D. P. Norton (1996). *The Balanced Scorecard*. Boston: Harvard Business School Press.

Kaplan, S. N. and M. Sorensen (2020). "Are CEOs Different?" NBER Working Paper.

Katelouzou, D. (2019). "Shareholder stewardship." In B. Sjafjell and C. M. Bruner, eds., *The Cambridge Handbook of Corporate Law, Corporate Governance and Sustainability*. Cambridge: Cambridge University Press, 581–595.

Katzenbach, J. R. and D. K. Smith (2015). *The Wisdom of Teams*. Boston: Harvard Business Review Press.

Khurana, R. (2004). *Searching for a Corporate Savior*. Princeton: NJ: Princeton University Press.

Khurana, R. and K. Pick (2005). "The Social Nature of Boards." *Brooklyn Law Review*, 70 (4), 1259–1285.

Kingsmill, D., J. Maeztu and J. Viñals (2021). "How Should Boards of Directors Deal with Corporate Purpose?" Discussion at the 2020 IESE ECGI Corporate Governance Conference. *Journal of Applied Corporate Finance*, 33 (2), 86–94.

Kirsch, A. (2017). "The Gender Composition of Corporate Boards: A Review and a Research Agenda." *Leadership Quarterly*, June.

Klarner, P., T. Yoshikawa and M. E. Hitt (2021). "A Capability-Based View of Boards: A New Conceptual Framework for Board Governance." *Academy of Management Perspectives*, 35 (1), 123–141.

Kochan, T. (2015). "The Leaders' Choice." *MIT Sloan Management Review*, September, 59–63.

Kotter, J. P. (2012). *Leading Change*. Boston: Harvard Business Review Press.

Kotter, J. P. and J. L. Heskett (1992). *Corporate Culture and Performance*. New York: Free Press.

Kouzes, J. and B. Z. Possner (1987). *The Leadership Challenge*. Hoboken, NJ: John Wiley.

La Porta, R. F., F. Lopez de Silanes and A. Shleifer (1999). "Corporate Ownership Around the World." *Journal of Finance*, 54 (2), 471–517.

La Porta, R., F. Lopez de Silanes, A. Shleifer and R. W. Vishny (2000). "Investor Protection and Corporate Governance." *Journal of Financial Economics*, 58 (1–2), 3–27.

La Porta, R., F. Lopez de Silanes, A. Shleifer and R. W. Vishny (1998). "Law and Finance." *Journal of Political Economy*, 106 (6), 1113–1155.

Larcker, D. F., A. L. McCall and G. Ormazabal (2015). "Outsourcing Shareholder Voting to Proxy Advisory Firms." *Journal of Law and Economics*, 58 (1), 173–204.

Larcker, D. F., G. Ormazabal and D. J. Taylor (2011). "The Market Reaction to Corporate Governance Regulations." *Journal of Financial Economics*, 101 (2), 431–448.

Larcker, D. F. and B. Tayan (2016). *Corporate Governance Matters*. Old Tappan, NJ: Pearson Education.

Leblanc, R. and J. R. S. Fraser (2016). *Handbook of Board Governance*. Hoboken, NJ: Wiley.

Lipton, M. (2019). "Purpose, Stakeholders, ESG and Sustainable Long-Term Investment." New York: Wachtell, Lipton, Rosen & Katz.

Lipton, M. (2017). *The New Paradigm*. New York: World Economic Forum and Wachtell, Lipton, Rosen & Katz.

Lorsch, J., ed. (2012). *The Future of Boards*. Boston: Harvard Business Review Press.

Malnight, T. W., I. Buche and Ch. Dhanaraj (2019). "Put Purpose at the Core of Your Strategy." *Harvard Business Review*, September–October.

Masclans, R. and J. Canals (2021). "Ingka." Case, IESE Publishing.

Masclans, R. and J. Canals, J. (2020). "Amadeus." Case, IESE Publishing.

Masclans, R. and J. Canals (2019). "Schneider Electric." Case, IESE Publishing.

Masclans, R., J. Tàpies and J. Canals (2020). "Fluidra." Case, IESE Publishing.

Mayer, C. (2021). "The Future of the Corporation and the Economics of Purpose." *Journal of Management Studies*, 58 (3), 887–900.

Mayer, C. (2020). "Ownership, Agency and Trusteeship." *Oxford Review of Economic Policy*, 36, 223–240.

Mayer, C. (2020). "Shareholderism versus Stakeholderism. A Misconceived Contradiction." ECGI Working Paper, 552.

Mayer, C. (2018a). *Prosperity*. Oxford: Oxford University Press.

Mayer, C. (2018b). "The Future of the Corporation: Towards Humane Business." *Journal of the British Academy*, 6 (1), 1–16.

Mayer, C. (2013). *Firm Commitment*. Oxford: Oxford University Press.

Mayer, C. and L. Zingales (2021). "Are Corporate Statements More Than Verbiage?"Special Session at the 2020 IESE ECGI Corporate Governance Conference. *Journal of Applied Corporate Finance*, 33 (2), 41–49.

McDonald, M. L. and J. D. Westphal (2003). "Getting By with the Advice of Their Friends: CEOs' Advice Networks and Firms' Strategic Responses to Poor Performance." *Administrative Science Quarterly*, 48 (1), 1–32.

McGahan, A. and M. E. Porter (1997). "How Much Does Industry Matter, Really?" *Strategic Management Journal*, 18 (1), 15–30.

McGrath, R. G. (2013). *The End of Competitive Advantage: How to Keep Your Strategy Moving as Fast as Your Business*. Boston: Harvard Business Review Press.

McNabb, B., R. Charan and D. Carey (2021). "Engaging with Your Investors." *Harvard Business Review*, 99 (4), 114–122.

McNulty, T. and A. Pettigrew (1999). "Strategist on the Board." *Organization Studies*, 20 (1), 47–74.

McNulty, T. and A. Pettigrew (1997). "The Contribution, Power and Influence of Part-Time Board Members." *Corporate Governance: An International Review*, 4 (3), 160–179.

Melé, D. (2009). *Business Ethics in Action*. Houndmills: Palgrave Macmillan.

Melé, D. and A. Corrales (2005). "Medtronic." Case, IESE Publishing.

Miles, R. H. (2010). "Accelerating Corporate Transformations (Don't Lose Your Nerve!)." *Harvard Business Review*, 88 (1), 68–75.

Milgrom, P. and J. Roberts (1992). *Economics, Organization and Management*. New York: John Wiley.

Millstein, I. (2017). *The Activist Director*. New York: Columbia Business School Press.

Minztberg, H. (2007). *Tracking Strategies*. Oxford: Oxford University Press.

Mocsary, G. A. (2016). "Freedom of Corporate Purpose." *BYUL Review*, 5 (4), 1320–1394.

Monks, R. G. and N. Minow (2011). *Corporate Governance*. New York: John Wiley.

Montgomery, C. (2012). *The Strategist*. New York: HarperCollins.

Moyo, D. (2021). *How Boards Work*. New York: Basic Books.

Neckebrouck, J., M. Meuleman and S. Manigart (2021). "Governance Implications of Attracting External Equity Investors in Private Equity Firms." *Academy of Management Perspectives*, 35 (1), 25–44.

Nooyi, I. and V. Govindarajan (2020). "Becoming a Better Corporate Citizen." *Harvard Business Review*, 98 (2), 94–103.

Nueno, P. (2016). *The Board in 2020. The Future of Company Boards*. Barcelona: LID Publishing.

OECD (2021). *Corporate Governance Factbook*. Paris.

OECD (1999). *Principles of Corporate Governance*. Paris.

Ormazabal, G. (2018). "The Role of Stakeholders in Corporate Governance: A View from Accounting Research." *Foundations and Trends in Accounting*, 11 (4), 193–290.

O'Reilly, C. A., K. Y. Williams and C. B. Barsade (1999). "The Impact of Relational Demography in Teamwork: When Differences Make a Difference." Academy of Management Proceedings, G1–G6.

O'Toole, J. (2019). *The Enlightened Capitalists*. New York: HarperCollins.

Palepu, K. (2012). "Focusing on Strategy to Govern Effectively." In J. Lorsch, ed., *The Future of Boards*. Boston: Harvard Business Review Press, 37–52

Palepu, K. and P. Nueno (2014). "Puig." Case, Harvard Business School Publishing.

Pearce, J. A. and F. David (1987). "Corporate Mission Statements: The Bottom Line." *Academy of Management Executive*, 1 (2), 109–116.

Pearce, J. A. and S. A. Zhara (1991). "The Relative Power of CEOs and Boards of Directors: Associations with Corporate Performance." *Strategic Management Journal*, 12 (2), 135–153.

Pérez López, J. A. (1993). *Fundamentos de Dirección de Empresas*. Madrid: Rialp.

Peteraf, M. (1993). "The Cornerstones of Competitive Advantage: A Resource-Based View." *Strategic Management Journal*, 14 (3), 179–191.

Pettigrew, A. (1990). "Longitudinal Field Research on Change: Theory and Practice." *Organization Science*, 1 (3), 267–292.

Pettigrew, A. and T. McNulty (1995). "Power and Influence in and around the Boardroom." *Human Relations*, 48 (8), 1–29.

Pfeffer, J. (1997). *The Human Equation: Building Profits by Putting People First*. Boston: Harvard Business School Press.

Pfeffer, J. (1972). "Size and Composition of Corporate Boards." *Administrative Science Quarterly*, 17 (2), 218–228.

Pfeffer, J. and G. R. Salancik (1978). *The External Control of Organizations: A Resource-Dependence Approach*. New York: Harper and Row.

Pick, K. and K. Merchant (2012). "Recognizing Negative Boardroom Group Dynamics." In J. Lorsch, ed., *The Future of Boards*. Boston: Harvard Business School Publishing, 113–132.

Piketty, T. (2014). *Capital in the Twenty-First Century*. Cambridge, MA: Harvard University Press.

Polman, P. and A. Winston (2021). *Net Positive*. Boston: Harvard Business Review Press.

Porter, M. E. (1996). "What Is Strategy?" *Harvard Business Review*, November–December, 62–78.

Porter, M. E. (1980). *Competitive Strategy*. New York: Free Press

Porter, M. E. and M. R. Kramer (2011). "Creating Shared Value." *Harvard Business Review*, January–February, 62–77.

Porter, M. E. and G. Serafeim (2019). "Where ESG Fails." *Institutional Investor*, October 16.

Post, C. and K. Byron (2015). "Women on Boards and Firm Financial Performance: A Meta Analysis." *Academy of Management Journal*, 58 (5), 1546–1571.

Pozen, R. C. (2010). "The Case for Professional Boards." *Harvard Business Review*, 88 (12), 50–58.

Pratt, M. G. and B. E. Ashfort (2003). "Fostering Meaningfulness in Working and at Work." In K. S. Cameron, J. E. Dutton and R. E. Quinn, eds., *Positive Organizational Scholarship: Foundations of a New Discipline*. San Francisco: Berrett-Koehler, 309–327.

Pucker. K. P. (2021). "Overselling Sustainability Reporting." *Harvard Business Review*, 99 (3), 134–143.

Pye, A. and A. Pettigrew (2005). "Studying Board Context, Process and Dynamics: Challenges for the Future." *British Journal of Management*, 16 (1), S27–S38.

Quinn, R. E. and A. V. Thakor (2019). *The Economics of Higher Purpose*. Oakland, CA: Barrett Koehler.

Rajan, R. G and L. Zingales (2001). "The Governance of the New Enterprise." In X. Vives, ed., *Corporate Governance*. Cambridge: Cambridge University Press, 201–227.

Rappaport, A. (1986). *Creating Shareholder Value*. New York: Simon and Schuster.

Ready, D. A., L. A. Hill and R. J. Thomas (2014). "Building a Game-Changing Talent Strategy." *Harvard Business Review*, 92 (1–2), 62–69.

Rey, C., M. Bastons and P. Sotock (2019). *Purpose-Driven Organizations*. Palgrave Macmillan.

Rey, C. and J. E. Ricart (2019). "Why Purpose Needs Strategy (and Vice Versa)." In C. Rey, M. Bastons and P. Sotok, eds., *Purpose-Driven Organizations*. Palgrave Macmillan, 47–58.

Ricart, J. E. and J. M. Rosanas, eds., (2012). *Towards a New Theory of the Firm*. Madrid: Fundación BBVA.

Roberts, J. (2004). *The Modern Firm: Organizational Design for Performance and Growth*. Oxford: Oxford University Press.

Rock, E. B. (2021). "For Whom Is the Corporation Managed in 2020? The Debate Over Corporate Purpose." *The Business Lawyer*, 76, Spring, 363–395.

Rock, E. B. (2020). "Index Funds and Corporate Governance: Let Shareholders Be Shareholders." *Boston University Law Review*, 100, 1771–1815.

Rock, E. B. (2018). "Institutional Investors in Corporate Governance," included in J. N. Gordon and W.-G. Ringe, eds., *The Oxford Handbook of Corporate Law and Governance*. Oxford: Oxford University Press, 363–386.

Roe, M. J. (2018). "Stock Market Short-Termism's Impact." *University of Pennsylvania Law Review*, 167 (1), 71–121.

Rosanas, J. M. (2008). "Beyond Economic Criteria: A Humanistic Approach to Organizational Survival." *Journal of Business Ethics*, 78 (3), 447–462.

Ross, S. (1973). "The Economic Theory of Agency: The Principal's Problems." *American Economic Review*, 63 (2), 134–139.

Rumelt, R. P. (2011). *Good Strategy, Bad Strategy*. New York: Crown Publishing.

Rumelt, R. P. (1991). "How Much Does Industry Matter?" *Strategic Management Journal*, 12 (3), 167–185.

Sakasai, Y., G. Ormazabal and J. Canals (2022). "The 2022 IESE Survey on Boards of Directors: Corporate Purpose, Culture and Strategy". IESE Publishing. Barcelona.

Salter, M. S. (2019). "Rehabilitating Corporate Purpose." Harvard Business School, Working Paper.

Schein, E. H. (2017). *Organizational Culture and Leadership*, 5th ed. San Francisco: Jossey-Bass.

Securities and Exchange Commission (1972). "The Financial Collapse of the Penn Central Company." SEC Staff Report to the Special Subcommittee on Investigations, Washington, DC.

Serafeim, G. (2020). "Social-Impact Efforts that Create Value." *Harvard Business Review*, 98 (5), 38–48.

Selznick, P. (1957). *Leadership in Administration*. New York: Harper and Row.

Shleifer, A. and Vishny, R. W. (1986). "Large Shareholders and Corporate Control." *Journal of Political Economy*, 94 (3), 461–488.

Siilasmaa, R. (2018). *Transforming Nokia*. New York: McGraw Hill.

Simon, H. (1991). "Organizations and Markets." *Journal of Economic Perspectives*, 5 (2), 25–44.

Simon, H. (1976). *Administrative Behavior*, 3rd ed. New York: Macmillan.

Simons, R. (2011). *Seven Strategy Questions*. Boston: Harvard Business Publishing.

Simons, R. and N. Kindred (2012), "Henkel: Building a Winning Culture." Case, Harvard Business School Publishing.

Srinivasan, S., D. W. Campbell, S. Gallani and A. Migdal (2017). "Sales Misconduct at Wells Fargo Community Bank." Case, Harvard Business School Publishing.

Srinivasan, S. and J. C. Coates IV (2015). "SOX after Ten Years: A Multidisciplinary Review." *Accounting Horizons*, 28 (3), 627–671.

Stempel, J. (2020). "Ex-Hertz CEO Settles U.S. SEC Charges Over Incentive Pay, Restatement." *Reuters*, August 14.

Storbeck, O., Morris, S. and Noonan, L. (2019). "The Day Deutsche Bank's Boss Decided on a Radical Solution." *Financial Times*, July 21.

Stout, L. (2012). *The Shareholder Value Myth*. San Francisco: Berret-Koehler.

Strine, Jr., L. E. (2019). "Towards a Fair and Sustainable Capitalism." Institute for Law and Economics, University of Pennsylvania Law School, Working Paper.

Strine, Jr., L. E. (2017). "Who Bleeds When the Wolves Bite? A Flesh-and-Blood Perspective on Hedge-Fund Activism and our Strange Corporate Governance System." *Yale Law Journal*, 126, 1870–1890.

Tapies, J. and J. L. Ward (2008). *Family Values and Value Creation*. London: Palgrave Macmillan.

Taylor, B. (2018). "What if Amazon's Next Big Innovation Was to Improve the Jobs of Its Blue-Collar Workers?" *Harvard Business Review*, online, June 7.

Teece, D. J., G. Pisano and A. Shuen (1997). "Dynamic Capabilities and Strategic Management." *Strategic Management Journal*, 18 (7), 509–533.

Thomsen, S. , T. Poulsen, C. Børsting and J. Kuhn (2018). "Industrial Foundations as Long-Term Owners." *Corporate Governance: An International Review*, 26, 180–196.

Tirole, J. (2017). *Economics for the Common Good*. Princeton, NJ: Princeton University Press.

Tirole, J. (2001). "Corporate Governance." *Econometrica*, 69 (1), 1–35.

Ulrich, D. and W. Brockbank (2005). *The HR Value Proposition*. Boston: Harvard Business School Press.

Useem, M. (2006). "How Well-Run Boards Make Decisions." *Harvard Business Review*, 84 (119), 138–148.

Vance, S. C. (1983). *Corporate Leadership: Boards, Directors and Strategy*. New York: McGraw-Hill.

Villalonga, B. and R. Amit (2020). "Family Ownership." *Oxford Review of Economic Policy*, 36 (2), 241–257.

Villalonga, B. and R. Amit (2010). "Family Control of Firms and Industries." *Financial Management*, 39 (3), 863–904.

Villalonga, B. and R. Amit (2009). "How Are US Family Firms Controlled?" *The Review of Financial Studies*, 22, 3047–3091.

Villalonga, B. and R. Amit (2006). "How Do Family Ownership, Control and Management Affect Firm Value?" *Journal of Financial Economics*, 80 (2), 385–417.

Vives, X. (2005). "Complementarities and Games: New Developments." *Journal of Economic Literature*, 43, 437–479.

Vives, X., ed. (2000). *Corporate Governance*. Cambridge: Cambridge University Press.

Vroom, G. and J. Gimeno (2007). "Ownership Form, Managerial Incentives and the Intensity of Rivalry." *Academy of Management Journal*, 50 (4), 901–909.

Wells, J. L., P. Berrone and P. H. Phan (2012). "Corporate Governance and Environmental Performance: Is There Really a Link?" *Strategic Management Journal*, 33 (8), 885–913.

Westphal, J. D. (1999). "Collaboration in the Boardroom: Behavioral and Performance Consequences of CEO-Board Social Ties." *Academy of Management Journal*, 42 (1), 7–24.

Westphal, J. D. and E. Zajac (2013). "A Behavioral Theory of Corporate Governance: Explicating the Mechanisms of Socially Situated and Socially Constructed Agency." *Academy of Management Annals*, 7 (1), 607–661.

Wiersema, M., A. Ahn and Y. Zhang (2020). "Activist Hedge Fund Success: The Role of Reputation." *Strategic Management Journal*, 41 (13), 2493–2517.

Wiersema, M., Y. Nishimura and K. Suzuki (2018). "Executive Succession: The Importance of Social Capital in CEO Appointments." *Strategic Management Journal*, 39 (5), 1473–1495.

Williamson, O. E. (1979). "Transaction-Cost Economics: The Governance of Contractual Relations." *Journal of Law and Economics*, 22 (4), 233–261.

Winter, J. (2018). "A Behavioral Perspective on Corporate Law and Corporate Governance." In J. N. Gordon and W. G. Ring, eds., *The Oxford Handbook of Corporate Law and Governance*. Oxford: Oxford University Press, 159–183.

Wong, J. C. (2017). "Uber CEO Travis Kalanick Resigns following Months of Chaos." *The Guardian*, June 21.

World Economic Forum (2020). "Measuring Stakeholder Capitalism" in collaboration with Deloitte, EY, KPMG and PWC. Geneva.

Wright, R. (2014). "Hertz to Restate Two Further Years of Results." *Financial Times*, November 14.

Yan, S., J. Almandoz and F. Ferraro (2021). "The Impact of Logic (In)Compatibility: Green Investing, State Policy and Corporate Environmental Performance." *Administrative Science Quarterly*, 66 (4), 903–944.

Yan, S., F. Ferraro and J. Almandoz (2018). "The Rise of Socially Responsible Investment: The Paradoxical Role of the Financial Logic." *Administrative Science Quarterly*, 64 (2), 466–501.

Younger, R., C. Mayer and R. G. Eccles (2020). *Enacting Purpose within the Modern Corporation*. London: Enacting Purpose Initiative Report.

Zingales, L. (2017). "Toward a Political Theory of the Firm." *Journal of Economic Perspectives*, 31 (3), 113–130.

Zingales, L. (1998). "Corporate Governance." In P. Newman, ed., *The New Palgrave Dictionary of Economics and the Law*. New York: Macmillan.

Zott, C. and R. Amit (2010). "Business Model Design: An Activity System Perspective." *Long Range Planning*, 43 (2–3), 216–226.

Index